TERRORISM AND AMERICA

TERRORISM AND AMERICA

FROM THE ANARCHISTS TO 9/11 AND BEYOND

DR BRYN WILLCOCK

AMBERLEY

First published 2019

Amberley Publishing
The Hill, Stroud
Gloucestershire, GL5 4EP

www.amberley-books.com

Copyright © Dr Bryn Willcock, 2019

The right of Dr Bryn Willcock to be identified
as the Author of this work has been asserted in
accordance with the Copyrights, Designs and
Patents Act 1988.

ISBN 978 1 4456 7660 9 (hardback)
ISBN 978 1 4456 7661 6 (ebook)

British Library Cataloguing in Publication Data.
A catalogue record for this book is available
from the British Library.

Typesetting by Aura Technology and Software
Services, India.
Printed in the UK.

CONTENTS

INTRODUCTION

The mention of the word terrorism, especially in relation to America, immediately brings forth the graphic images of 9/11, an event that pushed terrorism to the top of the political agenda, a position it has never fully relinquished. In truth, America has a long association with terrorism, an association that dates back throughout much of its history as an independent country. The early American Republic, without the protection of the British naval fleet, was soon forced to put aside millions of dollars to free its citizens from the Barbary pirates who held them captive after raids on US shipping in North Africa. This situation brought forth an early 'arms for hostages' deal, which had clear echoes two centuries later in Ronald Reagan's controversial deal to free American captives held in Lebanon. Whilst the first assassination attempt on an American president had occurred against Andrew Jackson back in 1835, it was the assassination of Abraham Lincoln in 1865 that ushered in a new kind of terrorism unique to America, Lincoln being the first of four American presidents to be slain whilst in office.

The invention of dynamite in 1867, followed by the growing rise in radical anarchist movements (many of the leaders of which had moved to America from Europe) saw terrorism grow significantly in the late nineteenth century, culminating in the Haymarket bombing of 1886. Labour unrest over poor working conditions and practices brought suspicion on the trades union movements by employers and politicians, giving rise to the idea that a secret association, the 'Molly Maguires', was committing acts of terrorism that included kidnapping, sabotage and even murder. Controversial investigations by the Pinkerton Detective Agency would lead to over 20 executions, but did nothing to end the anarchist era.

Many of the terrorist events covered in this book received considerable attention at the time that they were committed, but a significant number of these events were less well represented or even ignored in future years, with some American history texts choosing to simply leave out these negative aspects of America's past. Even with the wealth of material that has emerged since 2001 on the subject of terrorism, much of this material has failed to consider America's long and troubled relationship with terrorist acts. Most Americans would be unaware that a terrorist attack on New York permanently closed public access to the torch of the Statue of Liberty in 1916, or that the attack on Wall Street in 1920 (which killed 38 people) proved to be the culmination of the aforementioned anarchist era. It would also come as a surprise to many to find that the peak of terrorist acts in the US came in the early 1970s when there was an average of more than one terrorist attack per day. At this time, divergent terrorist groups protesting against American policy in Vietnam and American control of Puerto Rico, and civil rights groups, all attacked targets within the US, with women often taking a leading role in these movements.

Whilst internal threats had declined sharply by the late 1970s, as the Vietnam War came to end, and with many of the underground leaders now in jail, threats toward Americans from terrorist actions outside the US conversely saw a rise from the late 1960s. Some of these terrorist actions proved to be simply frustrating for the government. Hijacking aircraft to Cuba became so common in the 1960s that some pilots even carried plans of the layout of Havana airport. From 1968, a spate of aircraft hijackings, including multiple plane hijackings at Dawson's Field in 1970 (an activity replicated on 9/11) took place. These, together with other high-profile events such as the terrorist attack on the 1972 Munich Olympics (which played out in front of a global audience of half a billion people), forced President Nixon to move the threat of terrorism much higher up the political agenda. He set up a cabinet committee specifically to combat terrorism, having supported the Draft Convention for the Punishment of Certain Acts of Terrorism to the United Nations.

Rising threats to Americans overseas continued, most notably attacks on American personnel in Beirut in 1983, which killed nearly 300 servicemen. The activities of so-called rogue states such as Iran, Libya and North Korea, together with his belief that terrorism was being sponsored by the communist leaders in the Kremlin, led Ronald Reagan to declare a 'war on terror' in July 1985. In this Reagan adopted language which would be reflected in George W. Bush's 'war on terror' speech in 2002, but after a bombing raid on Libya's capital in April 1986, Reagan's war on terror simply fizzled out.

Since the 1970s terrorist threats have increasingly moved from the left wing of politics to the right, most graphically illustrated by Timothy McVeigh's bombing attack in Oklahoma in 1995, which killed 168 people (including 19 children). More than half of terrorist attacks that took place in America during the 1980s and 1990s were conducted by the extreme right (Lutz & Lutz, 2007, p. 113). Bill Clinton placed significant emphasis on the increased threat from terrorism, from terrorism, increasing the federal budget for anti-terrorism programmes, bringing in new laws, and directly targeting bin Laden in a controversial missile strike in 1998. There was a recognition from the president that Islamic terrorism now posed a serious threat to the US both internally (as seen with the first attack on the World Trade Center in 1993), and externally (as seen with the African embassy bombings in 1998). Despite this, most Americans still felt insulated from the threat terrorism posed to their security.

That insularity was shattered on 9/11, despite the fact that the pre-requisites for that fateful day had been coming together over the preceding decades. Since that time, terrorism has seldom left the political spotlight as America altered its internal and external approaches to dealing with the terrorism threat. Internal threats have been met via quickly passed legal measures such as the PATRIOT Act (2001), whilst externally America would engage in wars in both Afghanistan and, more controversially, Iraq. As will be highlighted, this threat has also featured heavily in presidential campaigns, as well as in the media and popular culture.

This book provides the opportunity to look back across America's long and troubled historical relationship with terrorism and to contextualise these events. All too often historians have perpetuated the myth that America remained largely untouched by terrorism until recent decades. It will be shown that many of these events did attract significant attention at the time they were carried out, and indeed were reflected in newspapers and political debates of the time. These events were often soon forgotten, or their importance downgraded, leading to a cultural amnesia on the subject of terrorism until the devastating experience of 9/11. After establishing what events and actions genuinely fall under the category of terrorism, we will undertake a historical journey to more fully understand the trends that have led to terrorism taking centre stage in America. History has some powerful precedents that contain important lessons.

TERRORISM: DEFINITIONS, TACTICS, MOTIVATIONS

How do we define terrorism? Whilst fraught with difficulty and lacking any clear agreement, it should be possible to set out a workable definition that will allow us to separate incidents of terrorism from acts of war, violence, or murder. From such a definition we can begin our historical journey through America's relationship with terrorism up to the present day. It is also necessary to define other aspects of terrorism that will feature in the following chapters. Who are terrorists, what are their motivations, and what methods do they use in order to try to achieve their goals? A short overview of the origins of terrorism is also necessary.

Walter Laqueur (1921–2018), who was the leading writer on the subject for many decades, has argued that the greatest myth surrounding terrorism is that it is a new phenomenon. This study will help in further dispelling this myth by showing that America's long and troubled relationship with terrorism predates the founding of the Republic in 1776. The threat from terrorism grew after the Civil War with the end of the nineteenth century bringing more systematic and organised forms of terrorism. Terrorism associated with anarchism, for example, spread from Europe to the US, when many of the anarchist leaders sailed across the Atlantic to advocate notions of 'propaganda by deed', ensuring that the twentieth century began, as indeed it would end, with the American government having to prioritise its policies to combat serious threats from terrorism.

Given America's long history with terrorism and the many diverse incidences that will be considered here, the question has to be asked why the subject has not been taken more seriously by many American history texts, and why America expresses profound surprise and shock when major terrorist events take place. The history books are often guilty of not giving full coverage to terrorist events, perhaps because they were considered to be aberrations in the historical narrative. One of the more recent authors to help correct the historical narrative is Beverly Gage, who has picked up on Richard Hofstadter's idea that Americans have a 'remarkable lack of memory' when it comes to recording acts of violence within their history (2009, p. 6). Gage also picks up on another key point that liberal historians, horrified by the excesses of McCarthyism, went out of their way to minimise past controversies over violence, terrorism and class conflict, (2009, p. 7). David Shi and the late George Tindall were rightly regarded as two of America's leading historians, their *America: A Narrative History* provides students with a solid and lengthy overview. However, terrorism is not mentioned under the final chapter when the events and repercussions of 9/11 are discussed. Howard Zinn, a notable left-leaning American historian, who provided a far more critical look at events from America's past in his *A People's History of the United States*, first published in 1980, does not mention terrorism at all, in an otherwise thought-provoking text.

The answer to the question why terrorism has not been more fully considered within many historical studies, as will be demonstrated, is that the threat levels from terrorism have not been consistent, but have risen and fallen. It was these gaps in terrorist activity which have led Americans to forget past events and lulled them into a false sense of security that terrorism was effectively a problem that had ceased to exist. This largely explains the sense of confusion when a new terrorist event has taken place. On 9/11 for example, there was initial bewilderment and incredulity that terrorists had taken control of planes, as the era of plane hijacks was considered to be long since past. Eric Foner, in his study *Give Me Liberty!: An American History* acknowledges that terrorism within America has a long history, but argues that following the end of the Cold War, Americans felt more secure against the threat of terrorist attacks than they had for decades (2009, p. 1040).

Any study of terrorism must naturally begin with a consideration of what is meant by the term. A precise definition, however, is likely to prove eternally elusive. Walter Laqueur argued that no definition could hope to cover all of terrorism's historical examples (2012, p. 6), and that any attempt to provide one would prove to be fruitless. The problem proves more complex given that perspectives alter significantly based on factors such as political ideology, time and geographical location. Although his role in the war or connection to the CIA should not be overstated, in the late 1980s Osama bin Laden was fighting on the same side as the US in seeking to remove Soviet troops from Afghanistan. There was common ground on a shared cause, an unlikely starting point for bin Laden to become America's most wanted criminal. Terrorism is not a specific ideology and so does not have a set of core beliefs. Whilst terrorist acts are usually focussed upon changing the political landscape, this is not always the case: groups such as the Ku Klux Klan are set upon *preventing* change and sometimes conduct actions that support the government in power.

John Richard Thackrah devotes several pages of his *Dictionary of Terrorism* to outlining various issues related to defining terrorism, noting that the emotive nature of the topic, and its use as a term within different kinds of negative political discourse, help cloud the issue (2004, pp. 75–79). The wide variety of causes and potential terrorist examples provide more complication. David Whittaker, in addition to noting that there are over 200 extant definitions of terrorism, has estimated that the number of terrorist groups in the world is more than 100, in over 70 countries (2004, p. 33). Given this diversity of groups, agendas and beliefs, it may initially seem as if it is all but impossible to create any meaningful or useful definition of terrorism.

It certainly does not help that within the US itself, the intelligence agencies give different, although not necessarily contradictory, definitions of what they consider terrorism. The Federal Bureau of Investigation (FBI) state that combating terrorism is their top investigative priority and they separate out international and domestic terrorism. They argue international terrorism is that 'perpetrated by individuals and/or groups inspired by or associated with designated foreign terrorist organisations or nations'. Domestic terrorism is regarded as that 'perpetrated by individuals and/or groups inspired by or associated with primarily US-based movements that espouse extremist ideologies of a political, religious, social, racial, or environmental nature' (FBI, 2018). The CIA defines terrorism as 'premeditated, politically motivated violence perpetrated against noncombatant targets by sub national groups or clandestine agents' (CIA, 2018). The American Department of Defense states that terrorism is 'the unlawful use of violence or threat of violence, often motivated by religious, political, or other ideological beliefs, to instil fear or coerce governments or societies in pursuit of goals that are usually political' (DoD, 2018). Alive to the dangers of perceptions of which groups may be targeted as terrorists, the US Department of Homeland Security details on its website recommendations from American Muslims on the need to avoid terrorist terminology that may simply conflate terrorism with Islam.

In truth, there are certain aspects that can be focussed upon to at least give us a framework by which we can judge what comprises terrorism, and what differentiates it from simple acts of violence or murder. Key, as the FBI and CIA definitions note, is the fact that terrorism has a political motivation. Such a distinction is made by authors such as Gus Martin (2013, p. 11) and Bruce Hoffman (2006, p. 2) and enables us to separate events such as the series of attacks carried out by George Metesky, 'the Mad Bomber', on New York during the period from 1940–56, or the 1927 Bath School Bombing, which killed 45 people and was carried out by Andrew Kehoe. Whilst the perpetrators utilised methods connected to terrorism (such as timed explosives), their actions were those of revenge and frustration, rather than any attempt to exert pressure for political change, as will be explored in chapter four.

The second benchmark set out by Martin (which is reflected in the FBI definition) is that the attacks must be on 'soft' targets – essentially those without military connections. The third and final criterion set out by Martin is that there must be an attempt to influence a target audience (2013, p. 11). A dramatic example of this came in Madrid in 2004, when a series of bombs killed 193 train passengers days before the Spanish election. This arguably resulted in the Socialist Party coming from behind to win the election, having committed to pulling Spanish troops out of the US-led coalition in Iraq. Under the second touchstone, the actions of Kehoe and Metesky meet the definition of terrorism, and those of Metesky possibly meet the third, but neither meets the political criterion. American presidents such as Richard Nixon have recognised that the political aspects of a cause may lend credibility to a terrorist attack and have sought to address this by simply equating deadly terrorist acts to those of murder.

These three criteria therefore provide a useful working definition of how we may classify acts within American history that qualify as terrorism. Whilst hardly exhaustive, they allow for a meaningful consideration of the impact that terrorism has had upon America. Such differentiation is not always clear cut and debates will always rage concerning what can be meaningfully included. For example, the actions of Stephen Paddock, who killed 58 people and injured over 500 others in a mass shooting incident in Las Vegas in October 2017, is a crime that lacks any obvious motive. Paddock meticulously planned his killings, yet there was no obvious rationale for his actions and an autopsy did not reveal any obvious medical reasons for his attack on a large crowd of people who were returning from a concert. As such, the killings cannot be ascribed to terrorism, since we lack any clear purpose for his actions actions (Wang and Berman, 2018). However, this did not stop the Amaq News Agency from reporting the totally unsubstantiated claim that Paddock was an Islamic convert who had carried out the attack on the behalf of Isis (Dearden, 2017). Whilst this was a frivolous claim, designed to keep the group relevant and in the public eye, it does highlight the problems of clear differentiation between terrorist acts and murder.

Aside from our three main criteria, more needs to be said about other aspects of terrorism, which will help guide any meaningful study. Nathan Yungher in his book *Terrorism: The Bottom Line* stresses that terrorism is never about the cause (as each side is equally convinced of the veracity of their beliefs) but is always about the methods used (2008, p. 5). Within terrorist activities, there are a great variety of potential methods utilised. However, as Griset and Mahan note (2003 pp. 197-201), the main 'conventional' activities include assassinations, kidnappings, hijackings and bombings. Inevitably, technology has facilitated the growth of the two latter examples. The invention of dynamite by Alfred Nobel in 1867 meant it was quickly utilised by anarchists in the late nineteenth century (see chapter three) who saw this as a powerful emancipator, one with the potential to physically destroy the capitalist regimes. Whilst the first recorded plane hijack took place in Peru in 1931, America would not face its first plane hijack until 1958. Despite a tightening of security, incidences of hijacking remained disturbingly high for most of the next decade, even if most of these incidents were peacefully resolved, as will be explored in chapter five.

More recently, these traditional terrorist methods have been augmented by the rise of cyber terrorism and suicide bombings, as well as the potential for the use of weapons of mass destruction, a nuclear, biological or chemical weapon attack. Whilst such attacks represent a very real possibility, and some of the actions America is adopting to prevent such measures will be looked at in chapter eight, it is worth noting that America has already suffered a bioterror attack, which took place in Oregon in 1984, infecting over 750 diners with Salmonella, although there were no fatalities. More notably, America suffered a wave of anthrax attacks shortly after 9/11, which were initially, if wrongly, linked to Islamic terrorism, as well as a ricin poisoning attempt via the US mail in 2013, which resulted in a 25-year prison sentence for the perpetrator James Everett Dutschke.

The League of Nations drew up a Convention for the Prevention and Punishment of Terrorism as far back as 1937, with signatories duty-bound to do all in their power to suppress any terrorist act with a political purpose (Whittaker, 2004, p. 5). This agreement, and indeed the League of Nations itself, was to be undermined by not having America as a member. The 1937 Convention, signed by 24 nations, including the USSR, never came into force (Durgard, 1974, p. 68). However, in 1949, the United Nations, with America as a founding member, did reaffirm the duties of the 1937 Convention, various conventions being added to the UN portfolio up to the present day. With terrible irony, the International Convention for the Prevention of Terrorist Bombings came into force less than four months prior to the 9/11 attack.

The lack of agreement regarding a concise definition inevitably hampers agreements on how to tackle the issues that arise from these conventions. Not only will different states define terrorism in different ways, they may also choose to enforce these conventions in different ways. Nevertheless, there has been a much greater international push since 9/11 to deal with the threat posed by terrorism and indeed, there has been some success in this regard. So whilst inevitably the perceived threat from terrorism has greatly increased since 2001, measures to clamp down on terrorism within America were sufficiently effective that by 2004, there were no recorded incidents of terrorist-related fatalities within the US. This of course did not rule out the possibility of future attacks, as the Boston Marathon bombing of 2013, or the 2018 pipe bombs located in the US mail, demonstrated.

Terrorism is not a neutral term, it is effectively a negative label that can be applied to individuals, organisations or states with whom one disagrees. As Brian Jenkins notes (cited in Whittaker, 2004, p. 7), the term is a moral judgement, and depends on your point of view. If a country such as America can successfully label its opponents as terrorists, then other countries will adopt that moral viewpoint to show support and solidarity. America, as the world's leading superpower, is able to dominate the agenda in terms of labelling states, groups or individuals who engage in terrorist activity. The adage that 'one man's heretic is another man's fighter for the true faith' is exemplified by the fact that it is usually the West, and more specifically America, that tends to define who the terrorists are. These definitions can alter over time. Figures such as Nelson Mandela and Gerry Adams were once directly linked to terrorism by western governments. Remarkably, Nelson Mandela was not actually removed from US terrorist watch lists until 2008 (Waxman, 2018). Adams' visit to the US in 1994 to meet President Clinton aroused fury from British Prime Minister John Major who told the president he was allowing entry to a man 'closely associated with terrorism for two decades' (Hornell and Roberts, 2018). Both Mandela and Adams went on to leading roles within their own political systems. Conversely, there was a push by America to term combatants opposing the Soviet invasion in Afghanistan as 'freedom fighters', something that would later haunt the US. Osama bin Laden moved from being a figure that America could support in Afghanistan to their most wanted terrorist following the 1998 African embassy bombings, as explored in chapter seven. Rapoport has stated that the number of people once regarded as terrorists who have won the Nobel Peace Prize is greater than the number of American presidents to do so (Rapoport, 2011, p. 118).

Whilst America does not formally keep a list of rogue states, as Griset notes, the Secretary of State is authorised to identify state sponsors of terrorism (2003, p. 48). As such, it has not been reticent about labelling countries as rogue states; although during the Clinton administration Secretary of State Madeleine Albright adopted the slightly less derogative term 'states of concern' (Cameron, 2005, p. 142). Such states have been highly diverse, but are usually states considered to be developing countries who actively support terrorism and pursue weapons of mass destruction (Lennon & Eiss, p. vii), although within such a definition would also fall some of America's allies. After 9/11, George W. Bush elevated concern about rogue states to be the most urgent issue facing America's national security interests (Homolar, 2010). In his 2002 State of the Union address he famously made the case that three states, Iran, Iraq and North Korea, formed an 'Axis of Evil, arming to threaten the peace of the world'. Whilst controversial, as we will explore further in chapter seven, the speech reflected Reagan's 'war on international terrorism' set out in 1985. In a speech in July of that year Reagan focussed on Iran, Libya and North Korea as terrorist nations. However, whilst Reagan's war on terror would largely be one of rhetoric, Bush's speech proved to be the prelude for his war to move beyond Afghanistan and into Iraq in March 2003. Whilst Bush tried to stress that America was not at war with Islam, such a message was increasingly lost, not least because, as Carolyn Gallaher notes, those commenting on terrorism issues frequently linked the term to Islam. (Gallaher, 2015, p. 317)

In 2017 Donald Trump made a speech at the United Nations saying that Iran, North Korea and Venezuela were the three countries that most seriously threatened the security of other countries. In addition, in late 2018, National Security Advisor John Bolton was referring to Iran as a 'rogue regime' as the justification for America withdrawing from a 1955 Bilateral Treaty of Amity. In reality, despite direct acts of terrorism being backed by countries that oppose American policy, these acts reaching a peak under Ronald Reagan, state-sponsored terrorism has declined sharply since the 1980s.

The fact that America is the nation imposing these rogue state labels onto other countries to which it is ideologically opposed has inevitably led to significant criticism and indeed the accusation that America itself is the true 'rogue state'. Fidel Castro stated that Cuba had faced more terrorist actions against them than almost any other nation on Earth at the hands of America (*Castro*, 2007, p. 252). Noam Chomsky has noted that America falls under the definition of a rogue state, explaining that the most powerful nations do not consider themselves bound by international norms (Chomsky, 2000, p. 1). This is best exemplified by the Reagan administration's criticism of, and refusal to accept, the World Court's decision that America owed Nicaragua substantial reparations, and that America should cease backing mercenary groups active in undermining the Nicaraguan government. Reagan had even included Nicaragua in his 1985 speech as a state sponsor of terrorism.

Chomsky has not been alone in putting forward the idea that America is the ultimate rogue state. Adam Jones has argued that in examining international involvement in mass violence 'no power approaches the United States when it comes to instigation of, and complicity in, conflicts and atrocities worldwide' (2006, p. 135).

Some authors have expanded this theme, creating works that focus on America's negative role in world affairs. William Blum in his *Rogue State: A Guide to the World's only Superpower,* first published in 2000, argued that American foreign policies, which included the deaths of many civilians and support of despotic regimes, provided the fuel for acts of terrorism against the US. The book gained notoriety when Osama bin Laden quoted from it in January 2006, a plug that would propel it into the bestseller lists. The book *Blowback: The Costs and Consequences of American Empire* by Chalmers Johnson was originally published in 2000, arguing that actions of the American government abroad effectively drove victims caught up in military actions to seek retribution against the US. After the events of 9/11 the book went through seven printings in just two months, Recent books by T. D. Allman, Clyde Prestowitz and Judith Blau et al, have all focussed on the idea or perception that America is effectively *the* rogue nation in the world.

The purpose of this study is not to explore the ideas surrounding whether America is ultimately a rogue state, but to help establish the rationale given by those who have conducted attacks on America and American citizens abroad. Given that terrorism is never random, or without cause, any study must seek to explain why terrorist events have taken place, whilst at the same time never seeking to justify or condone those events.

In its earlier incarnations terrorism was not considered a negative term. Alexander Berkman for example, who is considered in chapter three, was keen to stress that he was 'a terrorist by conviction' (Berkman, 1912, p. 10). From the 1970s onwards the more common pejorative usage of the term was exemplified by President Nixon calling student protesters against the Vietnam War 'terrorists' (Winkler, 2006, p. 192). For most of its modern existence the word 'terrorist' has been a negative term, people do not tend to attach such a label to themselves, although they can admit to terrorist actions in support of what they consider to be a higher cause. Being labelled a terrorist by America could even be seen as a badge of honour by some. Whilst governments see their actions as legitimate, so too do those carrying out terrorist actions. Ramzi Yousef, the man behind the first attack on the World Trade Center, stated at the end of his trial in 1997 that he was proud to be a terrorist (Reeve, 1999, p. 242). Following the 9/11 attacks, Osama bin Laden in an interview with Al-Jazeera's reporter Taysir Alluni in October 2001 stated that America practised 'ill-advised terrorism' whilst he practised 'terrorism that is a good act, because it deters those from killing our children in Palestine and other places' (Lawrence, 2005, p. 106).

This work is not a general history of terrorism, however, it is worth noting that terrorism predates the founding of America by many centuries, dating back to antiquity. Authors such as Randall Law or Andrew Sinclair take their studies back to pre-Christian times, although most historical surveys of terrorism list the *sicarii* (men of the dagger) as the first organised terrorist group. This sect were active in the Zealot struggle against the Roman occupation of Palestine during the latter part of the first century AD, attacking their victims with concealed short swords in crowded areas during daylight. One theme from this first historical example of terrorism that will reappear frequently in our later study is the rejection of foreign influence and the attempt to reclaim control of land and reassert traditional values.

The word 'terrorism' became popularised following the French Revolution. As Bruce Hoffman notes, at the time the term had a positive connotation (2006, p. 3), being associated with ideals of virtue and democracy. The *regime de la terreur* (1793–94) attempted to bring order from the increasingly violent upheavals of the revolutionary period that had begun in July 1789. Although the term would quickly transform into a negative one, Thomas Jefferson remained an ardent supporter of the French Revolution. Despite the revolutionary terror, in June 1795, in a letter to Tench

Coxe, he predicted success for a 'ball of liberty ... that we first put into motion'. That same year, British statesman Edmund Burke (1730–1797) identified that 'Thousands of those Hell-hounds called Terrorists, whom they had shut up in Prison on their last Revolution, as the Satellites of Tyranny, are let loose on the people' (Burke, 1991, p. 89) when discussing the release of prisoners to quell a potential rebellion in Paris. Burke, who had supported the American colonists in their revolutionary struggle, by opposing the French Revolution helped both to popularise the term and reverse positive conceptions of it.

As the next chapter will outline, there are arguments that incidences of terrorism have been carried out in the New World ever since colonial times. Less than two decades after the British established their first permanent settlement at Jamestown in 1607, Takaki has argued that the British were engaging in tricking the local tribes to drink poison, and by the eighteenth century were utilising a crude form of biological warfare, employing infected smallpox blankets to infect the Native Americans. Terrorist methods were utilised to remove the original settlers throughout the early nineteenth century, a period that also brought other incidences of racial and religious terrorism. Joseph Smith, for example, the founder of Mormonism, was killed by an angry mob shortly after announcing his political intentions to enter the presidential race in 1844. Just over a decade later events related to the American Civil War would lead authors such as Paul Finkelman to raise the question whether the violent actions of John Brown, in his quest to end slavery in the late 1850s, made him the father of American terrorism. Michael Fellman has argued that the killing of President Abraham Lincoln by John Wilkes Booth (himself inspired by the actions but not the motives of Brown) was in fact the last terrorist act of the Civil War. A new era of terrorism would open almost as soon as the war ended with the creation of the Ku Klux Klan in Pulaski, Tennessee, an organisation that would, according to Griset and Mahan, carry out deliberate racist terrorism for more than a century (2003, p. 89).

David Rapoport has put forward the idea that there have been four main terrorist waves: the anarchist wave (1878–1919), the anti-colonial wave (1920s–60s), the New Left wave (mid 1960s–1990s) and the religious wave (from 1979). Of these, America was significantly affected by the anarchist wave, which brought many prominent anarchists over from Europe. Johann Most, who was renowned internationally as an anarchist leader would become the quintessential image of a crazed terrorist, intent on utilising 'propaganda by deed' to undermine the American government. The combination of anarchists and radicalised workers movements saw America witness a significant rise in terrorism. Whilst the existence of a secret group of extremists intent on murder, kidnapping, bombings and sabotage that came to be known as the Molly Maguires can be challenged, America nevertheless faced very real terrorist threats from this time. These threats were underlined by both the assassination of President McKinley in 1901 (by Leon Czolgosz), as well as major bombing attacks such as that upon the Los Angeles Times building in 1910 (dubbed in the press 'The Crime of the Century'). This period culminated in the 1920 Wall Street bombing attack, which killed 38 people and came close to altering American history, given that John F. Kennedy's father was hit by the blast. These incidents, alongside major bombing attacks by those intent on keeping the US out of the First World War (such as the Preparedness Day Attack in San Francisco as well as an attack on Black Tom Island, New York, which damaged the Statue of Liberty), made this era of American history one that was especially marked by terrorism. A fuller consideration of these events is provided in chapter three.

By contrast, America largely escaped the second wave. Having broken free from British colonial control and having set up a republican constitution, others looked to America to support their calls for independence. Indeed, it is a sad irony of modern history, given the losses in the Vietnam War, that Ho Chi Minh was inspired by the American Declaration of Independence and had approached President Truman with a view to cooperation, a fact commented upon by Barack Obama when he met the then president of Vietnam, Truong Tan Sang, in July 2013. Despite acquiring significant overseas territories, especially from 1898, America, unlike older colonial powers, did not have to endure long liberation struggles, violence from which could have spilled over onto the American mainland. The main exception to this is the case of the Puerto Rican separatists, whose actions included opening fire on Congress, an attempted assassination of President Truman, and bombing attacks on American cities which did not fade away until the 1980s, as will be shown in chapter five.

America would have to increasingly face threats from terrorism, both at home and abroad due to other factors, many of which correspond to Rapoport's third and fourth waves of terrorism. Many on the New Left were inspired to action by America's increasingly controversial war in Vietnam, which (without the initial knowledge of Congress or the American public) would stretch into neighbouring Laos and Cambodia. Many radicals felt compelled to violent action in order to 'bring the war home' to the wider American public. A variety of notable groups made attacks on various American cities, such as the various Weathermen underground movements, as well as groups such as the Black Panthers. These groups were regarded as such a significant threat by the FBI that its legendary director J. Edgar Hoover launched some of the biggest manhunts in FBI history against the group's leaders. New leftists would be quietly added to Hoover's 'security index', a list of people to be rounded up at a time of national emergency (Gitlin, 1993, p. 378). This was also the era when increasing numbers of women became important figures within these underground groups. Figures such as Bernardine Dohrn and

Jane Alpert, who took leading roles in these movements, remain controversial figures in America, whilst JoAnne Chesimard, a member of the Black Liberation Army, has become the first woman to appear on the FBI's Most Wanted Terrorists List. These movements, and the rising prominence of female leaders within them, will be explored in chapter five.

Another key factor in the rising threat of terrorism against America came when it threw its military weight behind Israel during the 1967 Six-Day War. For many in the Arab world this engendered a powerful resentment, resulting in the radicalisation of groups and individuals who sought to take direct terrorist measures against the US. It was, for example, cited by Sirhan Bishara Sirhan as the motivation behind his assassination of Robert Kennedy (see chapter six). Despite some initial bewilderment at the 1993 attack on the World Trade Center, terrorists would quickly explicitly state that American support for Israel was the reason for their targeting of America. Simon Reeve, as chapter seven makes clear, stresses that Ramzi Yousef, the chief mastermind of this attack, always had the repression of the Palestinians as his central guiding motivation, despite the fact that he personally never visited Palestine (Reeve, 1999, p. 130).

Terrorists often attempt to appear as if they are extensions of the military. Terrorists justify clandestine attacks by arguing that they need to raise awareness for their cause and lack the numerical, logistical advantages of the state. As Hoffman notes, whilst warfare has proved far more devastating in terms of deaths and destruction, it is is often conducted according to certain rules and norms, such as the Geneva and Hague conventions (2006, p. 26). Terrorism moves outside the normal rules of warfare by often (but not always) targeting civilians, and refusing to abide by international diplomatic conventions. Warfare has certain codes and rules (which are admittedly not always adhered to) whilst terrorism lacks any such constraints. As these individuals, groups or even states who opposed the policies of the American government could not possibly defeat America in any kind of conventional direct military conflict, they would inevitably seek to apply pressure by engaging in unorthodox military activities. Terrorism is in effect the method by which the weak can attack the strong (Kolko, 2006, p. 83). Asymmetrical warfare is a term which highlights terrorist efforts to strike at unanticipated targets and arose from the belief that America simply could not be defeated in a traditional type of war (though it is not a term limited to terrorism). Asymmetrical warfare has been an increasing problem for more powerful states, as the weaker the opposing force the more likely it is to utilise unconventional means to compensate for its inferior position (Lennon & Eiss, 2004, p. 43).

It is important to differentiate between terrorists and groups who engage in guerrilla ('little war') tactics. Such forces often employ many of the same tactics as terrorists, and often work for political change. However, guerrilla forces can be differentiated from terrorists groups as they tend to be larger, often holding areas of territory, and operating essentially as military units, sometimes engaging in direct military combat. Yungher notes that guerrilla fighters must wear some kind of identifying symbol (such as a uniform) and must carry their weapons out in the open (2008, p. 12). This type of warfare has many successful historical examples, and America's failure to secure an outright victory during the Vietnam War gave inspiration to terrorist groups by showing that America was vulnerable to these forms of irregular warfare. Vietnam increasingly focussed attention on America being the real opponent in relation to the battle for social change in Third World countries. America's increasing military involvement in many areas of the world after 1945 extinguished it as a beacon of hope for those struggling for independence. Internationally, groups were increasing emboldened by America's failure to win the Vietnam War, despite all its logistical advantages. As Fidel Castro would note in 1997, Vietnam proved that it was possible to fight against the interventionist forces of imperialism and defeat them (Castro, 2006, p. 221).

It is important to note that the choices of targets by terrorists are not random, and Timothy McVeigh's actions are a demonstration of this. His decision to attack a federal building was to highlight opposition to federal control, since he saw himself as a patriot defending American liberties (Sinclair, 2003, p. 329). Targets are selected for their symbolic and propaganda value. So the threat to American cities has not been evenly spread; for example, New York is a city that has disproportionally suffered at the hands of terrorists, due to its high profile nature and significance, both in terms of politics, media portrayals and economic dominance. This was demonstrated by the targeting of the financial heart of the city in terrorist attacks in 1920, 1975, 1993 and 2001. Other cities such as Boston, Chicago, Philadelphia and San Francisco have also been subject to a disproportionate number of terrorist attacks. Overseas, American military personnel, embassies, businesses and private citizens have all been targeted in order to place pressure upon the American government's foreign policy strategy.

To gain media awareness, and therefore draw attention to a cause, is a key aspect of terrorism. As chapter two explores, during the Barbary Wars, American hostages would write letters to their families at home. Even in this early period, hostage takers were aware that holding hostages generates intense media interest, as there is a human interest aspect which readers can relate to. Hostage's letters would often be printed in newspapers, putting greater pressure on the American government to arrange their release. Terrorist actions were covered by national newspapers during the anarchist era, but it was the advent of television and a potentially global audience that further galvanised terrorist activity. The terrorist attack on the Munich Olympic games was viewed by a global audience of around half a billion (see chapter six).

The perpetrators of 9/11 were well aware that that media crews would scramble to record the attacks on the World Trade Center within minutes, and the fact that both attacks on the towers would be captured by TV crews meant the attack achieved maximum dramatic and distressing coverage.

Christopher Hewitt reflects in his study (2003, p. 15) that during the period from 1954–2000 foreign terrorism accounted for only 11.6 per cent of terrorist-related deaths, showing that domestic terrorist incidents were far more important within the US. He noted that white racist related terrorism accounted for more than half of those deaths, with a quarter of terrorist-related fatalities linked to black militant action. In their survey Borgeson and Valeri quote a RAND Corporation study from 2006 that revealed the average age of a domestic US terrorist was thirty nine, and that attacks had been predominantly conducted by males (87 per cent) who were likely to come from rural areas, be manual labourers and were 100 per cent white (2009, p. 2).

Since the early 1990s America has been especially affected by Rapoport's fourth wave of terrorism, the religious wave. He dates this from 1979, a starting point connected to the Iranian Islamic Revolution, when revolutionaries held fifty-two hostages at the American embassy for 444 days. James Kiras has described this as a watershed in transnational terrorism. He notes that the majority of transnational attacks since that time have been directed towards American citizens and symbols (Kiras, 2005, p. 484). These events would inspire a large number of new terrorist movements, points that will be considered in in chapter six. In reality the seeds of religious-based terrorism had been growing since the 1960s, gaining ground with the ideas of key figures such as Sayyid Qutb. Qutb has been described by Griset and Mahan as the most important thinker in the Muslim world over the last fifty years and his ideas increasingly found a receptive audience after his execution in 1966. James Toth has argued in his 2013 study of

Qutb that his legacy was a powerful one and created the mind-set that inspired the 9/11 attacks.

The end of the Cold War as the 1980s drew to a close had a number of important impacts upon terrorism worldwide. The collapse of the USSR saw threats from left-wing terrorism recede even further. In addition, Hoffman has noted the decline of ethno-nationalist/separatist groups as new states gained independence (2006, p85) and those still engaging in often bitter struggles to liberate their homelands had little opportunity or motivation to engage in international terrorism. By the 1990s however, there was a considerable expansion in groups connected to religious terrorism, a figure that has continued to rise ever since. This threat was far from ignored by President Clinton (see chapter seven). Indeed, Clinton became increasingly concerned about a major terrorist event on American soil and as Carol Winkler has noted, the president went on to make over a thousand speeches that mentioned terrorism.

The 1990s brought a number of serious attacks on the US both at home (including the first attack on the World Trade Center in 1993) and overseas (such as the African embassy bombing attacks in 1998). Despite Clinton's efforts to stress the importance of terrorism to the incoming president, the administration of George W. Bush did not initially place the threat from terrorism high on its agenda. This was important, as new forms of terrorism were bringing indiscriminate attacks aiming for maximum casualties and the use of extreme methods.

Whilst, as we have noted, religion is linked to the earliest examples of terrorism, it is clear, as Gus Martin has argued, that religion is also a central feature of New Terrorism (2013, p. 186). New Terrorism specialises in asymmetrical attacks, cell-based networks, indiscriminate attacks against 'soft' targets and threatens the use of weapons of mass destruction. There is of course much debate over what is actually novel about New

Terrorism (sometimes termed postmodern terrorism). Despite the rush to redefine terrorism after 9/11, there were many aspects that reflected traditional forms of terrorism. What was new was the size of the attacks and the level of death and devastation caused, 9/11 causing nearly 3000 deaths, which was a higher death toll than all the previous attacks within America during the previous half century. There was also over $50 billion of property damage. The insurance payouts meant increased premiums, there was lost revenue, an increase in unemployment, losses to the airline industry obviously, and a decline in share values. Randall Law has argued that the impact of 9/11 was so great that it simply clouded the origins of terrorism (Law, 2009, p. 5).

Chapter eight places the events of 9/11 into a historical context, the proceeding chapters having provided the background, and draws attention to the increasing rise in terrorist threats against the US. It highlights the fact that the methods utilised on 9/11 were largely not new and that the main motivations of the hijackers had been reflected in statements made after previous attacks on America, both at home and abroad. The official 9/11 Commission in their report indicated that had the American intelligence agencies worked differently, then the terrifying events of that day could have been avoided. This chapter will also provide the opportunity to look at how America reacted to the events of that day, both at home and abroad. Internal changes included controversial measures such as the PATRIOT Act, which greatly expanded the government ability to track communications, whilst external actions were even more controversial, with America entering into wars in both Afghanistan and Iraq, as well as setting up the Guantanamo Bay detention facility in Cuba. There will also be a consideration of how such measures, and indeed representations of terrorism by the media, have altered over time.

Perhaps the key aspect of the definition of terrorism is the central idea that terrorism has a political motive, a point driven home by both leading authors, as well as the American security agencies themselves. Providing such a definition allows us to separate terrorism from acts of violence, murder, warfare, or activities conducted by guerrilla groups. Terrorism is also classed as such because it tends to focus upon attacking civilians (soft targets) and there must be an attempt to influence a target audience, for example by bringing about a change of government policy.

The following chapters have been arranged chronologically in order to demonstrate that American history has never been free of terrorist incidents at home, and increasingly abroad. Whilst there have been historical periods when terrorism represented a much lower level of threat to America than at present, there was never an era when terrorism disappeared from the American narrative.

2

EARLY AMERICAN TERRORISM, 1776–1886

Whilst there can be debate about the extent to which early events both before and after the American Revolution can be regarded as incidences of terrorism, there were many incidences during this early period that fit into our definition. Terrorism within America predates even the founding of the Republic in 1776. As Yungher notes, US history is plagued by a long record of terrorism, which included the expulsion of the original inhabitants from their native lands and the establishment of slavery (2008, p. 120). The early years of the Republic saw targeted violence conducted against several groups, with the intention of denying those groups political influence. The large influx of new settlers into the US during the nineteenth century brought not only internal tensions, but specifically targeted campaigns. Mormon leader Joseph Smith would be killed by a mob anxious to quell his political ambitions. Fears over Catholic influence in politics help explain the vigorous crackdown on Irish workers in the coalfields of Pennsylvania and the trial and execution of various workers said to be associated with the Molly Maguires, a movement whose very existence is still debated. This period also brings the first assassination attempts against American presidents, starting with the attempted assassination of Andrew Jackson in 1835 and ending with the deaths of presidents Lincoln and Garfield. The case of slavery abolitionist John Brown, who attempted to lead the slaves to armed insurrection prior to the Civil War, provides for a fascinating debate between perceptions of terrorists and freedom fighters. The end of the Civil War in 1865 brought the creation of the Ku Klux Klan, whose first incarnation used violence, intimidation and murder to successfully prevent the racial equality envisaged by the Fourteenth and Fifteenth Amendments. So there are arguments that the Klan can be considered a terrorist organisation. This chapter will also consider the first terrorist actions against American citizens beyond the borders of the US.

Early skirmishes gave way to fierce battles as new settlers and native tribes fought over land and resources. Among such military conflicts there were notable incidents that clearly stepped outside the confines of war. In 1623, Captain William Tucker visited a Powhatan village in order to negotiate a treaty with the tribe. Once a treaty had been concluded, a toast was proposed and poisoned wine was served to the natives. In addition to the 200 Powhatans who died more or less instantly, around another 50 of the tribe were killed by Tucker's men, who took away parts of their heads as trophies (Takaki, 1993, p. 36). There is also an allegation that the British used an early form of biological warfare at the Siege of Fort Pitt. During a Native American uprising led by Chief Pontiac of the Ottawa tribe in 1763, Captain Simeon Ecuyer would give the tribe two blankets and a handkerchief laced with smallpox spores. This succeeded in decimating the tribe, who possessed no natural resistance to the disease, and made sure the British troops held on at the Fort (Robertson, 2001, p. 124).

Jennings certainly views the enforced removal of Native American tribes from their ancestral lands as an early example of state-sponsored terrorism, noting that 'It is sometimes difficult for citizens of the modern United States to fully comprehend the havoc wrought on Indian communities by the republic in its early years' (Jennings, 2015, p86). He cites an 1853 edition of the *Yreka Herald* which effectively called for the extermination of the original tribes. Indeed, a multifaceted campaign of terror was waged against the indigenous populations, with the sole intention of taking the lands for western expansion. The Indian Removal Act of 1830 saw Congress push the federal government to do more to free up the lands held by the various tribes. The Cherokee, increasingly targeted by the Georgia Guard, in an attempt to hold onto their lands took their case to the Supreme Court. Despite winning the case, the refusal of the federal government to enforce the decision meant that the removal could continue with impunity (Lutz, p. 30).

The continued expansion into Native American territory would in 1845 be termed by journalist John O'Sullivan, the 'Manifest Destiny'. In O'Sullivan's interpretation and that of Congress from 1846 it was given a providential underpinning. Tribes were driven off their lands by a mixture of force and fraud and whilst some tribes did fight back, the end result was always the same, with the native Americans removed from their lands. The War of 1812, effectively a rerun of the War of Independence against the British, saw the removal of the last real hope many native American tribes had of retaining their lands. The process of relocating the native American tribes continued throughout the nineteenth century. Yet, despite all these actions, Winkler notes the American Indians were the first group to be labelled as terrorists by the American government because they engaged in practices such as throat slitting and scalping against the colonial settlers (Winkler, 2006, p. 142).

The build-up to the American Revolution utilised forms of terrorism. This can be seen in the actions taken by the colonists to prevent the implementation of the Stamp Act in 1765. The campaign proved highly successful, with few willing to try to enforce the collection of the tax. Violence and intimidation were utilised, especially the practice of tarring and feathering, which proved highly effective in making the Act unenforceable. Such violent actions proved highly successful in changing British foreign policy.The repeal of the Stamp Act by Lord Rockingham in 1766 brought a reduction in tensions that was to prove only temporary and by 1775 British forces were engaging in military actions against American patriots, who responded to the British logistical advantages by engaging in guerrilla tactics and vigilante actions. Attacks against loyalists by William and Charles Lynch would give rise to the terms lynch law and lynching. The fear generated by orchestrated attacks and mob violence proved highly effective, even if by and large the actions did not result in the deaths of those being targeted. The war of 1812 brought atrocities on both sides, as both engaged in attacking non-military targets. There would be the burning of the town of York (now Toronto) as well as the British burning down the White House and the Capitol buildings.

After the War of Independence, America was faced with the task of protecting its citizens both at home, and more problematically given the absence of a navy, overseas. America soon found that task was complicated by attacks on American ships from the Barbary pirates who operated off the North coast of Africa. A lucrative kidnapping and ransom trade soon developed with the newly independent country. Congress may have feared the pirates, but they initially feared the cost of extended government more, and decided instead to allocate $80,000 per year to pay ransoms for American citizens caught by the pirates. This figure proved woefully inadequate and over a ten-year period some two million dollars had to be found to deal with the kidnappers' demands. There was even a system of pricing where a ship's master could fetch some $6,000, with lower sums for lesser crew members (Simon, 2001, pp. 30–31). The American prisoners were held in desperate conditions and wrote letters to the government to highlight their plight and gain support and sympathy in order to generate the money for their release. At the height of the pirates' activities, hundreds of Americans were held captive, creating significant pressure on the government to solve the growing problem. Jeffrey Simon has noted a clear connection between these events and the hostage crisis that would take place some two hundred years later under Ronald Reagan, where there was an attempt to appeal directly to American public opinion (Simon, 2001, p. 30). Kidnappers inevitably draw attention to the fact that countries are simply not able to protect their citizens at all times in all places, and states that are seen to be unable to protect their own nationals are seen as weak and vulnerable. America was at the mercy of actions taken against its own citizens thousands of miles from its own shores. The American ambassador to France, future president Thomas Jefferson, found himself involved in the hostage negotiations and despite his belief in smaller government, he became increasingly frustrated by the threat to American shipping and pushed for a strong response; but under John Adams the policy of paying 'tributes' continued, with Congress unwilling to take direct action (Leiner, 2006, p. 21).

By the end of 1790, the first American president George Washington was already addressing Congress regarding the need for a military solution to the problem via the creation of an American navy to help safeguard American shipping and civilians, but no immediate action was taken. America fell back on the policy of paying off the pirates, which in 1795 brought the first arms-for-hostages deal, when arms, as well as a million-dollar pay-off (alongside subsequent annual tributes) were agreed in a treaty with the Dey of Algiers. To put the amount in perspective, a million dollars was a sixth of the entire US budget. This resulted in the release of over a hundred American hostages, but the temporary 'victory' was soon negated by the capture of more Americans in what had become a highly lucrative business for the pirates. The same conundrum faced Ronald Reagan when dealing with the hostage takers during the 1980s.

Inevitably, only a military response would subdue the pirates who had little other incentive to desist. American anger over the actions of the pirates was one of the main reasons why America was able to overcome the reluctance of some to build up a navy, despite worries over the cost. The dangers posed by the pirates succeeded in uniting different sections of American opinion over the issue of an expanded military force. Actions taken by the US included a military attack on the Libyan capital, Tripoli. The same location would be the centre of a military strike by Reagan in 1986. The end of the threat from the pirates was achieved over a number of years and a series of wars, before the US finally proved to be triumphant in 1815.

Under the definition of terrorism set out in the opening chapter, it is clear that the pirates themselves were not terrorists. Their motivations were not political, since their aim was purely financial gain, if the ransoms were paid they had no interest in who governed America. The inclusion of the Barbary pirates here is because of their use of terrorist methods, kidnapping and enforced imprisonment to achieve their aims – and the reaction of America in taking the first proactive external steps to protect itself from these terrorist tactics. The events would provide a future echo of problems that America would face in the late twentieth century.

The early origins of terrorism in America have not attracted a large amount of academic attention, although this has been partly corrected in recent years by scholars such as Robert Kumamoto and Matthew Jennings. Jennings highlights various areas in which recognisable terrorist acts were committed in the early Republic. These areas include actions against Native Americans during the invasion of British North America, against Mexico in the 1840s, against newly arrived immigrants to the US, and over the issue of slavery.

The war against Mexico (1846–1848) may seem a surprising inclusion, but Jennings includes this because of the way in which the combatants, the vast majority of whom were volunteers, attacked civilians and ignored the established customs of warfare. Whilst the regular army tended to stay within these rules of warfare, the volunteers would engage in sexual violence, robbery and murder of innocent civilians (Jennings, 2015, p. 87).

In 1798, America, caught up between the warring powers of Britain and France, would pass the Alien and Sedition Acts, which meant aliens could be imprisoned at will by the government during times of war. They also controversially criminalised seditious writings. As Douglas Bradburn (2008) has noted, these acts generated significant opposition. The patriotic fervour of the time raised tensions and brought reprisals against those who did not seem to represent the new 'national character' of America. The Federalists in particular were keen to push an ideal that American citizenship could only be granted to 'true Americans'. There was an attempt to create a homogeneous vision of American citizenry in order to secure America against threats of war or sedition.

The Alien and Sedition Acts would be a clear antecedent to the Sedition Acts (1917 & 1918), Executive Order 9066, which imprisoned Japanese Americans during World War Two, and the PATRIOT Act of 2001.

A pamphlet entitled *What Is our Situation. And what are our Prospects? A Few Pages for Americans, by an American* written by Joseph Hopkinson (whose father had written the first national song, 'Hail Columbia') stated that true Americans must focus on enemies within the country: 'The great source of all our political evils and misfortunes ... is the facility with which foreigners acquire the full and perfect rights of citizenship.' He also noted that emigrants represented 'none but the vile and the worthless, none but the idle and discontented, the disorderly and the wicked' (1799, p. 20). Such notions brought large petitions of support to the Adams government, but his failure to go to war with France in 1798 destroyed his chances at the 1800 election. Such tensions and patriotism were easily whipped up in times of potential conflict and could be employed against political opponents.

In a new and excellent study, Mel Ayton has traced the various assassination attempts against the early American presidents, noting that many presidents after Jackson faced them, indeed some faced multiple attempts, which were often kept secret to shore up confidence in the presidency and to prevent copycat actions. Many of the would-be assassins were either suffering from mental illness, or were seeking to redress failed lives by seeking fame or infamy by their actions. As such, only those attempts against presidents and others in authority which had political motives will be assessed in this and later chapters, except possibly for the first, below.

The first attempt to assassinate an American president would take place in January 1835 against Andrew Jackson, by then a relatively old and an increasingly sick man. The president's would-be assailant was British-born Richard Lawrence, who tackled the president on the steps of the Capitol Building. Lawrence had a history of mental illness, which often resulted in violence, and was even declared insane by a doctor who treated him for a minor medical ailment (Ayton, 2017, p. 33). Jackson was attending the funeral of Warren R. Davis of South Carolina. As the president left the service, Lawrence fired a pistol at close range. Not for the first time in his life, Jackson had to attack an assailant, this time he beat Lawrence with his cane Lawrence, armed with a second pistol, fired again, but remarkably this gun also misfired and Lawrence was quickly overcome by those on the scene, who included Davy Crockett. Jackson's near miss was all the more remarkable given that tests on the pistols revealed that they were properly loaded and worked as normal when later examined.

Lawrence was soon put on trial and found not guilty by reason of insanity within just five minutes of the jury retiring to consider their verdict. This should represent a clear-cut case of an action which simply cannot fall under the umbrella of terrorism and yet both sides of the political divide would soon seek to make capital out of the event. Jackson's opponents soon accused him of staging the attack, especially as it seemed unlikely that two pistols could misfire. Conversely, Jackson's allies were not against using threats against the president to bolster support for him (notably death threats published in the *Globe* newspaper, who also interviewed Lawrence and declared him sane).

Jackson himself openly accused his rival Senator George Poindexter of Mississippi of being behind the attack and a Senate investigation was called, which found no evidence of a connection between Poindexter and Lawrence (Rohrs, (1981).

A more political dimension can certainly be made out in the case of Joseph Smith, who published the *Book of Mormon* in 1830. Smith originally began his church in New York, before local tensions forced him to move to Ohio and then Missouri, where violence erupted, pushing the group to Nauvoo in Illinois. It was not just Smith's religious beliefs that provoked local animosities. Smith stated that he expected the overthrow of the nation within a few years, anticipating that a 'kingdom of Saints' would follow (Turner, 2012, p. 105) and soon he began exercising some political authority within the city, even arguing that he was permitted to veto certain state and national laws (Lutz & Lutz, 2007, p. 20). When Smith and his followers moved to destroy a printing press that had published negative stories about him, he was seen to be attacking the constitutional right to free speech. Such actions led to his arrest, along with his brother, Hyrum. Smith was fatally shot on 27 June 1844 by an armed mob whilst imprisoned in Carthage Jail (Western Illinois). This would lead Brigham Young to take the Mormon community to Salt Lake City. What is interesting about the death of Smith was that it took place after he had announced that he would be standing in the 1844 US presidential election as a third party candidate. Smith argued for a 'theodemocracy, where God and the people hold the power' and a Council of Fifty helped plan out his presidential campaign. Fears that there could be a Mormon takeover, or that he could influence the course of the election, give the actions of the 'mob' a political motive, with the suspicion that the event was orchestrated by others, perhaps even leaders within the Whig Party keen to preserve the political status quo. The fact that those accused of Smith's murder were soon acquitted seems to give weight to this idea.

The first half of the nineteenth century gave rise to terrorism committed by both sides of the slavery divide. During the first half of the century riots targeted black communities, often forcing people out of their homes in cities such as New York, Washington D.C. and Philadelphia. The northern states remained ambivalent about the end of slavery and those who advocated its removal faced the threat of violent reprisal. One dramatic example of this came when the pro-abolitionist Illinois newspaper editor Elijah Lovejoy was shot dead in November 1837.

Few figures encapsulate more aptly the adage one man's heretic is another man's fighter for the true faith than John Brown (1800–59). As Robert Maxwell notes, for some in the northern states Brown would be the inspiration for a holy war against slavery, whilst in the South he provided proof that the two sides of the slavery debate could not exist in the same state (Maxwell, 1979, p. 22). Brown's actions at Harpers Ferry would provide a final spark that would plunge America into the Civil War. The key issue would be that of slavery, which provided the potential for terrorist acts to come to fruition as both sides of the divide increasingly moved towards violence and murder in order to further their desired outcome.

Brown's life had seen much hardship and many business failures across several states before his hatred of slavery brought him toward violent actions, which it can easily be argued fall within the category of terrorism. Brown first came to prominence via his actions in Pottawatomie during the struggles that broke out over the future slave status of Kansas. In May of 1856, in retaliation for pro-slavery forces attacking Lawrence in the northeast, Brown attacked Pottawatomie Creek, some fifty miles to the south, dragging out five residents in the middle of the night and then stabbing them to death in the nearby woodland. The random nature of selection of those too far away to have taken part in the events in Lawrence, and who did not possess slaves, means that Brown effectively targeted innocent civilians in a political cause, fitting the criteria of terrorism. Brown went into hiding, re-emerging from time to time to help free further slaves, until his decision to try to make a second, far more important intervention.

Brown's lawyer, George Hoyt, attempted to prove mental instability at the trial via nineteen affidavits from those who knew Brown, which, if successful, would have simply reduced the actions to those of a madman, rather than someone who clearly knew both the seriousness and consequences of his actions. Although at his trial Brown would deny violent intent, he eagerly accepted the martyrdom that his sentence provided, refusing suggestions of rescue and openly stating that his blood would advance the cause further than any of his other actions (Oates, 1984, p. 336). His final written statement ahead of his execution stated that the 'crimes of this guilty land will never be purged away; but with Blood'. In both 1856 and 1859 Brown had utilised violent actions and encouraged others to rise up and join those actions. It was this willingness to advocate violence that for Gilpin firmly places Brown in the category of terrorist. Brenda and James Lutz share this assessment (Lutz & Lutz, p. 140). Michael Fellman argues that Brown's use of terrorism even viewed through the prism of defeating slavery should not lead us to the conclusion that Brown was what we today term a 'freedom fighter'. Fellman notes that Brown was content to kill innocent victims and his acts splintered

American society, helping to spark the Civil War (Fellman, 2010, p. 18). Once Brown and his sons formed an active group to combat slavery, Brown effectively became a terrorist. Over a century later Brown's actions provided inspiration to the Weather Underground movement who saw him as an iconic figure in American history (Burrough, 2015, p. 362).

Davidson and Lytle state that for every Emerson or Thoreau who pronounced the raid the work of a saint, a southern fire-eater condemned the venture as the villainy of all northerners (1992, p. 145). Among the latter group was John Wilkes Booth, who came to watch Brown hang. Booth could hardly have been further away in terms of Brown's political beliefs, but he soon noted the impact of Brown's actions and the propaganda value of the trial and martyrdom, and this helped inspired Booth's own act of terrorism in conducting the first assassination of an American president.

Lincoln had suffered a long history of presidential assassination threats and indeed the Pinkerton Detective Agency was brought in to offer protection to the new president. As the president during almost the entirety of the Civil War, it was not surprising that Lincoln would face elevated threats to his safety, even if he remained largely reluctant to up the level of his own security. The first ever successful American Presidential assassin would be John Wilkes Booth, who first made an abortive attempt to kill Lincoln during his second inauguration day on March 4.

Robert Maxwell Brown has argued that partly by accident, but also featuring as a direct cause, the Civil War saw a move towards the adoption of political assassination (Maxwell, 1979, p29). One of the curious aspects of Booth's plan to kill the president was that this was part of a wider conspiracy with two other potential assassins. George Atzerodt was planning to assassinate Vice President Andrew Johnson but he found he was unable to carry out the deed; Lewis Powell attempted to kill Secretary of State William Henry Seward, and succeeded in badly wounding him (both would-be assassins were later hanged). Booth's actions were made easier by the fact that Lincoln's own protective guard simply swanned off to a local saloon. Booth himself was an actor who enjoyed sufficient fame as to be known to the president, and his occupation also afforded him easy entry to Ford's Theatre, where earlier he had drilled a hole in the door of the presidential box to better gauge the position of the target. Shooting Lincoln in the head, Booth jumped out of the presidential box onto the stage in front of the shocked audience (breaking his leg in the process), allegedly shouting the phrase 'Sic semper tyrannis' ('thus always to tyrants'). One hundred and thirty years later, in his arrest photos Oklahoma bomber Timothy McVeigh would be wearing a T-shirt containing Thomas Paine's words 'The tree of liberty must be refreshed from time to time with the blood of patriots and tyrants.' Thomas Goodrich comments that Booth never saw himself as committing a terrorist act, but a man who considered himself as attempting to emulate his father and act in glory and honour (Goodrich, 2005, p. 43).

After the shooting, Booth managed to hobble out of the theatre onto his horse. With the War Department offering a $50,000 reward and his picture being posted up around the surrounding areas, evading capture was all but impossible and he was killed in a shoot-out at Garrett farm on 26 April. The dying president was ferried across to a small bed in the Peterson House directly across from the theatre, where he passed away a few hours later. There was no sustained attempt to create a greater level of security for future presidents, as the event was seen as exceptional and presidents still wanted to maintain an air of openness and accessibility.

For Goodrich and Fellman, the actions of both Brown and Booth had an important additional dimension, so important to terrorism. This was the ability to inspire others to follow the cause and imitation would indeed follow, and Lincoln would be one of four American presidents to be slain by gunfire.

The American Civil War had an interesting repercussion in terms of the history of terrorism in that it killed off any potential desire for areas of the country to break away into independent nations. Many countries, not least the United Kingdom and Spain, have suffered terrorist attacks by groups wanting to achieve either independence or alternative governmental structures. The one exception to this is the Puerto Rican independence movement, which undertook an intermittent, violent campaign in America from 1950 until the 1980s, as explored in chapters four and five.

The actions of Booth were to be characterised by some as the work of someone who was mentally unbalanced, despite the obvious political motivation. Even well into the twentieth century, it proved very difficult to get Americans to accept there could be a rational political purpose as the explanation behind the assassination of political leaders (Clarke, 1981, p. 99).

Gilpin argued Booth 'inaugurated a broader kind of terror, a unique American terrorism that served a formal political party, underwrote the social, economic and political hierarchies of the South, and virulently fought to forestall change.' (Gilpin, 2015, p145). The end of the Civil War in April 1865 may have signalled the end of the military campaigns, but soon leading white southerners would find ways of regaining their powerbase and preventing former slaves from exercising their newly won social and political freedoms. Just one year after the end of the War the Ku Klux Klan came into existence. The group, albeit in various incarnations and revivals, has existed, with some gaps, from its founding in Pulaski, Tennessee, until the present day. The group's central motivation was to maintain white supremacy and prevent the successful implementation of the Thirteenth Amendment, which abolished slavery and involuntary servitude in 1865. The group had a clear political agenda to deprive the former slaves of gaining any form of political or social equality. Daniel Goldberg has argued that the Klan were a terrorist group intent on the violent overthrow of the Reconstruction governments established in the South (Goldberg, 1999, p. 117). It is worth noting that the Klan also attacked whites, especially those who supported the Republicans, or who showed sympathy with the former slaves.

The first organised convention took place in Nashville in May 1867, which anointed Nathan Bedford Forrest, who had fought in the Confederate Cavalry, as the first 'Grand Wizard of the Invisible Empire'. Tactics of the Klan in the post-Civil-War era included lynching, burnings, beatings and harassment, and given that these tactics were conducted for political purposes, to hold and maintain political power, the group, and indeed its later reincarnations, ably fits the definition of a terrorist organisation.

In 1870 the Klan murdered North Carolina senator John Walker Stephens, fearing his effectiveness as a radical Republican, popular among the former slaves. The group rose in importance during the 1870s, so much so that even President Ulysses Grant, whose two terms as president (1869–77) personified limited government, felt compelled to urge Congress to pass legislation to curtail the Klan, in opposition to liberal Republicans. During 1870–71 three Enforcement Acts were passed, with the Klan as the main target, which even allowed for a temporary passing of martial law and use of federal troops, giving the opportunity to scatter the Klan. The Acts did have some limited success in curtailing some of the activities of the group and even the first Imperial Wizard, Nathan Bedford Forrest, believed it was time to end the Klan. Inevitably, both then and in later decades, prosecution of Klan members proved extremely difficult, not least as many officials from the southern states were members, their features hidden behind white robes. Local enforcement officials were highly reluctant to investigate the group's activities, assuming they had any desire to do so at all, and all-white juries were clearly biased towards defendants or intimidated by threats of violence. However, the actions of President Grant and Congress in rounding up and prosecuting Klansmen did prove effective. In addition, the end of the Reconstruction era in 1877, when northern forces withdrew from the southern states, also took away much of the impetus for the group's existence and the original Klan effectively died out.

Eric Foner has clearly stated that the Klan was a terrorist association (Foner, 2009, p. 549). He argues that the group offers us an example of mass terrorism, noting that some thirty former slaves were murdered, along with a white Republican judge, in Meridian, Mississippi, in 1871, and in 1873 in Colfax, Louisiana, hundreds of former slaves were murdered. Edward Hyams has argued that the terrorist campaign conducted by the KKK enjoyed considerable success in that the group achieved their central aim of white supremacy by effectively disenfranchising over half of southern voters for over a hundred years, thereby denying the African American population the protection of the laws of the republic (Hyams, 1975, p. 13). At this time the Klan were not the only organisation spreading fear in the communities, as groups such as the 'Jayhawkers', 'Regulators' and 'Black Horse Cavalry' also operated, for much the same reasons as the Klan.

The end of the first incarnation of the Klan did not bring an end to terrorism. Political violence rose significantly during election years. The peak years for lynching, a term that by this point has come to mean extrajudicial execution, would be during the 1890s, and the vast majority of victims would be former slaves. Whilst lynching of former slaves would comprise one of the most graphic incidences of racial repression at this time, it was not the only example. The end of the nineteenth century also saw the Chinese population targeted. Roger Daniels has argued that at this time no group, aside from Native Americans, suffered as much violence as the Chinese communities (Daniels, 1988, p. 58). Chinese immigrants were beaten and murdered, and a number of cities experienced anti-Chinese riots; the Los Angeles riot of 1871 saw twenty-one Chinese shot, hanged or burned alive (Daniels, 1988, p. 59). Violence increased following the 1882 Chinese Exclusion Act. James and Brenda Lutz have described the persecution of the Chinese community as among the worst examples of communal terrorism in American history (Lutz & Lutz, 2007, p. 45).

One of the most intriguing examples of terrorism in America to occur during this period concerns a terrorist group that some authors, such as J. Walter Coleman, have argued was a fabrication. Much controversy surrounds discussion of the Molly Maguires. The group have been identified as 'a secret society of Irish miners with loose ties to the Irish fraternal association called the Ancient Order of the Hibernians' (Kumamoto, 2014, p. 253). Irish immigration into America rose dramatically during the years of the potato famine in the 1840s. It rose from about 170,000 during the decade from 1830–39 to over 656,000 from 1840–49, peaking at over 1 million from 1850–59 (Tindall & Shi, 2013, A116).

Such a large influx of Catholic immigrants caused significant tensions and resulted in riots breaking out in several US cities, one of the largest being in Philadelphia in 1844, where Catholic sectors were attacked for a period of three days over a dispute regarding the use of proscribed Catholic bibles in city schools (Lutz & Lutz, 2007, p39). Across New England anti-Catholic violence became increasingly common in the 1850s. Fear of Catholics gaining a political foothold resulted in the emergence of the American Party, better known as the 'Know-Nothing Party' as it emerged from a secret society. The party stood on a vigorously anti-Catholic platform and utilised violence in their political campaigns in order to suppress voting. In the 1850s they became a formidable political force, winning the governorship of Massachusetts, as well as winning mayoral positions in Philadelphia, Chicago and San Francisco.

In 1856, an election marked by violence and intimidation, they gained 21.6 per cent of the popular vote, being represented by former Whig president Millard Fillmore.

The suspicion of and violence against the Catholic communities was fertile ground for the industrial suppression of these new labourers, who often worked in enterprises such as coal mining. It was very much in the interests of the wealthy and the influential members of society to minimise unrest and keep the work force in line via suppression of any possible disputes and by removing any internal threats to the smooth running of their business operations. This was to be greatly facilitated by the creation of the Pinkerton Detective Agency in Chicago in 1850.[1]

Labour disputes in America proved to be considerably more violent than those in Europe. Louis Adamic wrote that given the labour situation that prevailed at that time, it was quite natural for organised terrorism to arise (Adamic, 2008, p. 17). From the 1860s America began experiencing significant labour unrest and such struggles provided a major source of terrorism. Worker movements gave a voice to discontent and made militant activism possible, especially in trades such as the coal mining industry in Pennsylvania. Walter Laqueur has stated that the Molly Maguires represented an example of working class terrorism (2008, p. 11). The Molly Maguires were an alleged secret association who were responsible for murder, kidnapping and sabotage, against both those who owned and operated the mines, and also against fellow workers who were not of Irish origin and Roman Catholic. The name itself began appearing in American newspapers in 1857. Robert Kumamoto has argued that no incidents of American terrorism have been shrouded in as much mystery as the violent events of this time. Since virtually no concrete evidence of such

---

1   Allan Pinkerton had been appointed Chicago's first police detective in 1849; his agency had 20 offices across the US by 1906, and the organisation continues to the present day.

as association exists, there is little agreement on whether such a movement was real, or a fiction perpetuated by mine owners and politicians keen to provide a justification to suppress potential worker unrest or rebellion. There is for example, no agreement on whether there was even a real person by the name of Molly Maguire, although the origins of such a movement could potentially be linked to the landlord and peasant disputes that had prevailed in Ireland.

Franklin Gowen, a hugely controversial figure, headed the powerful Philadelphia and Reading Railroad Company and during his time in control came the Great Railroad Strike of 1877, a violent dispute caused by wage reductions. At least ten workers were killed. Gowen certainly had a vested interest in exploiting fears about worker uprisings and turned to the Pinkerton Detective Agency to infiltrate the worker movement. James McParland would spend two-and-a-half years undercover, up to March 1876, and would provide much of the, often suspect, testimony against members of the Molly Maguire movement.[2] His infiltration of the group led, apparently, to the group's demise (Bulik, 2015, p. 288).

Tellingly, it would be Allan Pinkerton himself who wrote the first text on the Molly Maguires, *The Molly Maguires and the Detectives*, in 1877. The book ran to over five hundred pages, stressing the dangers of the movement to American society. The seventh chapter, for example, entitled 'Bloody record of the Mollie Maguires', sets out a record of various murders, which the author described as 'skilfully planned and relentlessly carried out, and the bleeding bodies and evidences on the ground of a deadly struggle were all remaining to tell the tale of cruelty' (1877, p. 71). Pinkerton would also compare the Maguires to the Thugs[3]

---

2   His name would appear as McParlan in Pinkerton's book.

3   Thuggee, from which we derive the word 'thug' were a group that robbed and killed travellers across parts of the Indian subcontinent for several hundred years, before the takeover of British forces in the nineteenth century.

and argued that a tough response was need to combat the threat. Laqueur has argued that the movement was initially seen as linked to communism (2012, p. 15), which, whilst false, fits in with first Red Scare that will be further explored in the following chapter.

Unsurprisingly, and based on the 'evidence' provided by McParland, various workers found themselves subjected to unfair trials and twenty workers were hanged between the years 1876–78. Those executed included the so-called 'king of the Maguires' John Kehoe, who would be pardoned in 1979. McParland's evidence would also result in a further twenty-five imprisonments for members of the Maguires. Bulik has stated that the early apologists for the prosecutions that took place portrayed those hanged as primitive terrorists who brought Old World methods of resistance into the New World (Bulik, 2015, p. 7).

It was not until the 1930s that an alternative perspective was put forward that in fact, it was the workers movements and the coal workers themselves that had been subject to terror tactics, and that any violent responses against the employers should be seen in that light. (Although even in the 1940s authors such as Anthony Bomba were prepared to place the blame for various unsolved murders on the group.)

Whilst Louis Adamic had no real doubts about the existence of the group, even believing that there was a real figure of Molly Maguire (Adamic, 2008, pp. 12–13), some later authors were less keen to accept this. In 1969 Charles McCarthy concluded that any suggestion of a movement was little more than a hoax, although ironically this was the same year that Hollywood made a high profile movie about the group starring Sean Connery as Kehoe and Richard Harris as McParland, *The Molly Maguires* (it flopped). Labour leader and author Sidney Lens in 1973 would also state that the movement was no more real than fairies.

However, more in-depth research for the period of the 1870s does reveal that there were many incidents taking place at this time which do indeed fit into the category of terrorism. The *Miner's Journal* (Pottsville, Pa., 1837–69) would list six murders between the years 1863–68 that they attributed to the Maguires (out of a total of fifty murders). A further ten murders were to be attributed to the Molly Maguires between the years 1870–75.

Some of the most recent research into the group has included that by Kevin Kenny, whose 1998 book, *Making Sense of the Molly Maguires*, argued that whilst there was no widespread terrorist threat, there was a pattern of 'sustained but sporadic' violence by workers (1998, p. 285). In the end Kenny does not deny the existence of the group, or that they did conduct assassinations. Even more recently Kumamoto has argued that the Maguires were guilty of murder and industrial espionage, although suggestions of a widespread conspiracy were clearly overstated. He concludes that the Maguires were the 'quintessential American terrorists' (2014, p. 279).

It seems logical to deduce that at this turbulent time that there was some loose form of organisation engaging in violence, kidnapping, sabotage and murder. In order to fit our criteria for terrorism, the group must have a political motive rather than just one of revenge or an attempt to pressure employers. Evidence of a wider political goal can be seen not only with an attempt to garner better worker conditions but also in the attempts to gain power in the political arena, something that Adamic argues the Mollies achieved within Pennsylvania where their concentrated numbers brought them a strong power base, which he argues allowed them to improve living conditions for miners across the region (Adamic, 2008, pp. 16–18). One reality is that whatever group did exist during these years, any danger it represented and any terrorist incidents that it carried out were much exaggerated by figures such as Pinkerton, who stood to gain financially from creating the idea that he had been responsible for breaking up a significant threat to American society. Like the anarchist threats that will be covered in the next two chapters, those in positions of power gained both authority and prestige by claiming to eradicate threats within the state, as well as maintaining their support base within the business community, for whom a compliant workforce maximised profits.

Just sixteen years after the death of Lincoln, an unguarded President Garfield was assassinated by Charles Guiteau, just four months after assuming office. Guiteau shot the president in the arm and then the back at the railway station in Washington D.C. on 2 July 1881. The president hung on in great pain but died on 10 September. Although authors such as Robert Maxwell Brown and Charles Rosenberg have stressed that Guiteau was suffering from mental illness; the jury refused to believe – despite his eccentric performance in court and his claim that he had been ordered to conduct the killing by God – that Guiteau was insane and found him guilty of murder. Complicating the issue was the fact that Guiteau was a stalwart Republican who backed the patronage system. He had offered to work in support of the Garfield campaign, although his help was refused. A new president could potentially have reversed Garfield's reforms, so there was in theory a political motive behind Garfield's slaying. Some rejected the idea that an American president could be slain for political purposes out of hand. A contemporary article by William R. Smith written in 1881 stated that 'The idea of a political conspiracy, encompassing the life of a great party leader for party purposes, *must not* be entertained in this country' (Clarke, 1981, p. 83). Smith was at least correct in this case, as after his hanging on 30 June 1882, an autopsy revealed that Guiteau was suffering a brain disease (Tindall & Shi, 2016, p. 720).[4] As such, despite Guiteau's modest link to a political cause, his mental state at the time of the assassination makes it impossible to classify his act as one of terrorism. Oddly, despite his actions and the public support

---

4   Presidential assassin Leon Czolgosz also had his brain examined for signs of
     brain disease, but this remained unconfirmed.

for the death penalty, Charles Guiteau did not attract the universal hatred of later presidential assassin Leon Czolgosz. He would be given the opportunity to have a fair trial and fully address the court. He even received scores of support messages including one that stated 'All Boston sympathises with you. You ought to be president' (Drinnon, 1961, p. 74).

The claim that the forced removal of indigenous inhabitants of North American lands were subject to terrorism is naturally controversial, as is the notion that aspects of terrorism accompanied both the 1812 War, the Mexican War and the religious disturbances of the middle of the nineteenth century. These are potentially open to more debate than the later examples of terrorism that will follow. However, this chapter has demonstrated that within these historical events terrorist tactics were utilised, both by and against the government and its citizens. It is notable that terrorist activity took place on both sides of the slavery divide, with the actions of both John Brown and James Booth, as well as the early incarnation of the Ku Klux Klan. Whilst perhaps not the final word, recent research has suggested that the Molly Maguires, or at least some form of loose affiliation, existed during the 1850–1870s that engaged in terrorist actions. Although such actions were quickly exploited for political and economic gain by employers and agencies who stood to gain from hyping up both the threat from the groups and their role in removing that threat. As will be seen, the idea of hyping up a terrorist threat for political gain would be a common thread in American history.

3

THE ANARCHIST ERA

The anarchist era represents a time when an increasing number of high-profile terrorist attacks took place on American soil. As we noted in the opening chapter, this era corresponds to David Rapoport's first wave of terrorism, and is a time when terrorist attacks heavily impacted American society. The last decades of the nineteenth century had proved especially violent in parts of Europe with many anarchist groups successfully targeting heads of state. America attracted a number of high-profile anarchist thinkers who journeyed over from Europe, many with the express desire of attacking capitalism. The end of the Civil War saw America enter a period of economic boom, which Mark Twain famously labelled the 'Gilded Age'.[5] The period from 1880–1900 saw America take over as the world's leader in industrial output, and whilst there was growing wealth for many workers, disparities of wealth grew alarmingly. There was era of the rise of the 'robber barons' such as John D. Rockefeller and Andrew Carnegie, whose enjoyment of economic and political power brought vast wealth, whilst working conditions, despite improvements in some areas, remained poor for many employees. There was therefore much

---

5   *The Gilded Age* (1873) was actually co-written by Twain and Charles Dudley Warner.

opportunity to exploit workers' unhappiness and grievances over their pay and conditions.

Anarchism, a term first used in 1840 by Pierre-Joseph Proudhon,[6] means the absence of authority or government, and its link to terrorism came via the methods some were prepared to advocate in order to achieve this end. It is important to outline that most anarchists, including Proudhon and such figures as Leo Tolstoy, were opposed to the use of violence to achieve their aim of the creation of an anarchist society (Novak, 1954, 176).[7] Though Staughton Lynd and Andrej Grubacic have argued that despite many historical differences, both Marxism and anarchism have a shared predilection for terrorist violence. They argue that terrorism (that directed at civilians as well as combatants) is something that anarchists have considered necessary to create a new society (2008, p. 232). In reality, anarchists have always been divided over the issue of force since the concept is essentially humanitarian and therefore opposed to violence. Leading anarchist author Peter Kropotkin (1842–1921) who pushed the idea of 'propaganda by word' was aware of the paradox of utilising violence to achieve anarchist aims, but was also keen to point out that governments seldom hesitated to use violence against those they considered enemies of the state (Novak, 1954, p. 177).

For most politicians, security services, and journalists there was rarely any attempt made to differentiate an anarchist from a communist, a socialist, a trade unionist, or indeed a terrorist. The fact that many of the leading figures in the anarchist movement in America were foreign and often rallied support from newly arrived workers created a situation where many anarchists were viewed with deep suspicion, which always limited their impact

---

6   Proudhon (1809-65) is perhaps most famous for declaring that 'property is theft' in his work *What is Property?*

7   William Godwin (1756–1836) was the first person to call himself an anarchist, although Tolstoy never directly did so.

and influence. It would also, as we will see, make it easier for the security services to detain and deport some of these key anarchist leaders as the movement reached its final stages in the Red Scare that followed World War One.

In 1848 Karl Marx and Friedrich Engels had published their *Communist Manifesto*, which implored the working men of the world (the proletariat) to unite together to break the chains of their oppression. That same year many came to the US to escape from government crackdowns following the failed revolutions in the Austrian Empire, Sicily, France, Germany and Italy. By 1872, the International Workingmen's Association (which Marx had helped to create in London) had moved its headquarters to New York City. Marx argued that the socialist revolution might happen peaceably in America (and potentially Great Britain). Many more Germans arrived following Bismarck's Anti-Socialist law in 1878, where even socialist members of the Reichstag would find themselves under arrest.

As Philip Taft and Philip Ross note in the book *Violence in America*, this era represents a bloody period of labour history, with some governors even calling upon President Rutherford B. Hayes to give federal assistance to employers to deal with strikers in West Virginia in 1877; something the president acquiesced to (1979, p. 190). Riots and strikes became prevalent in many states. As Richard Jensen notes, anarchists did not initially call for terrorist tactics, but this changed as a result of the harsh social environment in which many workers found themselves (2010, p. 116). Trades unions would find themselves in a difficult position. Many trade union leaders feared violence and recognised that was often counter-productive, since employers could often call upon greater financial resources, security measures, the potential to fire workers, and rally the press and high-level politicians to help defend them.

Key to the increased threat from terrorism was dynamite, invented by Alfred Nobel in 1867. By 1875 Nobel had created the even more powerful gelignite. Dynamite gave the terrorists a weapon of almost unimaginable power. This helped lead to what became known as 'the decade of the bomb' (Barton, 2015, p. 308) as anarchists could now leave explosives in public places, which inevitably endangered innocent civilians.

The first actual anarchist society in America, The Social Revolutionary Club, was founded in 1880 in New York. This group upheld the principle of 'propaganda by deed', focussing on the need for direct action. They were the first to fully make use of dynamite, and would celebrate Tsar Alexander II's assassination in 1881 by the left-wing revolutionary group *Narodnaya Volya* (Party of the People's Will), who were one of the first modern terrorist organisations in the world. Four months later in London, an international congress of anarchists endorsed the use of terrorism as 'propaganda by deed', the idea that violence was necessary to create change, first argued by the Italian anarchist Carlo Pisacane (Barton, 2015, p. 306). At a Chicago conference in 1881 a resolution was adopted which recognised 'the armed organizations of workingmen who stand ready with the gun to resist encroachment upon their rights, and recommend the formation of like organizations in all states'. However, as Taft and Ross indicate, the attempt to unite the scattered groups of social revolutionaries was unsuccessful (1979, p. 189). 1883 brought the Pittsburgh Manifesto, with contributions from Albert Parsons and August Spies, who would both be executed for the events at Haymarket. The document had obvious Marxist leanings and pushed for the destruction of the existing class structure by direct action. Spies edited the *Arbeiter-Zeitung*, the German-language anarchist newspaper, from 1873; Parsons edited *The Alarm*, an anarchist newspaper that defended the use of dynamite, referring to it as 'the emancipator' – 'of all the good stuff, that is the stuff' (quoted in Adamic, 2008, p. 35). As Carl Smith points out, Parsons had not always been in favour of the use of violence, but his involvement in the railroad strike of 1877 led him to become 'a social outlaw' to the business elites of Chicago (Smith, 1996, p. 109). Even his wife, Lucy Parsons, would in the pages of *The Alarm* exhort the poor not to give into their situation but to use the opportunities presented by dynamite against the rich.

The anarchist leader with the greatest impact at this time was Johann Most, who was born in Augsburg, Bavaria, in 1846. Most was imprisoned in both Austria and Germany for agitating against the ruling classes. A crackdown on socialists in Germany led him to move to Britain where he would also spend time in prison for openly calling for the assassination of Russian Tsar Alexander II (Gay & Gay, 1999, p. 147), after which he was invited to the US to undertake a lecture tour. Most's arrival in 1882 was seen as a triumph for New York City's German workers, with those of German stock making up a significant portion of organised labour at this time. Most set about giving talks to try to rally the masses, addresses which included information on the making of bombs and poisons. It was Most who stressed the importance of direct action to undermine the political system. He published his newspaper *Freiheit* (which can translate as either freedom or liberty) in 1879, initially in London, before bringing it to the US, the readership of the journal peaking at around 25,000 copies (Laqueur, 2012, p. 56). For Most, speeches and demonstrations were not enough; violence was required to create the physical overthrow of the political system. Most therefore became 'the leading apostle of terrorist acts' (Anderson, 1998, p. 89) by further championing the notion of 'propaganda by deed' over notions of 'propaganda by thought'. For Most this concept was a key aspect of revolutionary activity. As Novak points out, such deeds were to have an educational value, reminding people of their ongoing oppression and the need to overthrow their governing systems (Novak, 1954, p. 177). He also notes that whilst officially printed literature could not incite people to direct action, once such actions had been committed there could then be a more open consideration of the events and an attempt to explain or justify them (Novak, p. 176).

Most was to be depicted as the very image of a mad anarchist bomber. As Clymer notes 'with his bushy beard and gesticulatory speaking style' he became 'the prototype for the ubiquitous caricatures of anarchists as unkempt and wildly buffoonish figures that appeared in mainstream newspapers' (Clymer, 2003, p. 8). Due to an infection as a child, part of his jawbone was removed, leaving him permanently disfigured, helping to make illustrations of Most even more sinister. As the most feared and vilified man of the time, contemporary cartoons such as those featured in *Harper's Weekly* would depict Most as holding a sabre or a gun (in addition to showing him as a coward after the events at Haymarket). Most would ironically find work in an explosives factory in Jersey City, which helped him to pioneer new techniques, such as letter bombs (Laqueur, 2012, p. 59). Curiously, despite Most's writings and speeches, he never personally seems to have practised the art of violent protest and was not a hands-on practitioner.

It is hard to define how much impact Most had within America. Many newspapers did not report the content of his speeches, so his statements struggled to reach a wider audience. As Randall Law has commented, since most anarchists were of foreign origin, they already attracted suspicion from many. Whilst there were several thousand anarchists at the height of the movement, and many more would have shared some sympathy with some of their values, the vast majority of Americans viewed anarchism with deep distrust. James Green does note that 6,000 people turned out in Chicago in 1882 to hear Most speak against the evils of capitalism and the class war being waged against the poor (Green, p. 95).

Perhaps the greatest significance of Most lay in his impact on others in the anarchist movement. His beliefs for example inspired Emma Goldman, who would go onto become the most prominent anarchist in America. Emma Goldman represented a more uncompromising anarchist figure. Dubbed 'Red Emma' and the 'Anarchist Queen', Goldman found herself portrayed as the most dangerous woman in the US and its most visible anarchist (Gay and Gay, 1999, p. 91). She became more radicalised by the events at Haymarket. Goldman was born in June 1869, in Kovno, Russia, to Jewish parents.[8] Her parent's marriage and most of Goldman's childhood was an unhappy one. With her sister Helena's help, she was able to move to the US at the end of 1885. Goldman would meet Most in the summer of 1889 and he became her chief guide and mentor, Most even inviting her on a lecture tour to New England, where the two were housed in a boat that Goldman considered most luxurious. Most helped stir up public feeling ahead of events at Haymarket. In 1885 he published his handbook, *The Science of Revolutionary Warfare*, which proclaimed that 'the hour of battle is near.' In July of that year police had violently moved against workers during a streetcar strike, where even passers-by were subjected to physical attacks. Newspapers seemed to be able to discover a terrorist plot in almost every district and helped foment what was effectively the first 'Red Scare' amongst the American public (Jones, 2015, p. 134).

Whilst Chicago had not suffered from any anarchist bombing attacks, it was the city in which the anarchists had the greatest influence during the 1870s and 1880s. By 1885 the city's businesses were deeply worried about workers joining anarchist movements (Green, 2006, p. 144). The city also had an active Socialist Labour Party. The economic elites had powerful support from the newspapers who set out to demonise the anarchist movements and question their allegiance to the US. They were however powerless to prevent a wave of worker unrest that came to be known as the 'great upheaval'. In 1886, 1,400 strikes hit 11,562 businesses with as many as 60,000 people walking out, an unprecedented figure in either the US or Europe (Green, 2006, p. 145).

---

8   Now named Kaunas, it is the second largest city in Lithuania.

The events at Haymarket, Chicago's wholesale produce area, on 4 May 1886 are highly controversial and the full details of what happened that evening will never be known. This was the first time in the US that dynamite was used for the destruction of human life. James Green argues that Haymarket marks American's first experience with what is now known as terrorism, noting that the anarchists made serious threats to use dynamite against their enemies in order to terrorise the authorities and the public (Green, 2006, p. 360). Mary Barton has referred to the Chicago Haymarket bombing as the most famous act of anarchist terrorism during the 1880s, with the subsequent trial of eight suspected anarchists causing an international sensation (Barton, 2014). Anarchists had become more involved with the worker's struggle when they backed the call for an eight-hour working day. When striking workers from the McCormick Harvester Machine Company were viciously attacked by over 200 police (several workers being killed), August Spies, who had witnessed the deaths of some of the workers, led the anarchist call for a protest meeting in Haymarket Square the following evening. Spies fatefully wrote that had the workers been armed with guns, or even a single bomb, then they would have been spared the violence that was inflicted upon them. It did not help Spies that the previous year he had shown a large stick of dynamite to a reporter, stating his wish to place it under the Board of Trade building (Smith, 1995, p. 114). Tensions were high throughout the day, with strikes across Chicago creating a potentially dangerous atmosphere in the city. Although many spectators had already filtered away, Captain William Ward ordered an end to the meeting, to which Samuel Fielden, then speaking, objected, declaring the meeting peaceful. It was during this attempt by the police to end the meeting at around 10:20 pm that a bomb was thrown, prompting the police to open fire. In the ensuing melee, not helped by the heavy rain, seven police would eventually lose their lives with sixty-seven injured

(Adamic, 2008, p. 53). At least three civilians died, although this figure was likely to be higher, and no one recorded the figure of civilians injured. In the darkness, smoke, panic and confusion it is likely that the police shot at each other, indeed, this was the belief of Spies as well as other spectators.

Clymer notes that the *New York Times* 'linked the bombing to the most notorious and reviled advocate of terrorism in America' (Clymer, 2002, p. 36) and it is unsurprising that Most found himself arrested soon after the Haymarket bombing for the offence of holding an unlawful assembly. Many Americans equated anarchism to terrorism, and associated both with trades unions, causing the latter to lose considerable support and forcing them to publicly distance themselves from the anarchist movement. A huge manhunt was to follow and almost anyone connected to, or suspected to be part of, the anarchist movement was arrested or questioned; which means that in many ways this was America's first attempt to create a counterterrorism policy. Police used intimidation and bribery to bring charges against eight men, who included August Spies.

The mockery of a trial saw the defendants have little hope of reprieve, even though some of the accused had not even been at the scene and none were identified by credible witnesses. It was made clear that anarchism itself was on trial, and as known anarchists they were simply guilty by association. The fact that seven of the eight accused were foreign-born only helped rally the newspapers to denounce the suspects even more; in the run-up to their executions it was reported that there were some 20,000 armed and dangerous anarchists in the city of Chicago waiting to rampage (Clymer, 2002). Newspapers stressed the idea that the city had become so invaded by outsiders that it was now effectively no longer a part of the US. By 1890 around 450,000 of Chicago's population of 1.1 million were born abroad (Smith, 1995, p. 149).

Michael Schaack, who was born in Luxembourg, played upon nativist fears when he referred to the anarchists as 'exotics'. It was he who led the investigation into the events at Haymarket and he would stress his role in breaking up a huge terrorist network. Schaack could not resist printing his own book, *Anarchy and Anarchists*, in 1889 to buttress his own image, much as Allan Pinkerton had done with the Molly Maguires. The accused actually played along with this notion of a larger plot, as they argued that it was they who were the victims of a conspiracy, blamed for an event that the capitalists had in fact orchestrated. They would have stressed this point even further had they known businessmen had paid Schaack to hire informants to help seek out subversive elements (Smith, 1995, p. 126).

William Black in his closing statements for the defendants would invoke the actions of John Brown. He argued that the attack of John Brown on Harpers Ferry could be compared to the socialist attacks on the evils of modern capitalism, and was even able to remind the judge of his own stated support for Brown's actions (Smith, 1995, p. 154). Schaack would compare the anarchists to savage Indians, describing anarchist women as both crazy and bloodthirsty 'squaws' who had no role in the real America. Just as with Joseph Hopkinson's pamphlet on identity, the focus quickly became on who were 'real' Americans. All foreigners were potentially terrorists. The fact the Crow Indian War was coming to an end and that Geronimo had just been captured gave Schaack the opportunity to conflate the Native Americans and foreigners as two edges of the same sword threatening the state (Smith, 1995, p. 150, p. 338).

Although the public mood against the defendants was beginning to change, newspapers continued to call for the death penalty to be carried out. The outcry against the ultimate sanction spread internationally, with George Bernard Shaw organising a petition that gained the signature of Oscar Wilde (Adamic, 2008, p. 57).

There was also an attempt to take the case to the Supreme Court, but this was rejected unanimously on 2 November 1887. With all legal avenues exhausted, four of the anarchists would be hanged (one had already committed suicide). In 1893 Illinois Governor John Peter Altgeld concluded belatedly that all eight defendants had undergone an unfair trial and gave the remaining three prisoners absolute pardons. That same year a memorial was erected in memory of those executed in what Carl Smith has called one of the most shameful proceedings in American legal history (Smith, 1995, p. 122).

Also inspired by Most was Alexander Berkman, who utilised Most's instructions from his *Science of Revolutionary Warfare* on how to make an explosive device to attempt to assassinate Henry Frick, the chairman of the Carnegie Steel Company. The device failed to detonate, possibly because of Most's poor instructions, and another method had to be followed. On 23 July 1892 Berkman stormed into Frick's office in Pittsburgh where he shot Frick twice, as well as stabbing him in the leg.[9] In his memoirs, Berkman attempted to claim that the attack was 'the first terrorist act in America' (Berkman, 1912, p. 59). Frick was targeted because he had hired 300 Pinkerton agents to protect against striking workers during the Homestead Strike, resulting in violent battles and the death of ten workers. Frick also used his political influence to persuade the governor to send in eight thousand national guardsmen to bring in martial law and allow the plant to reopen (Anderson, 1998, p. 182). Whilst Berkman's actions proved to be very much an isolated incident of violence conducted by an anarchist, fear of anarchism and worker unrest was such that in 1894 President Cleveland requested more security due to his fear of an attack (Jensen, 2014, p. 250).

---

9   Frick survived the attack, becoming something of a folk hero, and died in 1919.

Johann Most opposed Berkman's actions, creating a rupture between him and Goldman. Indeed, the two would fall out in dramatic fashion. Goldman's biographer Alice Wexler suggests that Most's criticisms may have been inspired by jealousy of Berkman. It is possible that this influenced his increasingly outspoken attacks on both Goldman and Berkman. Goldman so objected to Most's accusations that the attack on Frick had been staged using a toy pistol that she came to one of his lectures and sat on the front row. As Most rose to speak she directly challenged him, when he refused to directly confront the issue, she produced a horse whip and repeatedly struck Most on his face and neck in full view of the audience, before being forced out of the hall (Goldman, 1970, p. 105). This brief but sensational event was widely reported at the time and whilst Goldman would later regret her actions, it graphically reflected divides in the anarchist movement.

The assassination of William McKinley in September 1901 was one of the most infamous terrorist acts committed by the anarchists. It shattered the notion that America was somehow immune to the wider threat of anarchist violence that had so affected other countries. McKinley's assassin was Leon Czolgosz, a Polish-American. Whilst McKinley did have the protection of bodyguards, the attack took place at the Temple of Music in Buffalo, New York State, where hundreds had gathered to meet the president. Czolgosz was able to mingle with the crowd and conceal his gun in a bandage in his right hand; as the president finished shaking his assailant's left hand, Czolgosz shot him twice. Given many people carried white handkerchiefs that day to mop their brows in the summer heat, the bandage did not look out of place, and the security services were unable to stop him firing. Czolgosz was a self-proclaimed anarchist and his weapon of choice was a .32 calibre Iver Johnson revolver.

This was highly symbolic as the same make of weapon had been used to assassinate King Umberto of Italy in July 1900

(McCann, 2006, p. 27). The King had been assassinated by Gaetano Bresci, who had actually travelled from Paterson, New Jersey, where he had worked as a skilled silk weaver, to carry out the attack. Paterson was an industrial city which attracted a significant number of anarchists. As Jenson notes, despite Bresci's radicalism, he was free from any investigation or prohibition, and the local police chief even naively stated that there were no anarchists within his city, despite the fact that the city represented something of a hotbed for anarchist sympathisers (Jensen, 2015, p. 445).

The death of McKinley occurred during a time when many high-profile assassinations were taking place internationally and Ayton notes that there is some evidence to suggest that anarchists were attempting to assassinate McKinley prior to Czolgosz's individual actions (Ayton, 2017, p. 163). The closing years of the nineteenth century and the beginning of the twentieth saw seven heads of state assassinated, creating the first international push for concerted action to address the growing terrorist threat. Germany and Russia, both significantly affected by the movement, called for anti-anarchist measures to be agreed and enforced internationally. Accepting that the issue of anarchist violence was bigger than a single country, an international protocol was created in 1904, but the US, very much still directed by its isolationist instincts, did not sign it, and Congress, with southern representatives worried about the expansion of federal power, simply failed to agree on any legislation outside of tighter controls on immigration. Some individual states, including New York and New Jersey, did move to make the support of movements who supported the overthrow of government a crime, with most other states eventually following this lead (Barton, 2015, p. 320). Unsurprisingly, following the death of McKinley, despite Roosevelt's initial reluctance to accept the constraints of more security there was finally a recognition of the need for greater protection of presidents and increased intelligence gathering on potentially subversive anarchists. The Bureau of Investigation was established in 1908. Such actions were long overdue and highly necessary. Appleton notes that there would be over one hundred attempts to kill public officials in the US during the twentieth century (2000, p. 495).

As McKinley lay dying, the soon-to-be president Theodore Roosevelt wrote to his friend Henry Cabot Lodge, 'We should war with relentless efficiency not only against anarchists, but against all active and passive sympathisers with anarchists' (Avrich, 2012, p. 167). This war was meant in a moral sense rather than a literal one, although McKinley's death brought a great surge of violence in the US against suspected anarchists. Despite the fact that he did not initiate the legislation, Roosevelt did sign into law the Immigration Act of 1903, which allowed the deportation of anarchists within three years of their arrival, as well as banning alien anarchists from entering the country. This was the first time since the Alien and Sedition Acts of 1798 that America had utilised a political test for immigration and citizenship. Although the act proved difficult to enforce and did not have a major impact, it enjoyed the support of most Americans.

As soon as Czolgosz was arrested newspapers reported not only that he had been inspired by the words of Emma Goldman, but that the two had collaborated prior to the event. In fact, they met very briefly on two occasions prior to Czolgosz's act (Jensen, 2014, p. 242). Following his arrest, the *New York Times* called him a 'rabid anarchist' and the press would quote from his police interview the inspiration for his actions: 'I am an Anarchist. I am a disciple of Emma Goldman. Her words set me on fire' (Kemp, 2018, p. 149). Despite intense questioning over seventeen days and even a physical assault, the police eventually concluded that there had been no collusion; although Goldman's link to and highly controversial defence of Czolgosz meant the cause of anarchism would forever be linked with the presidential assassin. The *New*

York World openly declared that Goldman had 'inspired McKinley's assassination' and the *New York Journal* even claimed Goldman was a paid agent of the Tsar (Drinnon, 1961, pp. 87–88). Despite the fact that Goldman renounced violence after the failed assassination on Frick, and the fact that she offered to nurse the ailing president after the attack, in an increasingly nationalistic age she increasingly came to be seen as a 'national enemy'.

The influence of newspapers during this era, who pushed the idea that Czolgosz was an illiterate, weak-minded foreigner, easily inspired by the dangerous and anti-democratic ideas of anarchism, should not be underestimated. The age of anarchism coincided the first age of mass journalism, which soon helped to whip up mass hysteria over the supposed threats from anarchist forces. William Randolph Hearst and Joseph Pulitzer were bitter rivals who built up major newspaper empires with record readerships in the days before radio, and both engaged in 'yellow journalism', the tactic of creating eye-catching headlines with little or no research into the actual story being covered. Clymer (2002) argues that through repetition the media pushed people into believing that events at Haymarket were clearly a terrorist act, something made easier in the absence of genuine information about the real perpetrators. By the end of the nineteenth century the *New York World* was pushing circulation figures over 600,000. Although in May 1889 New York anarchists called for the assassination of President Benjamin Harrison during his visit to the city (Ayton, 2017, p. 124) newspapers would inevitably exaggerate the dangers and threats, rallying their readers against dangers to the political system posed by anarchists, radicals, socialists and foreigners, as well as whipping up popular outrage against those accused of violent actions. It must be stressed that at no stage in the anarchist era did the movement ever possess the means to overthrow the state, despite claims by some politicians to the contrary.

Whilst Most would find himself back in prison for republishing an inflammatory article following the death of McKinley, he openly condemned the assassination of the president. Most had been moving away from calls to revolutionary violence since the 1890s, especially acts of individual terrorism (Avrich, 1995, p. 4), indeed he stated that he no longer found terrorism to be effective in promoting his cause (Gay & Gay, 1999, p. 148). By the 1890s both he and other leading anarchist figures, such as Peter Kropotkin, had openly denounced terrorism.

Czolgosz, bearing the signs of physical beatings both immediately after his attack and during his detention, was soon put on trial, facing a charge of first degree murder. With clear witnesses to the event and a confession, the trial was unlikely to last long; it was concluded within three days. Czolgosz was unsurprisingly sentenced to death, and inflamed the authorities yet further at his execution by exclaiming that he was not sorry for his actions and that the late president was the real 'enemy of the good people' (Clarke, 1981, p. 100). The verdict and sentence on Czolgosz was not without controversy. As Richard Jensen notes, many commentators have questioned the sanity of the assassin (2014, p. 246), not least owing to the claim he made to his family that he was going to die soon, and wished to depart with a blow to the political system. Most leading anarchists, including Goldman, stated that he was not actually an anarchist. Naturally, any verdict that indicated that Czolgosz was insane would have negated the assassination as an act of terrorism and placed him at the same level as would-be presidential assassins such as John Shrank or Richard Lawrence, who spent their remaining days in mental asylums. Ironically, opposition in Congress still meant that a federal law related to assassinating, or attempting to assassinate a president was not passed until the death of John F. Kennedy.[10]

---

10 The assassination of John F. Kennedy on November 22, 1963 is not covered in this work. Even if one accepts that the assassin was Lee Harvey Oswald, Oswald's own assassination forty-eight hours after his arrest meant that there was no trial, and without a confirmed assassin or motive, a discussion here would merely add to the reams of speculation that have engulfed the events ever since.

Whilst the influence of figures such as Johann Most was waning long before his death in 1906, and whilst support for anarchism declined steeply in the wake of McKinley's death, there were others who helped breathe new life in the concept of 'propaganda by deed'. Only a month after McKinley's assassination, Luigi Galleani, an Italian anarchist, who had already spent time in prison in his homeland and who harboured an intense hatred for capitalist exploitation, arrived in the US. Over the next few years, he and his circle of followers would be behind the most audacious acts of terrorism in America's history; and yet, as Jeffrey Simon notes, they are largely forgotten in that history (Simon, 2008). Galleani settled in Paterson, New Jersey, where he soon became involved in supporting striking workers at the silk mill (Gay & Gay, p. 85). During the strike action he was shot, and had to flee to Canada to avoid arrest over the charge of inciting a riot. Living under a pseudonym in Vermont, he published *Cronaca Sovversiva* (The Subversive Chronicle), which, despite a modest print run of around 5000 copies, gained significant influence in the anarchist movement in the US and beyond. Many were to be inspired by Galleani's writings, which in 1905 included the publishing of instructions on how to make bombs, although the instructions were inaccurate and had to be corrected in later editions (Law, 2009, p. 121).

The Industrial Workers of the World (IWW),[11] is a union which is still in existence. Formed in Chicago in 1905 and led by 'Big Bill' Haywood, they would become known as the 'Wobblies', their militant tone making them the most feared worker's association of the time. Haywood would be implicated in the murder of the former governor of Idaho, Frank Steunenberg, who was killed in grisly fashion returning home on 30 December 1905 by

---

11 Minutes from the founding convention are now on line at https://www.iww.org/history/founding.

dynamite planted on his front gate. This killing made national news. It was the first time in American history that dynamite had been employed in an assassination. Steunenberg, who had previously enjoyed trade union support, had called upon President McKinley for help from federal troops; African American troops brought in from Texas added an extra element of racial tension (Adamic, 2008, p. 93). More than a thousand miners were rounded up and placed into detention centres, and martial law was introduced to quell the miner's dispute. Investigating the crime was none other than James McParland of the Pinkerton Detective Agency, no doubt interested by the $15,000 on offer for the arrest of the perpetrators. He engaged in controversial interrogations of suspect Harry Orchard and forced a confession that linked senior figures of the Western Union of Miners to the crime (Irwin, 2015, p. 231). Amidst the clamour against those standing trial, President Roosevelt could not resist a populist interjection and described the accused as 'undesirable citizens' (Johnson, 2018, p. 43), although this only further galvanised the workers movements. Luckily for Haywood, he was able to call upon the services of Clarence Darrow (1857–1938), who would go onto to become one of the most infamous lawyers in American history. Darrow, somewhat sidestepping actual questions of guilt, was able to argue that the whole workers movement was on trial, and that any crimes committed were morally justifiable. Haywood and others were exonerated and the notoriety of the trail and its verdict allowed Haywood to rally support for other causes.

There were certainly writers keen to stress the link between trades unions and terrorism. The *Outlook* magazine of February 1912 printed an article by Walter Woehlke entitled 'Terrorism in America', specifically linking trades unions to both violence and terrorism. Woehlke overstated any such link, but his comments were set against a background of rising terrorist activity. Jeffrey Simon (2001, p. 42) states that over 100 dynamite explosions had taken place on bridges, factories and plants across the US between the years 1906–11. Whilst these explosions rarely resulted in a loss of life, they did create a climate of fear, which, as discussed in chapter one, is a central rationale of terrorist activity. Employers were required to be on their guard, needing to employ extra security measures and live with the constant prospect of attack if they did not meet the demands of the unions.

Towards the end of 1908 there was to be another anarchist scare, and a number of anarchist attacks took place. A Chicago police chief was injured at his home by an anarchist (who was killed during the attack), and another would-be anarchist bomber blew himself up whilst targeting police officers at a socialist rally in New York City. (Jones, p. 136). However, as Jensen notes (2014, p. 91) attacks were not at this time directed toward the government, partly because Roosevelt had long stressed his progressive credentials and tried to distance himself from the interests of Wall Street to a much greater degree than McKinley had done.

It was to be the attack on the Los Angeles Times building on 1 October 1910 that brought the question of the resurgence of terrorism to the forefront of American life. The bombing and subsequent fire caused by a timed detonation of sixteen sticks of dynamite killed twenty-one people and injured hundreds more, as well as causing an estimated $500,000 of damage. The explosion was so powerful it threatened the structural integrity of the building. The newspapers across America covering the attack on their front pages soon dubbed the bombing, 'the crime of the century'. One of the most recent studies on the events of that day is *Deadly Times: The 1910 Bombing of the Los Angeles Times and America's Forgotten Decade of Terror* by Lew Irwin. He points out that despite the scale of the attack, as a child he was unaware of the events of that day because of the lack of coverage in history texts that he read in school or college (2015, p. ix), another example of an important terrorist event being excised from American history.

Since 1886 the paper had been owned and run by Harrison Gray Otis, a man who was staunchly against organised labour. Otis had been personally targeted on the day of the newspaper attack, other bombs were discovered at his home. Police soon linked the explosives that had been used to an extremist association, the International Association of Bridge and Structural Iron Workers (IABSIW). The clandestine attacks by the IABSIW were conducted ostensibly out of desperation and the weak position they faced against the forces of capitalism, although Adamic notes that the average wage for members of the American Iron Workers (AFL) rose from $2.50 for ten hours work to $4.30 for eight hours work between 1905-10, following the 150 or so bombing attacks carried out on buildings and bridges in the US and Canada (Adamic, 2008, p. 141). It is arguable therefore that terrorist-related tactics by radical workers could ultimately lead to improved conditions and therefore be classed as a success.

Two brothers would stand trial, John and James McNamara, who were able to secure the services of Clarence Darrow; he felt somewhat obliged to accept the case. With so much evidence against them, Darrow persuaded them to change their initial plea to guilty in connection to nineteen counts of murder. This was a decision which would save their lives, but ultimately antagonise the labour unions for whom he had worked so diligently for eighteen years (McRae, 2009, pp. 36–37).[12] Despite the guilty plea Darrow refused to condemn actions which he believed were in defence of the welfare of his class. James would plead guilty to setting the explosive charge and would spend the rest of his life in San Quentin State Prison. As Irwin notes, he became a hero to the

---

12 The trial cost Darrow his professional standing as he faced two subsequent trials for allegations of bribery. Despite being acquitted on the first, with the second deemed a mistrial, Darrow still faced bankruptcy.

most radical socialists and communists worldwide (2015, p. 335). John would be sentenced to fifteen years for setting explosives at the Llewellyn Iron Works Plant in Los Angeles, bombed during Christmas 1910. He left San Quentin after nine years. Both brothers died in 1941.

Whilst many Americans did abhor the actions of the McNamara brothers, not least because of their confessions, which served as a major blow to the workers unions that were organising appeals and fundraising for them, the bombing did serve the same purpose as many terrorist attacks in that it drew public attention to the cause. In fact, President Taft set up an Industrial Commission which 'played an important role in educating public opinion about the realities of labor-capital conflict' (Simon, 2001, p. 42). In 1912, nearly forty union leaders associated with the International Association of Bridge and Structural Iron Workers were convicted of conspiring to transport explosives on passenger trains across state lines. Clymer argues that the attack on the Los Angeles Times building marked a move away from attacking unoccupied structures (Clymer, 2003, p. 176).

In 1911 police investigated a potential anarchist plot to kill President Taft, when anarchist John Steele stated that he had heard from others within the movement that Taft would soon be targeted for assassination. In 1912 police also investigated two other potential anarchist plots to kill the president, although these were never fully substantiated (Ayton, 2017, pp. 202–203). Dynamite remained a powerful potential tool with which to attack the state and a plot was discovered to use explosives to blow up a bridge on which the president's train was due to pass, close to Santa Barbara. Frank Ryan, who was the International Iron Workers president, was arrested along with 53 union officials in what was dubbed the 'dynamite conspiracy'. Although a $5,000 reward was offered to catch those responsible for planning the explosion, they were never found.

In October 1912, just three weeks ahead of the presidential election, Theodore Roosevelt would be targeted by an assassination attempt during a rally in Milwaukee. His assailant was John Schrank, who shot Roosevelt from less than 30 feet away, with the bullet going through his overcoat, glasses case and the manuscript of his speech. Remarkably, Roosevelt, although bloodied and with the bullet lodged under his ribs, went on to deliver his planned speech, stating that 'it takes more than that to kill a Bull Moose' (cited in Miller, 1992, p. 530). Although Schrank was opposed to the idea of Roosevelt serving a third term as president, this potential political motive was discounted and he was put on trial for murder but found to be insane. He claimed to be have been inspired by the ghost of McKinley, and was duly committed to a mental asylum, where he died in 1943. Such a verdict therefore removed any possibility that this was a terrorist act.

After a lull in anarchist bombings, 1914 saw the beginning of a resurgence. To counter this threat New York founded a secret policing group which was referred to as the 'anarchist squad'. Despite the fact that the police managed to infiltrate these anarchist groups, the bombings continued, with attacks on St Patrick's Cathedral and St Alphonsus Church (where a group of homeless activists had previously been arrested), a courtroom in the Bronx and another targeted in Lower Manhattan (Jones, 2015, p. 136).

In 1914 Galleanists planned an attack on John D. Rockefeller Jr[13] following his suppression of workers in the Colorado mines, where a strike turned bloody and resulted in the deaths of thirty-three people. With further deaths, President Wilson despatched Federal troops to help end the strike, but Rockefeller still refused to recognise the union. The dangers implicit in the creation

---

13 This was the son of John D. Rockefeller (1839-1937), founder of the Standard Oil Company and widely considered to be the richest American, and possibly the richest man, ever to have lived.

of homemade explosives were literally brought home when an explosion collapsed a tenement on Lexington Avenue, Harlem, on 4 July, panicking holiday crowds, with police finding three anarchists in the rubble (Jones, 2015, p. 146). This setback did not prevent a series of bombs being planted across New York.

Jeffrey Johnson has argued that after 1916, terrorist events over the next few years were essentially carried out by followers of Galleani. Whilst there were probably only around fifty to sixty active hardcore members of the group, their use of new and surprise tactics, coupled with their skilful exploitation of the media, made them a powerful force in America, even as their numbers dwindled towards the end of the decade.

Key to the resurgence of terrorist activity was the outbreak of World War One in July 1914. Tensions rose dramatically leading to a wave of violence ahead of America's entry into the war in April 1917. A good example of this tension is the attempted assassination of America's leading financier J. P. Morgan on 3 July 1915 by Erich Muenter. Using the alias Thomas Lester, he called at the Morgan residence and threatened the butler with two guns. Morgan tackled the intruder and was shot in the process, but he, along with other servants, managed to restrain the attacker, who was also armed with dynamite. Giving his name as Frank Holt, it was later revealed that his real name was Erich Muenter, a man with a PhD from Cornell University who had even taught at Harvard. It was later revealed that the day before, an explosion in the (empty) Senate reception room was also set by the same man, which McCann states was the first known attack on American soil against a federal government target that was intended to influence foreign policy (McCann, 2006, p. 45). Meunter's actions were soon revealed to be a protest at Morgan providing substantial war loans to the United Kingdom, as he revealed in interviews following his arrest, although he never faced trial as he committed suicide in prison on 6 July.

Far more dramatic actions against American involvement in World War One took place in San Francisco less than a year later. San Francisco had long been a stronghold of the trade union movement. The Preparedness Day Parade was always going to be controversial since it pitched the anti-war union movements (notably 'the Wobblies') against pro-war forces. Not a single union was due to march in the parade that day. Not only was isolationism still a strong impulse in the US, but with the parade being organised by the Chamber of Commerce, there was always the implication that joining the war would serve merely to further business or imperialistic interests. At 2.06 pm on 22 July, half an hour into the parade a four-inch pipe bomb containing metal rivets and bullets to increase the level of carnage exploded, killing ten people and injured forty more.

As with the Los Angeles bomb attack, this event has also attracted more scholarly interest in recent times, with many history books having previously ignored these events. A new study by Jeffrey Johnson looks at the events in the context of the radicalism of the time. He concluded that this attack marked the height of 'progressive era' terrorism (Johnson, p. 126). The main suspect in the case would be Thomas Mooney, seen as the foremost radical in the city, and a friend of leading Socialist Eugene Debs. Mooney's trial and sentencing would only add to the controversy of the tragic events.

Mooney had been born in Chicago in 1882, spending his childhood around the Indiana coal areas and later moving to San Francisco. Mooney had been labelled a 'labor agitator' and was noted for his sympathies for extreme socialist doctrines, making him 'a man to fear', and he had previously been implicated, but not found guilty, of plots involving explosives (Johnson, 2018, p. 54). After the attack Mooney was quickly sought out and arrested and he was charged along with four others (including his wife) with murder. Opposition rapidly gathered, raising a huge amount for the defence of the accused, but Mooney was sentenced to death on the basis of highly suspect witness testimony. Adamic, writing of events during the 1930s, was in no doubt that there was no direct evidence to link Mooney to the attack (Adamic, 2008, p. 196). The campaign to commute Mooney's death sentence became so significant, both at home and internationally, that President Woodrow Wilson eventually contacted Governor Stephens to pursuade him to commute the sentence. One of those chiefly responsible for arousing international pressure was none other than Alexander Berkman, who had eventually served twenty-two years imprisonment for his attack on Frick, but who quickly rejoined Emma Goldman as leading figures in what was now a much reduced American anarchist movement. Berkman had moved to San Francisco and was quickly implicated in the plot. As the years went on, the trial judge, ten living jurors and the District Attorney all moved to petition California for a pardon, but this was refused and Mooney did not secure a final release from San Quentin until 1939, by which time he was in poor health. Mooney died in March 1942, and there remains no agreement on who conducted the attacks in San Francisco.

Another major attack in connection to America's potential involvement in the war took place in New York just eight days later. This attack, one of the biggest ever explosions in a major metropolitan area, is even less widely known about than the events in Los Angeles, with comparatively few authors bothering to record the events of the evening. One of the few to cover the events in detail is Jules Witcover in his book *Sabotage at Black Tom*. He states that the explosions that night rocked a nation believing itself far removed from the terrors of the Great War (1989, p. 162). Black Tom Island itself was actually a landfill site, connected to the mainland by a mile-long pier. Today it is part of Liberty State Park.

A series of fires had already been reported ahead of a massive explosion at 2.08 am that resounded across the city. Thousands of windows shattered, those still on the streets were knocked off their feet, sleepers were knocked out of their beds, fire and burglar alarms were set off across the city, phone lines went down between New York and New Jersey, and the whole sky lit up as if it were daylight. The explosions were so powerful that the underground Hudson tubes were jolted, the cemeteries at Bay View and New York Bay had vaults disturbed and monuments toppled, whilst those on the Brooklyn Bridge experienced the structure swaying alarmingly, as well as shattered windscreens. Those arriving at Ellis Island and those living on riverboats had to be evacuated. (Witcover, 1989, pp. 12–13). The explosion would measure 5.5 on the Richter Scale, thirty times more powerful than the collapse of the World Trade Center in 2001 (Roberts, 2016). Disturbances were reported in five different states, even as far away as Philadelphia, some eighty miles distant. Only the timing of the attack, and an element of luck, meant that the confirmed death tally was just five, one of which was a ten-week-old boy thrown from his crib in Jersey City. Hundreds more were injured. The *Jersey Journal*, whose external clock was stopped at 2.12 am by flying debris, suggested in their headline that day that the initial death toll would be around fifty people. The attack also made international headlines, the *Daily Mirror* in Britain featuring the story on their front page on 15 August.

The attack on Black Tom was far from random. Despite having very little security, Black Tom Island was the storage and shipping depot for explosive powders and munitions created for the Allied powers in Europe, a fact that led some initially to deduce that the explosions were an accident. On the day of the attack some two million pounds of munitions would be detonated and the depot was completely destroyed. In the end, after much investigation, the explosions were traced to sabotage by Germany, in a case that would rumble on through the decades leading up to World War Two and beyond. The events were a deliberate attempt to influence American decisions about the war, clearly making them political acts. In a curious aside, Ronald Reagan related in his first autobiography, *My Early Life*, that as a young child he would excitedly recite the events of Black Tom to his family (1965, p. 12).

One of the legacies of the explosions that day was from the shrapnel that hit the Statue of Liberty, which is situated opposite the site and which sustained around $100,000 of damage. It was this terrorist incident which would close the torch area of the statue forever to tourists, in the same way that 9/11 would close the crown.[14] A further legacy was that West Germany would pay compensation for the attack to America, starting with a $3 million payment in 1953, not completing the final payment until 1979. Security was understandingly tightened, with Secretary of the Treasury William G. McAdoo ordering increased funding for the secret service. Counter-intelligence and naval protection were stepped up (Carlisle, 2004, p. 76).

The event at Black Tom would prove not to be an isolated one. There was already an organised network of saboteurs created by the German government who were financing and planning attacks on the American mainland. From May 1915 to April 1917, nearly 100 explosions or fires took place on merchant ships or munitions plants from New York to California, although not all would have been direct acts of sabotage (Schwab, 2012).

On 11 January 1917 another massive explosion ripped through the Canadian Car and Foundry Company's plant at Kingsland in New Jersey. The company had already increased security, but with insider assistance the attack proved devastatingly effective. The plant produced millions of shells for the Russian military forces and it is thought that around half a million three-inch explosive shells burst into the air as people began to flee from

---

14 Although the Crown did reopen to limited numbers of tourists and under strict security measures on 4 July 2009.

neighbouring towns as the complex was destroyed, although without loss of life (Witcover, 1989, p. 192).

The FBI website does mention the events at Black Tom noting that the attack quickly led to the passing of the Espionage Act and the Sabotage Act. The Espionage Act (1917) would prove to be highly controversial, especially amongst those who argued that the act ran counter to the First Amendment, which includes the right to free speech and press. The Act set out stiff punishments of twenty years imprisonment and fines of up to $10,000 for those who tried to interfere in military enlistment. Charles Schenk, general secretary of the American Socialist Party, tried to use the First Amendment as a defence against the Act, but in the judgement against him, Oliver Wendell Holmes stated that there was a 'clear and present danger' in allowing any actions that harmed the conduct of the war effort (Lowe, 2005, p. 185). Inevitably, the Act was used against anarchists and radical unions such as the IWW. The Wobblies suffered greatly as many leading figures were sent to prison, the movement's leader Bill Haywood avoiding a twenty-year prison sentence by fleeing to Russia, where he died in 1928; some of his ashes were buried at the Kremlin. Even in the 1920s large numbers of members of the IWW remained in jail as 'political prisoners' (Preston, 1966, p. 8).

The Sedition Act of 1918 was more draconian, not only moving against those accused of disloyalty or threatening the military effort, but anyone seen to be disloyal towards the state could be charged. This allowed the government to prevent distribution and publication of anarchist literature, as well as break up anarchist movements or meetings. Once more this legal change brought most actions against those considered radical or socialist, as will be seen in the case of Eugene Debs. In truth, many workers did go on to support the war, along with key figures such as Clarence Darrow. However, the damage to the union movement, now linked in various ways to terrorism, socialism, communism and the anti-war movement, was very real and membership declined sharply. It was still as high as 4.9 million in 1920, but by 1923 had declined by about a third.

A series of bomb explosions rocked America 1917–19. For example, a number of bomb attacks in Milwaukee, where Theodore Roosevelt had almost met a premature end in 1912, resulted in the conviction of eleven Italian anarchists (Lutz & Lutz, 2007, p. 80). At the end of April 1918, a new anarchist plot was uncovered. Over thirty identical package bombs had been sent out in the mail. It was described by the *New York Times* as 'the most widespread assassination conspiracy in the history of the country' (Simon, 2008, p. 202). Inspired by Johann Most, who had once advocated the technique of parcels containing explosives, the attempt to create a simultaneous attack (all the parcels were intended to arrive on 1 May) represented a major upsurge in terrorist tactics. Most parcels were sent to leading capitalists such as J. P. Morgan and John D. Rockefeller, and national and local government officials. The packages were mailed from New York and marked with 'Gimbel Brothers Department Store'.[15] Although only two packages were actually delivered, a maid at the home of Senator Thomas Hardwick had her hands blown off when she opened the parcel. For Jeffrey Simon, the targeting of Rayme Finch, who had investigated the Galleanists, was a clear indication that it was individuals from this group who were behind the attacks (Simon, 2008, p. 201). With all parcels identical, police were able to prevent the majority of the parcels reaching their intended recipient. For one, Attorney General Alexander Mitchell Palmer, these growing attacks represented both a threat to established order as well as

---

15 Gimbels' Stores were well known at the time and remained a noted brand in the US until the 1980s, although most would remember the name from the Christmas movie *Miracle on Thirty Fourth Street* (1947). The store was attacked by small scale explosives in the late 1970s by members of FALN (see chapter five).

an opportunity to seize the political initiative, as he was intent on taking the 1920 nomination for the Democratic Party to replace the ailing President Wilson.

Having failed via the American postal service, on 2 June 1919 the anarchists targeted the cities of New York, Washington, Cleveland, Boston, Philadelphia, Pittsburgh and Paterson (New Jersey) with a series of larger, hand-delivered bombs. These bombs were largely aimed at the home addresses of politicians, judges and mill owners and resulted in injury and one death in New York. The bombs exploded within two hours of each other, revealing an orchestrated approach and a well-planned campaign. Pink anarchist leaflets called 'Plain Words' and signed by the 'The Anarchist Fighters' were found at the various bombing sites, warning that there would be future bloodshed against the capitalist class. This was an attempt to strike fear into the capitalist hierarchy, a notable facet of terrorism at this time. The most significant of these attacks was at the home of Attorney General Alexander Mitchell Palmer where Galleanist supporter Carlo Valdinoci, carrying two guns and twenty pounds of dynamite, accidently blew himself up whilst attempting to light the fuse. Palmer, who had just moved away from the window, managed to escape injury. Across the street future president and first lady Franklin and Eleanor Roosevelt were just arriving back home and felt the force of the blast as their windows blew in, part of the scalp of the bomber landing on their car (Pietrusza, 2007, p. 145).

Palmer was able to take advantage of the fear of a major organised nationwide conspiracy to orchestrate the rounding up and expulsion of scores of suspected anarchists. Palmer indicated that he wanted to move against 60,000 'red' radicals, of which he considered Emma Goldman to be the most dangerous. The idea that these 'reds' had formed a 'Great Conspiracy' was given added weight by the young and energetic J. Edgar Hoover, now promoted to Special Assistant to the Attorney General in the Bureau of

Investigation.[16] In truth, many of these latter terrorist events were never traced to any specific individuals. Galleani and many of his closest associates were deported on 24 June 1919, which prevented a full investigation into their potential role in the bombing attacks.

In the end, despite much investigation, those behind the attacks were never brought to justice, despite the media outcry that included headlines such as 'Reds Planned May Day Murders'. The Red Scare was a myth; the communist movement in 1919 amounted to no more than 70,000 people, less than 0.1 per cent of the population (Reynolds, 2010, p. 323). The vast majority of these members were born outside of the US. The socialist movement fared better, with Eugene Debs the effective leader of the movement standing five times for election 1900–1920, his support peaking at 6 per cent of the vote in 1912. In 1918 Debs was imprisoned for ten years for charges under the Espionage Act.

Freeberg argues that despite a desire by President Wilson to pardon those who were imprisoned for opposing the war, Attorney General Mitchell Palmer pushed the president not to pardon Debs because he believed it would be seen as a capitulation to terrorism (2009, p. 161).[17] Despite his imprisonment Debs secured over 900,000 votes in the 1920 election, a fact that seemed remarkable at the height of this second, and far more serious, Red Scare. Such figures show that despite the prevalence of terrorist attacks during this era, no radical movements within America represented anything that could be considered a genuine threat to the state.

America would oppose the communist takeover during the Russian Civil War and refused to recognise the USSR when the

---

16 Hoover would head the FBI from 1924–1972 becoming one of the most powerful figures in America during the twentieth century.

17 Eventually Palmer would urge President Wilson to pardon Debs at the end of his term of office, but Wilson refused to do so and he was eventually released by President Harding on Christmas Day, 1921.

war ended in 1922. Palmer was supported by the media, which widely reported the mail bombings. The *New York Times* were quick to overstate the threat declaring that there was 'a bold plot against the American Government and the forces of law and order', singling out the anarchists, bolshevists and the IWW as those intent on assassinating officials.

Against such a background Palmer organised a series of raids across the US from 7 November 1919, with an even bigger round-up of thousands of alien radicals taking place from 2 January to 6 January 1920. The raids enjoyed popular support: at that time, as now, violent crimes, especially those connected to terrorism, create a situation in which government can take firm and decisive action despite controversies over the abandonment of legal safeguards. Arrests were often violently conducted without warrants and thousands were detained together in highly unsanitary and overcrowded conditions without trial. Around 800 were eventually deported (Reynolds, 210, p. 324). These raids and deportations comprised America's first systematic attempt at counterterrorism (Borgeson & Valeri, 2009, p. 95).

On 21 December 1919 at 4.20 am 249 'anarchists' would be removed from America on the aging army transport the *Buford*, amongst them Emma Goldman and Alexander Berkman, who were separated during the voyage. It had been a long legal challenge, stopping just short of the Supreme Court (Drinnon, 1961, p. 220). Once Emma Goldman was thrown out of the US, the animus drained from the anarchist movement and the anarchist presses effectively closed, although Goldman was allowed a brief return to the US in 1934.

The actions of Palmer attracted much support from those who believed such a response necessary to protect the state from further terrorist attacks. It could indeed have provided a strong basis for Palmer's attempt to gain the presidency, had he not overreached himself. He openly stated that May Day 1920 would bring a mass 'red' uprising, which both the local authorities and the media fully bought into. When nothing of note took place, Palmer's bluff had been called and his credibility was gone.

The years from 1886 to 1920 represent a high water mark in American terrorism, incorporating some of the biggest terrorist attacks on the American mainland, which in terms of casualties and impact would only be superseded in the 1990s. Whilst many of these incidents have at least managed to attract some scholarly attention in recent years, they remain largely underrepresented in American history books, many of which start any discussion of terrorist events in the 1990s. This was an era of violence and upheaval and amidst the clamour to address worker conditions and the intense inequality of the age, it is clear that some of this violence spilled out into what can be defined as terrorism. As the years passed, attacks became more deadly, with many incidents designed to maximise casualties rather than just targeting specific individuals or locations. The outbreak of the First World War in Europe only heightened tensions further and the anarchist era coalesced with a violent campaign to keep America out of the war. Dominant in the final years were the supporters of Luigi Galleani, whose call to propaganda by deed was far more direct and destructive than any campaign led by Johann Most. Galleani's supporters would carry out the biggest terrorist attacks of this era, indeed with the biggest attack yet to come. In the end, a mixture of new legislation, the clampdown on and expulsion of many anarchist, socialist and radical union leaders, increasingly organised police and security forces and a growing government focus against the communist threats via a second 'Red Scare', all combined to end this major era of terrorist violence. Despite the prevalence of terrorism during the period from the 1880s to 1920, these incidents would soon fade from memory. The anarchist era was seen as nothing more than an aberration.

4

FROM WAR TO AN UNEASY
PEACE, 1916–1968

This chapter continues our chronological journey and provides an opportunity to show that as the wave of anarchism that had hit America since the 1880s came to an end in the 1920s, the number of major terrorist attacks significantly declined. This gave the appearance of quieter years in America, but there remained significant terrorist threats. Attacks against presidents and Congress, a rise in violence caused by a resurgent Ku Klux Klan, in addition to the activities of lone wolf terrorists, mean that this period was still significant in looking at the history of terrorism in America. By the 1950s, America would also face growing threats against the airline industry, as it entered a period where skyjackings became an issue for the first time. The end of this period would also see the US having to deal with its citizens being held hostage by countries to which it was in ideological opposition. The chapter begins by looking at the end of the anarchist era in the US, which encompasses both the biggest terrorist act on American soil to date, as well as the most notorious anarchist trial in American history, that of Nicola Sacco and Bartolomeo Vanzetti. The end of the anarchist period was contemporaneous with the second incarnation of the Ku Klux Klan, whose re-emergence can be linked to the film *Birth of a Nation*, as well as internal and external tensions created by World War One.

The year 1920 would bring the biggest terrorist attack on the American mainland until the Oklahoma bombing of 1995. The Wall Street bombing represents the last great terrorist act of the anarchist era, and was again to strike at the heart of capitalism, Wall Street in New York. Just before midday on 16 September, a horse-drawn wagon was parked up just across from the J. P. Morgan building. The driver of the vehicle quietly departed the scene, which became one of carnage as high explosives surrounded by metal casings exploded. People were to be engulfed in the fireball, mown down by flying metal debris or cut by the many imploding windows. The construction of the bomb and the timing of the attack indicated the bomber's intention to maximise casualties. Soldiers quickly rushed in to protect the Assay Office and police began to investigate the gruesome scene. This act of anarchist violence even resulted in the Stock Exchange being closed for the first time in its history. William J. Burns, who headed the Bureau of Investigation, aided by J. Edgar Hoover, then beginning a career that would lead him to becoming the first director of the FBI, would both quickly adjudge the bombing as perpetrated by communists (Jensen, 2014, p. 360), showing how American security services were already beginning to view the success of communists in Russia as a possible threat to the security of the US.

In the end no one would be convicted of this act of terrorism. After an extensive study, in 1991 Paul Avrich would point the finger squarely at Mario Buda (who also went under the name of Mario Boda) and authors such as Bruce Watson, Mike Davis and Beverly Gage have all agreed that Buda was the most likely culprit. Buda was an Italian immigrant anarchist, a supporter of Luigi Galleani who saw himself as the 'avenging angel' of imprisoned anarchists Sacco and Vanzetti (Davis, 2007, p. 2). Buda would never be charged in connection to the bombing, indeed he did not even feature in the Bureau's investigation, returning to Italy shortly after the attack. Mike Davis argues Buda had initiated a new form of terrorism in the form of a prototype car bomb, a highly effective and relatively cheap means of bringing huge levels of destruction, and a method that would be expanded and perfected in the decades to come. America would suffer from deadly truck bomb attacks both at home and overseas in the coming decades, as will be explored in chapters seven and eight. Despite the death toll, and national outrage, memories of the crime soon dimmed. Today an information board on Wall Street commemorates the events of that day and states that thirty people lost their lives, although most of the information discusses the power and prestige of the J. P. Morgan family. Pockmarks in the Wall Street facade have also been left unrepaired as a reminder of events.

A detailed and highly recommended study of these events has recently been published by Beverly Gage, who places the final death toll at thirty-eight and with 143 seriously wounded (Gage, 2009, p. 161). American history could have been altered significantly had Joseph Patrick Kennedy, then a stockbroker, and father of future president John Fitzgerald Kennedy, been closer to the explosion; as it was, he was one of many swept off their feet by the force of the impact. As in previous attacks, anarchist literature was found close to the scene warning of more death if all political prisoners were not freed and signed the 'American Anarchist Fighters' (Simon, 2008, p. 205). William J. Flynn investigating the bombing found uncovering a motive easier than prosecuting a suspect.

Just nine days before the bombing two anarchists were to be indicted for murder in one of the most controversial legal cases in American history. For Flynn, the two events were directly related.

Despite the high-profile attacks, the reality is that the expulsion of so many leading anarchists via the controversial Palmer Raids was bringing the anarchist era to an end. Anarchist violence was all but over, but would have one final cause célèbre in the case of Sacco and Vanzetti. Bartolomeo Vanzetti and Nicola Sacco were noted anarchists and supporters of Galleani, both originally born in Italy before moving to Boston in 1908. There were also links between the pair and Mario Buda, as well as failed anarchist assassin Carlo Valdinoci, his sister Assunta later going to live with the Sacco family, creating at the very least guilt by association.

On 5 May 1920, just days after Attorney General Mitchell Palmer had whipped up a surge of fear over a May Day uprising, Vanzetti and Sacco were arrested for a robbery in South Braintree, Massachusetts, where two people were shot dead. As noted in the previous chapter, this period in American history represented the height of the second 'Red Scare' and both men faced a hostile court. The trial judge, Webster Thayer, was even heard to call the defendants 'those anarchist bastards' (Johnson, 2018, p. 128) a statement which hardly boded well for an impartial trial. Neither of the two accused had criminal records, but both were armed upon their arrest.

Allegations of bias coupled with doubts over evidence supplied and retracted statements by witnesses made the case disturbing even for those for whom anarchism was anathema. Soon the outcry over the verdict was international, with support from such figures as Bertrand Russell and H. G. Wells. Upton Sinclair and John Dos Passos waited outside Charleston Prison for word that the 'good shoe maker and poor fish peddler' were dead, giving an even higher profile to the case.[18] Sacco and Vanzetti had become two of the most famous people in the world, with major protests against their sentence held as far afield as London, Paris, Tokyo, Johannesburg and Sydney. In Argentina, there were demonstrations and even a plot to

18 Sinclair would publish his book *Boston: A Documentary Novel*, based on the events of the case in 1928. Dos Passos more firmly believed that the men were innocent.

assassinate Herbert Hoover during a visit to the country in revenge for the deaths of Sacco and Vanzetti (Ayton, 2017, p. 245).

After years of legal wrangling, millions believed the men either innocent or felt that they had not received a fair hearing during their trial. As Avrich notes, no case in the US at this time received such widespread attention. It deeply divided America (Avrich, 1994, p. 89). Gage states that the executions appeared to be the grim culmination of the anti-anarchist frenzy that had started back in the 1880s. However, even as late as 1925, police were still uncovering plots by a small remaining core of anarchists to assassinate President Calvin Coolidge. Norman Klein, the leader of a small anarchist group, was finally tracked down to Florida after a three-month manhunt, having threatened the life of both the president and figures such as John D. Rockefeller and Henry Ford.

During the weeks before their execution, on 23 August 1927, and encouraged by Sacco and Vanzetti themselves, a series of bomb attacks rocked the US, with attacks in Philadelphia, Baltimore and New York. A parcel bomb destined for the governor of Massachusetts was intercepted. Attacks were also recorded in other countries around the world. For example, there was an attack on the US Embassy in Buenos Aires, as well as a bombing attack on two American banks in the city, which killed two people and injured twenty-three (Jensen, Routledge, p. 124). The executions nevertheless marked the final hurrah for anarchist-backed violence and terrorism in the US. In a postscript to these events, Massachusetts Governor Michael Dukakis, not without some controversy, declared that the pair had been unfairly tried and convicted on the fiftieth anniversary of their executions. Although Adamic still lists some fifteen attacks, out of around a hundred explosions that took place in 1929, as likely to be linked to labour-related terrorism (Adamic, 2008, p. 238), it is clear that from this period onwards, threats from anarchism were essentially forgotten as public attention increasingly turned to the threat and fear of communism.

The anarchist era, coupled with American entry into the war and the Red Scare that immediately followed, all combined to create a surge of nationalism which helped revive the Ku Klux Klan. This second era of the Klan begins in 1915 aided by the release of D. W. Griffith's film *Birth of a Nation* based on the book *The Clansman* by Thomas Dixon published ten years earlier. The film made the Klan appear to be a noble organisation and portrayed it in a romantic and chivalrous light, with Klan members rescuing women from the dangers posed by the bestial former slaves (Sinclair, 2013, p. 150). The film was the first cinema blockbuster, taking some $60 million and being crucial to cementing the rise of Hollywood as the core of the American movie making industry (Wade, 1987, p. 120).[19] It has also been described as the most controversial film ever made (Goldberg, 1999, p. 117).

This film's success encouraged William Joseph Simmons to revive the Klan. He and a group of associates set fire to a cross on Stone Mountain, Atlanta. Simmons took the opportunity to sell regalia and charge membership fees, but the movement did not grow in any great numbers until 1920, when Simmons engaged the help of two publicists. This new version of the Klan no longer accepted men as members simply because they were white, members now had to be both white and Protestant. The group still engaged in unchecked vigilantism, just as it had done in its previous incarnation (Tuman, 2003, p. 57). The idea that foreign influences were undermining American society, coupled with patriotic fervour caused by the First World War, the Red Scare, and setting up of the League of Nations, led to a rapid resurgence of the group. The fact that the population of the US rose from 31 million in 1860 to 105 million in 1920, and that many of the immigrants

---

19 President Woodrow Wilson would watch the film at the Whitehouse and was impressed by what he saw. The film continues to be controversial, as seen in 2019 when Lillian Gish's name was removed from an on-campus theater at Bowling Green State University because of her appearance in the picture.

were now from eastern Europe, rather than Nordic immigrants (whose arrival was still encouraged even after the 1924 National Origins Act), only exacerbated nativist tensions.

The resurgent Klan, which had an estimated 4.5 million members by 1924, now began to spread its influence into the northern states, indeed, Indiana claimed some 350,000 members, the most of any state (Zinn, 2008, p. 279). One reason for this expansion was the fact that the First World War had driven African Americans into the northern states in much greater numbers than ever before, with some 750,000 arriving there to take advantage of opportunities brought about by increased demand for workers and temporary slowing of immigrants into the US (Wade, 1987, p. 151). This created anger and suspicion in many northern cities, leading to racial tensions and riots. The new Klan therefore moved beyond its southern male origins, bringing in more than half a million female members. The Klan would enjoy the support of many Democrats and were far more visible in American life. The fact that their membership included police officers and that the group rarely targeted wealthier classes, meant that their tactics of violence and intimidation were seldom investigated and prosecuted even more rarely (Lutz & Lutz, p. 86). Wyn Craig Wade has even stated that President Warren G. Harding was inducted into the movement during a ceremony held at the Whitehouse headed by William Simmons (Wade, 1987, p. 165). The Klan engaged with politics at every level and following the 1924 election the *New York Times* contained the headline 'Victories by Klan Feature Election: Order Elects Senators in Oklahoma and Colorado, Governors in Kansas, Indiana and Colorado'. Al Smith, the Democratic Governor of New York, attacked the group as unpatriotic and un-American, accusing President Calvin Coolidge of failing to condemn the activities of the group in order to maximise his election chances.

Famously, some 45,000 Klansmen and women, no longer masked, paraded down Pennsylvania Avenue, Washington D.C., in 1925.

However, the focus of the Klan would expand from concentrating on African American repression to now include an emphasis on preventing political power going to Catholics and Jews, as well as attacking recent immigrants (Gilmore, p. 134). As part of an attempt at a broader appeal their targets also included bootleggers and even wife beaters. In recent research Sarah Churchwell has noted that Fred C. Trump, the father of Donald Trump, was one of six people arrested and detained at a Memorial Day parade in 1927 in which the Klan took part, the other five arrested that day all being 'avowed Klansmen', strongly suggesting that this version of the Klan has a connection to the father of the forty-fifth American president (Churchwell, 2018, p. 295). This Klan was notable in having an organised, legitimate political front, but the group also contained extremists who were prepared to engage in violence to promote their aims. Klansmen would whip African Americans who attempted to vote or oppose the Jim Crow Laws.

This second incarnation of the Klan would fade quickly for a variety of reasons: the 1924 Quota Bill addressed immigration concerns, prohibition was failing and there were a number of high-profile scandals, most notably the trial and imprisonment of Indiana Grand Dragon David Curtiss Stephenson on second degree murder charges relating to his brutal kidnapping, rape and torture of Madge Oberholtzer, alongside bribery and corruption. Stephenson would agree to turn state's evidence and exposed Klan corruption via a series of documents that showed just how much political power the Klan wielded in Indiana, leading to prosecutions of John Duvall, the Mayor of Indianapolis, an indictment against Governor Ed Jackson and a fine for the entire Indianapolis city council. Such damaging revelations led to the Klan being down to just thirty thousand members by 1930 (Gilmore, p. 135). Tensions remained throughout this period, as did the continuing desire to keep political and social control over those not viewed as real Americans.

During the 1930s, the Black Legion were another white supremacist group who engaged in violence, intimidation and murder. The group had links with the Silver Legion of America, a fascist group founded by William Dudley Pelley in 1933 in response to the rise of Hitler, showing that the appeal of fascism, so damaging to Europe in the 1930s, was not totally absent from the American scene. Much of the inter-war violence in the US centred around racial or religious violence, for example some 242 racial battles in forty-seven cities took place during the early 1940s (Lutz & Lutz, p. 88). However, in 1944, this version of the Klan was forced to surrender its charter when it failed to pay its tax arrears.

Whereas the violence of the anarchist era had been aimed at overthrowing or at least ameliorating the evils of capitalism, violence committed by the KKK and other splinter groups was essentially aimed at supporting the government and maintaining the social order. As such, much of the violence was targeted not just at African Americans, Jewish and Catholic communities, but also at the trades union movements. For the IWW, because they were especially targeted, a ban was placed on the organisation, ironically legitimated by the argument that this was the best way to protect members from attack. Lynching, which had peaked during the 1890s, a time of economic dislocation, still continued, and race riots fomented by white groups became a noted facet of inter-war America. Indeed, not only did lynching continue in the 1930s, but there were incidents recorded after World War Two (Miller, 2013, p. 160).

The success of the civil rights movement, via the Brown v Board of Education decision in 1954 in which the Supreme Court ruled against educational segregation, and the Montgomery Bus Boycott that desegregated buses in Montgomery, Alabama, and which brought Rosa Parks and Martin Luther King to prominence, alongside the election of the first Catholic president

John F. Kennedy in 1960, saw a return of the Klan. This later incarnation focussed on the activities of the civil rights groups, reducing the anti-Semitic and anti-Catholic emphasis of the Klan's second incarnation. Klan membership and violent activities grew as some whites moved to stop African Americans from securing equal rights, something that had seemed an unattainable goal after the Plessy v Ferguson decision of 1896 that ruled states could provide separate facilities for whites and African Americans. A bomb attack on a Baptist church in Birmingham, Alabama, in September 1963, which killed four girls aged between eleven and fourteen, saw four Klansmen accused of the act. The last conviction, against Bobby Cherry, would not be finalised until 2002, just two years before his death.[20] The Klan also specifically targeted the Freedom Riders, civil rights activists who rode interstate buses into the southern United States in 1961 and subsequent years to challenge the non-enforcement of the US Supreme Court decisions *Morgan v. Virginia* (1946) and *Boynton v. Virginia* (1960), which ruled that segregated public buses were unconstitutional. In addition, they committed arson attacks on churches, synagogues and houses. The campaign to prevent greater equality via violence and intimidation did not prove to be as successful as it had in the past. This was down to the determination of President Johnson, who made civil rights a key platform. A series of key laws, which included the Civil Rights Act (1964), Voting Rights Act (1965) and the Housing Act (1968) were among many passed in an attempt to finally secure rights denied to non-whites. President Johnson was keen to allow J. Edgar Hoover, with whom he got on well, to target and infiltrate the Klan during the 1960s. Whilst this may have deterred many from active membership, the Klan remained a force in the campaign to prevent racial equality, with Hewitt listing some 588 violent incidents reported 1955–1971 (2000, p. 17).

---

20 One suspect was never charged.

The 1927 Bath School bombing was one of the most significant internal attacks in twentieth-century American history. The tragic events took place on 18 May. It was a very well planned attack. Andrew Kehoe, a farmer from Michigan, who had already killed his sick wife in the preceding hours, rigged dynamite in the basement at various places in the school. Kehoe had been elected school treasurer and became the school handyman, giving him time and opportunity.

The first explosion of 500 pounds of dynamite took place at 8.45 am. Whilst his explosive devices were triggered in the north wing, Kehoe had also planted another 500 pounds in the south wing, which failed to detonate. However, the school was not to be spared further bloodshed as Kehoe then drove to the school with yet more explosives, which he detonated after calling over the school superintendent Emory Huyck, who was busy helping the injured. When the carnage had ceased, forty-five people were dead, including Kehoe; of those, thirty-eight were children, with another fifty-eight injured. Bath town hall had to be turned into a morgue, such was the number of deaths (Burcar, 2011, p. 88).

These tragic events, which Mike Davis notes are 'curiously repressed in the national memory' (2007, p. 14) commemorated today by a historical marker, deserve to be fully remembered as they comprise the greatest mass murder of children by an individual in American history. Arnie Bernstein in his often gruesome study of the events looks at how they compare to other terrorist attacks within the US, but despite the use of terrorist methods to accomplish murder and destruction, this event cannot be considered to be one of terrorism. Kehoe's motives were of revenge, he faced a foreclosure on his farm and he believed his financial difficulties were down to local taxes levied to fund a new school at Bath, something he had opposed. There were no political motives and he had no desire to influence any target audience.

Kehoe would not be the only person who employed terrorist techniques in order to satisfy a desire for revenge. From 1940, New York City would be targeted by a series of pipe bomb attacks by an unknown perpetrator who would be dubbed the 'Mad Bomber'. The bombs were frequently located in populated areas of the city and targets included Grand Central Station and the Empire State Building. In the end, thirty-three bombs were planted (or located), of which twenty-two exploded. These attacks reached a crescendo in 1956–7 when a number of bombs were left in various sites around the city. The design of the bombs made clear that they were from the same source, but police had no clear leads as to who this might be. On 2 December six people were injured by a bomb in a movie theatre and during that Christmas period there were 138 bomb alerts (Winick, 1961, p. 26) as well as over one hundred hoax bomb calls in January 1957, following the police decision to go public about the bombs that were being planted in public locations.

With no suspect, no motive for the bombs could be ascertained, but over time the bomber would signal his grievances to various newspapers before a crucial lead was gained when the bomber sent a letter that was printed on the *New York Times* front page on 26 December, and other letters followed. The letter echoed previous communications regarding a grudge against the Consolidated Edison Company, who had failed to grant him a pension after he had sustained an injury and the attacks were an attempt to draw attention to the plight of those in such a position.

With TV, radio and newspapers all joining the quest to uncover the bomber, an extensive search through company records eventually led, on 22 January 1957, to the arrest of George Metesky, a fifty-four-year-old former Edison employee. Footage of Metesky's arrest show him smiling and waving to the assembled press and he would state that he was not sorry to have conducted the bombing attacks.

It is clear that Metesky's actions provoked fear within New York, and his actions injured fifteen people, but his cause, such as it was, could hardly be considered political and soon Metesky would be regarded as insane, not even standing trial for his actions.[21] There are, however, a couple of additional points of interest. Firstly, Metesky would once again highlight the threat posed by, and difficulty of capturing, those who conducted 'lone wolf' terrorist actions, a fact that will be brought out much more fully when assessing the actions of Unabomber Ted Kaczynski in chapter seven. Secondly, a study by Charles Winick provided some fascinating information about American public perceptions of terrorists at this time. When asked about who they believed the bomber to be, those surveyed argued that the bomber must be male, foreign, a communist/socialist and the biggest percentage suggest he must be an atheist, since they could not envisage someone with religious beliefs planting bombs; and 16 per cent of those surveyed stated that they had some sympathy for the bomber. Over half those surveyed believed that the bomber was a communist or socialist, but few people, only 9 per cent, suggested that the bomber could be an anarchist (Winick, 1961, p. 29) showing just how distant threats from the anarchist era now seemed. Metesky's actions would not go unnoticed by others, who certainly found inspiration in his bombing campaign. Sam Melville, who helped kickstart an era of intense radicalisation within America in August 1969, grew up during the era of Metesky's bombings and they became something of an obsession for him: he spray-painted the message 'George Metesky was here' onto buildings.

One area where technology has significantly transformed the tactics utilised by terrorists is in the growth of the airline industry.

---

21 Metesky was eventually released in 1973, thanks to a legal loophole, and then lived quietly until his death in 1994.

International hijacking by definition involves more than one country, and when passengers are included in the equation a great many countries can have an interest in the outcome of a a single terrorist event. The first ever confirmed plane hijacking took place in 1931 in Arequipa, Peru, with the perpetrators wishing to seize the aircraft to drop propaganda leaflets. The aircraft's pilot, Byron Richards, was hijacked twenty-eight years later when his plane flying from Phoenix was taken over by Leon Bearden, who tried unsuccessfully to fly to Cuba, thus making Richards the first person to be hijacked twice. 1933 brought the first recognised incidence of the detonation of a bomb aboard an aircraft, in Indiana, killing its seven passengers, although the rationale for this bombing has never been discovered (Simon, 2001, p. 46). The ease with which bombs could be placed on aircraft was cruelly exposed by John Gilbert Graham, who on 1 November 1955 placed a bomb containing twenty-five sticks of dynamite in a package, which he wrapped and presented to his mother to take on board, informing her it was a Christmas gift. His mother was due to visit her daughter in Alaska and the bomb would detonate soon after the plane departed from Denver. All forty-four people on board the plane were killed. This act of matricide would be for no other reason than the collection of the insurance money, Graham having taken out a $37,500 insurance policy from a vending machine at the airport just prior to the flight. President Eisenhower was horrified by Graham's actions, but at this time there was not even a specific charge connected to the blowing up of an aircraft. This was quickly remedied in 1956 when there would be an act passed which provided for the death penalty for anyone found guilty of bombing an aircraft, bus or a commercial vehicle. Surprisingly, despite many copycat threats being made, tighter security at airports was still several years away, partly because more practical detection equipment was still being developed.

The event was a sad foretaste of what was to follow, even if in this case the murders were simply for money.[22]

In 2008 it was revealed that the first international hijacking from American soil had taken place fifty years earlier on 1 November 1958, when Cubana flight 495 that took off from Miami International Airport bound for Cuba was hijacked by members of the 26 of July Movement, attempting to take military supplies to Fidel Castro, who was at this point edging closer to an overthrow of the Batista Regime. An FBI investigation, an NBC Miami special – and members of his own family – pointed the finger at Edmundo Ponce de Leon, a naturalised US citizen who died whilst still being investigated in 2011. The hijack ended disastrously when the plane was unable to land on a short runway and ran out of fuel, landing in the sea and killing fourteen.

The 1960s was the hijack decade. And thenceforth hijacking would become one of the most important terrorist tactics of the modern age. During this decade around 90 per cent of all hijacked planes were flown to Cuba, a situation which frustrated both the American and Cuban governments sufficiently that by 1973 the two sides signed the first agreement between the two countries since Castro took office in 1959. The major era of American-Cuban hijackings began in May 1961, when a plane leaving Florida was hijacked by Antulio Ortiz. He demanded that the aircraft be flown to Havana. July 24 brought another hijack, also to Cuba. This resulted in a greater diplomatic incident because Fidel Castro was unwilling to return the plane, although he quickly arranged the release of those who had been on board. Following yet another hijack to Cuba on 9 August America began to suspect, wrongly as it transpired, that Fidel Castro was orchestrating these events to embarrass the US. On board this aircraft was Columbian

---

22 Despite an attempt to plead insanity, Graham was found guilty of the murder of his mother, the only charge that could be brought, and he was executed in the gas chamber on 11 January 1957.

foreign minister Julio Ayala, who was a noted critic of Castro. The Cuban leader would later state that he regarded such acts as being conducted largely by those who were mentally unstable, and dismissed the notion that these were political actions (Castro, 2007, p. 341).

John F. Kennedy took only modest steps to meet this new terrorist threat. He did not move to take direct action against Cuba, but tightened security instead. For the first time metal detectors were brought in at airports, cockpit doors were locked and there would be a $10,000 reward for capturing hijackers. 1963 brought further, limited, international measures.

This 'quieter period' also encompasses two major presidential assassination attempts, which both inevitably came close to altering the course of American history. Giuseppe Zangara, an Italian immigrant who later stated that he was trying to assist the poor people of the world, armed with an eight dollar pistol, took five shots at present-elect Franklin Roosevelt on 15 February 1933 in Miami. Zangara had first hatched a plan to assassinate outgoing president Herbert Hoover, but changed his mind when he discovered Roosevelt's travel plans. Roosevelt, who was to be was the last president inaugurated during March rather than the now traditional 20 January, came perilously close to assassination, despite the fact that Zangara, just 5 foot 1 inch tall and standing on a rickety chair, had his aim pushed upwards by spectator Lillian Cross. Zangara continued firing and emptied the gun, by which time he had struck six people (Shappee, 1958, p. 104). Chicago mayor Anton Cermak died on 6 March of his injuries. Zangara provides another example of lone-wolf terrorism, in that no other person was ever connected to his crime. At his trial he expressed no remorse.

Question marks inevitably remain regarding his mental status. After his arrest his explanation was that he intended to kill the president-elect as he was opposed to all rulers; however, whilst this explanation has a trace of anarchist-related rationality to it, his follow-up comment that he hoped to get relief from the constant pain in his stomach, which became a constant refrain through his trial, suggested a less balanced psychological mindset, as did his request of the trial judge to up his original sentence of eighty years to a 'round' one hundred. Nevertheless, county physician Dr E.C. Thomas had originally pronounced him sane, and Zangara pleaded guilty to the charges.

Following the death of Cermak a second trial saw another guilty plea and a sentence of death by electrocution. Interestingly, the presiding Judge Thompson took the opportunity to call for Congress to pass tighter gun laws to prevent would-be assassins arming themselves (McCann, 2006, p. 73) James Clarke has categorised Zangara as a nihilist who effectively believed in nothing, unlike such figures as Charles Guiteau, who believed their actions ordained by a higher power (Clarke, p. 95). In his last statements Zangara lamented the crimes of capitalism, but his own motivations may have been to gain attention: he was angry because no one photographed his execution on 10 March 1933 (Shappee, 1958, p. 110).

The 1950s saw terrorism strike at the very heart of American democracy with attacks directed at both the president and Congress. Puerto Rico had been taken over by America in a war with Spain in 1898. The same war brought American control of both Cuba and the Philippines. The Philippines gained independence in 1946, but there was little prospect of this for Puerto Rico, the citizens of which became citizens of the US on 1 March 1917. Such a designation did not sit happily with every Puerto Rican, some of whom questioned America's right to control the island and pushed for it to become a sovereign nation in its own right. In 1948, the passing of Law 53 attempted to silence those calling for independence by making it a crime to call for the violent overthrow of the Puerto Rican government (Hunter, 2005, p. 211). Those pushing for Puerto

Rican independence were always in the minority and over the next three decades would increasingly move towards terrorist methods to promote their cause. The movement for an independent Puerto Rico would be the only violent independence movement within the US during the modern era.

By the late 1940s the White House was in such a poor condition that President Truman was forced to move out for four years whilst major structural renovations took place. He took up residence at Blair House, situated across from the White House, known as 'The President's Guest House'. The building did not afford the same amount of security as the White House, offering much easier access from the street. The events that took place on 1 November 1950 are again largely unknown to Americans today. Stephen Hunter's 2005 book is the most comprehensive study, Hunter noting early in the book that few Americans remember the assassination attempt, one that came uncomfortably close to success.

At around 2.20 pm two Puerto Ricans, Griselio Torresola and Oscar Collazo, intent on rallying the cause of their island's independence, decided to assassinate Truman, having discovered that he was resident at Blair House rather fortuitously from a cab driver. Truman had retired upstairs for an afternoon nap when the gunmen attacked the security forces at the house. Truman's decision not only to look out of the window but actually open it and look down at the unfolding events could easily have proved fatal, as he was in clear view for Torresola to shoot from a distance of 30 feet (Hunter, 2005, p. 240).

Torresola, having shot security officer Joseph Downs and policeman William Coffelt, was in a position to move into the house, but was shot in the head and died instantly, the last heroic act of the dying Coffelt.[23] Oscar Collazo wounded police officer Donald Birdzell before he was shot, although not seriously and

---

23 Coffelt's badge is still displayed at Blair House.

he was arrested at the scene. Truman carried on his events for the day, a Pathe newsreel shows the president smiling as he reached Arlington National Cemetery, but the shootout, which lasted for just over half a minute, clearly did shake the president. At a news conference the following day Truman simply dismissed reporter's questions stating that there was 'no story' and that he was never in danger (Truman, 1965, p. 695). However, Stephen Hunter goes as far as to suggest that the experience may have led Truman not to stand again in 1952. Truman, preoccupied with events following the outbreak of the Korean War, does not dwell on the events in his memoirs.

Torresola's accomplice Oscar Collazo refused an insanity plea at his trial (as advised by his own council) which could have led to him avoiding the death penalty, because he was keen to make sure the events on behalf of the Puerto Rican cause were not delegitimised by the suggestion that the would-be presidential assassins were mentally unstable (McCann, 2006, p. 91). James Clarke has argued that the case of Collazo and Torresola represents one of the clearest examples of a political motive of any attempted president assassination. Indeed, Collazo used the trial to reel off a tirade of abuse about how the US had exploited his country both politically and economically. Worries about the impact on public opinion meant that Coffelt's widow was even persuaded to visit the island in 1951.

Collazo was duly found guilty of assault with intent to kill and was sentenced to death, but this was commuted a week before it was due to be carried out on the orders of President Truman. Collazo would be freed by President Jimmy Carter in 1979 and he moved back to Puerto Rico. Unsurprisingly, presidential security would be increased after the attack, including armour-plating the presidential limo and providing it with running boards for the secret service, and the president no longer walked to Blair House or took a regular pattern of walks. These measures proved insufficient to prevent the death of President John F. Kennedy in November 1963, not least because no security agents were riding on the running boards of the president's car.[24]

Despite some evidence that the actions of Griselio and Collazo were part of a larger movement, linked to Pedro Campos, a leading figure within the independence movement, there remains some debate about the extent of a wider conspiracy and Collazo did not publicly discuss any such information before his death in 1994. Certainly, those supporting Puerto Rican independence would launch an even more dramatic attack at the seat of American government on 1 March 1954. The date is significant as this was the day on which Puerto Ricans were granted American citizenship thirty-seven years previously.

Four armed Puerto Ricans made their way to the viewing gallery of the House of Representatives whereupon they opened fire on the 240 representatives in the chamber, then waved a single-starred red, white and blue flag, shouting 'Viva Puerto Rico libre!' (Romero, 2010). Remarkably, only five representatives were seriously wounded by the thirty shots that they were able to fire, most notably Michigan Representative Alvin Bentley, who was shot in the chest but survived the attack.

Jeffrey Simon notes that the attacks in 1950 and 1954 were the first time that terrorism was directed against US targets on American soil, in order to impact upon specific foreign policies (2001, p. 52). The events resulted in 179 arrests, with 21 people being tried. Despite getting so close to the heart of American politics, as Simon points out, the events in the Cold War – not least in Korea – seemed much more important, and the events were even

---

24   The events of Kennedy's death at Dealey Plaza, Dallas, on November 22, 1963 are not covered in this book as, unlike other presidential assassinations, we do not know for certainly who the assassin(s) were and therefore we cannot ascribe a motive to the actions which may categorise them as terrorism. The assassination of Robert Kennedy is considered in chapter six.

viewed by John Foster Dulles through the prism of communist subversion, rather than as acts of terrorism connected to the cause of independence.

The group that attacked the House was led by Lolita Lebron. *Time* magazine noted upon her death at the age of 90 in August 2010 that she was likely to be remembered as both a hero and a terrorist, personifying the notion that one person's freedom fighter is indeed viewed as a criminal by others. Lebron was sentenced to fifty-six years in prison and served twenty-five before she was released by Jimmy Carter. Even in old age, and back on her native island, Lebron never apologized for her actions and never gave up the struggle, stating angrily late in her life that she was not a terrorist, but was fighting American terrorism (McCann, 2006, p. 96). Even at the age of 81 she was arrested and imprisoned for protesting against the American military base on the island of Vieques. (Martin, 2010).

The 1950s would close with the Eisenhower administration having to deal with American servicemen being held in East Germany after an American Army helicopter strayed into East German airspace and was forced to make a landing. The nine servicemen were turned over to the Soviet military, who, to Eisenhower's frustration, pushed them back to East Germany, a country which the US did not recognise. Although keen not to give into pressure, Eisenhower pushed for some flexibility via a soft approach (Eisenhower, 1981, p. 355). The situation was further complicated by the fact that China and the Soviet Union were also holding American servicemen captive at the same time (Simon, 2001, p. 53). To add yet more complexity, there was also to be the taking of some forty-seven American citizens, including thirty servicemen, by Cuban rebels led by Raul Castro.[25] The hostages

---

25 Raul Castro (1931-) is Fidel's Castro's younger brother, and was later leader of Cuba from 2006–2018.

provided high-profile publicity for the Cuban rebels, as well as putting pressure on the Americans not to supply the Batista regime with weapons. The rebels argued that Batista was using American weapons to bomb their positions. The servicemen would also possibly become human shields if America chose to strike against the rebels. Despite the fact that there were calls for retaliation from both Democrats and Republicans, who feared they could be seen as being ineffective against terrorism, Eisenhower trod warily. Whilst condemning the taking of hostages, as well as statements from John Foster Dulles[26] that America would never give into blackmail, the president confirmed that no arms were being supplied to Cuba, which certainly seemed to indicate a victory for the rebels. Eisenhower, eschewing ultimatums, attempted to win over public sympathy for the hostages and this softer approach paid off when the Cuban rebels, also by now looking for a resolution to the crisis, released all the hostages unharmed on 18 July 1958. Given that the actions of the Cuban rebels were instrumental in pressuring Eisenhower not to further supply the Batista regime, and the fact that the regime fell at the start of 1959, the taking of American hostages proved to be a highly successful tactic.

The period from the 1920s to the 1960s, whilst quieter than the one that preceded it, was still punctuated by terrorist activities. The dramatic Wall Street Bombing and the trial of Sacco and Vanzetti represented the end of the anarchist terrorism that had been part of American life since the 1880s. However, as one terrorist threat subsided, another soon took its place, as the resurgent Ku Klux Klan emerged to promote racial supremacy and feed on nativist sentiments created both by the nationalism of America's entry into World War One, as well as unrest created by the large-scale movement of former slaves into the northern states. The second coming of the Klan was therefore wider in terms of the

---

26 John Foster Dulles (1888–1959) was Secretary of State from 1953 to 1959.

number of states where it enjoyed significant political influence, and expanded its campaigns of violence to prevent political power falling into the hands of Jewish or Catholic representatives. Whilst the influence of the Klan dipped markedly in the 1930s and 1940s, it was clear that the success of the Civil Rights movement allowed a third, modern incarnation of the Klan to gain support, which still used violence in a continuing attempt to prevent progress towards racial equality.

It was this seemingly quieter era which also saw the rise of skyjacking and the use of explosives against aircraft. Whilst the actions of John 'Jack' Gilbert Graham, as well as those who engaged in the initial skyjacking attacks against American aircraft from the late 1950s onwards did not all carry out their actions with political motives, the events proved to be an ominous foretaste of future events. The 1950s also brought the first attacks by Puerto Rican separatists, who came close to killing both members of Congress and President Truman; further groups would emerge to continue the armed struggle on the American mainland during the 1960s. The era would end with another precursor to more serious terrorist events when Americans would find themselves held by governments that America did not recognise in East Germany and China, as well as by rebels in Cuba. Such events would also provide an antecedent for future hostage situations with rogue states that America would soon have to address.

5

FROM LEFT TO RIGHT: THE RISE AND FALL OF US DOMESTIC TERRORISM, 1968–1980

Whilst bombings and assassinations have been common enough in the country's historical experience,[27] never before had they been so concentrated nor accompanied by such outpourings of radical rhetoric against militarism, capitalism, racism and oppression. Carolyn Gallaher calls the 1970s the heyday of domestic terrorism within America, with a staggering 450 terrorist attacks reported in America during 1970 (Gallaher, 2015, p. 325). The FBI went further by stating that there were 2,500 bombings on American soil in an eighteen-month period between 1971–72, which, if true, is more than five a day. J. Bowyer Bell and Ted Gurr argued that by this time terrorism had become 'trendy' in both word and deed (1979, p. 329). Bombings became so common that the public seemed almost resigned to their frequency. Despite the prevalence of attacks, this era has been, according to Bryan Burrough, 'all but ignored by historians', something he addresses in his highly detailed 2015 book *Days of Rage: America's Radical Underground, the FBI and the Forgotten Age of Revolutionary Violence*. Laura Kalman

---

27 One of the most high-profile examples was the assassination of controversial Louisiana Senator Huey Long in 1935. Long clearly had presidential hopes, but was shot by the relative of a judge he was attempting to remove.

suggests that during the 1970s Americans became fixated on terrorism. This concern was in part due to anxiety about America's declining position on the world stage (Kalman pp. 2010, 60–61).

Whilst there is no attempt in this chapter to list all of the groups and individuals committing violent actions during this era, and no suggestion that all violent attacks were political, there were some key driving forces that motivated the main actors conducting terrorist activities. The volume of attacks was dow-n to the coalescing of a number of political causes. The most important of these causes was the growing radicalism caused by America's involvement in the Vietnam War, a war which Nixon soon illegally extended into neighbouring Laos and Cambodia, galvanising American youth into a hitherto unknown violent upheaval and a desire from radicals to bring the brutality of the war home to America itself. Another source of terrorist actions stemmed from more strident forces within the civil rights movement, who pursued campaigns of violence that would engage the attention of FBI director J. Edgar Hoover. He deemed groups such as the Black Panthers the greatest threat to American security. This period would also bring a resurgence of terrorism that sought to push Puerto Rico towards independence, and their violent attacks, coupled with those of other groups such as Croatian and Cuban nationalists, all helped to explain why this period represented the peak of terrorist attacks in American history.

Another reason that terrorism was increasingly prevalent at this time was the easy availability of explosives, which could be bought openly or stolen from construction sites where there was comparatively little security. The period from 1969–70 saw some 975 bomb explosions, 3355 incendiaries and 1175 unexploded bombs. These figures were compiled by the Alcohol, Tobacco and Firearms Division of the Treasury Department, with around a quarter of the explosions believed to have been conducted for political motives (Graham & Gurr, 1979, p. 335). Dynamite was easily stolen from building sites which maintained little security.

New York City alone would experience some four hundred bomb scares in just a twenty-four-hour period (Nixon, 1979, p. 470). Unsurprisingly, Nixon would stress the importance of inserting anti-bombing legislation into the Organised Crime Bill put forward in October 1970.

It is important not to underestimate the galvanising force that American involvement in the Vietnam War had on terrorist movements both internally and externally. Many youths became radicalised by a war where hundreds of thousands faced a military draft, including such figures as Mohammad Ali, who fought a long legal campaign to avoid conscription on religious grounds that went all the way to the Supreme Court ruling in June 1971. Anger and outrage only intensified when it was revealed that the war was being illegally expanded into the neighbouring countries of Laos and Cambodia, a fact only admitted by Nixon on 30 April 1970, which pushed the students into protest mode.

The bombing had actually begun in March 1969, and by the time of Nixon's admission, some 110,000 tons of bombs from 3600 flights had been dropped onto Cambodia (Gitlin, 1993, p. 378). Jeremy Varon has stressed the importance that the Vietnam War had in creating a general climate of radicalism that extended well beyond the US. Many were concerned about oppression in the Third World and felt a connection with wider protest movements, although in reality groups in America never possessed any significant international connections that may have created a greater threat to American security. Whilst there is no suggestion that this era, the peak in terms in home-grown terrorist attacks, could ever have resulted in a violent overthrow of the United States government, the rhetoric of the New Left was often couched in pre-revolutionary terms. Many of the left made the mistake of imagining that far more people wanted violent change than was actually the case. It is notable that the Nixon administration kept to hand martial law proclamations if it became too difficult to keep order in any American cities under normal conditions (Thomas, 2016, p. 285).

The biggest opposition group to the war were the Students for a Democratic Society (SDS), which briefly enjoyed a membership of over 100,000. It was founded by Freedom Rider Tom Hayden who helped pen the 'Port Huron Statement', which centred on civil rights (although it would fail to unite whites with African Americans). Inevitably its focus became increasingly anti-draft and it opposed the large military expansion in Vietnam. By 1968, with the death of Martin Luther King, the chief advocate of non-violence, gunned down by James Earl Ray, coupled with mass uprisings that seemed to be taking root in countries such as France, where student protest grew into a situation which did threaten to overthrow the political elites, the idea of a genuine revolution within America seemed a real possibility. Factions within the SDS were becoming increasingly radical, inspired by Dr Ernesto 'Che' Guevara (1928–1967), the poster boy of the revolutionaries, who advocated violence to bring down corrupt and oppressive governments in order to liberate the people. Guevara was one of the few revolutionaries who gained support inside and outside America, both before and after his execution in Bolivia in 1967. Bomb-making manuals began to circulate amongst the SDS and bomb incidents rose during 1968. John Jacobs, one of the early leading theoreticians of the group, argued that there needed to be a 1969 equivalent of John Brown, the implication being that the movement was just awaiting a violent initial spark.

The Weathermen, (later, the Weather Underground), would become the radical splinter group from the SDS, taking their name from the Bob Dylan song *Subterranean Homesick Blues*. The group would be the biggest terrorist organisation of the era in terms of membership, believing that America had become racist and repressive and was now guilty of the kind of militaristic imperialism that she had once broken free from. They believed that the time was ripe to call upon the people to rise up and spark a revolution. Their first bombing target, in October 1969, was revealing: they attacked the statue erected in memory of the police killed during the 1886 Haymarket bombing (see chapter two). The statue had to be rebuilt, only to be destroyed a second time by the movement a year later, provoking anger from the city's mayor, Richard J. Daley

The period 8–11 October 1969 brought the 'Days of Rage' in Chicago. This began with a commemoration of the martyrdom of Che Guevara and involved around 600 youths, with 287 arrests (Varon, 2004, p. 82). The group stated that they wished to 'bring the war home' which became their mantra, but the turnout was disappointing and they were soon heavily outnumbered by police, although seventy-five police officers were injured in the disturbances (Gitlin, 1993, p. 393). Police heavy-handedness included beatings, and most notably the brutal death of Fred Hampton in December 1969. Hampton was the twenty-one-year-old chairman of the Panthers in Illinois, who was killed when police fired eighty-two bullets in his apartment (Nacos, 2010, p. 65). The media portrayed the event as self-defence, even though there was little sign that Hampton fired back and was sleeping in a room with his wife and child. It was this event that partly radicalised the Weathermen movement. A group of hardcore members decided to go underground at the start of 1970, a task made easier by the roaring trade in fake identities brought about by draft avoidance of the Vietnam War. However, a disastrous accident in March 1970, where three leading members of the movement blew themselves up in a Greenwich Village townhouse, not only led many to leave the movement but also led to a much greater interest in the group being taken by the FBI.[28] The group

28 A series of explosions not only destroyed the townhouse but damaged adjoining properties including the home of actor Dustin Hoffman, who was photographed outside the still burning apartment.

would look to target military and corporate targets, as seen with their attacks on the National Guard Headquarters in Washington D.C., as well as the New York City Police Headquarters, the Presidio army facility in San Francisco, and the Harvard Center for International Affairs. Even before the Weathermen moved underground at the end of 1969, police and security agents were already moving in on the association.

J. Edgar Hoover, who had monitored the group since its inception, certainly believed that the Weathermen underground movement was part of a nationwide terrorist offensive and was linked to wider protest movements. In his memoirs Richard Nixon agreed and looking for validation of his belief in a wider terrorist movement quoted a 1977 *New York Times* article, which stated that there had been direct support for the group from both North Vietnam and Cuba, the latter country aiding the group's escape from the FBI (Nixon, 1979, p. 471). Despite the possibility of such links and the truth (at least in terms of the sheer volume of terrorist incidents) of Nixon's argument that America faced an epidemic of unprecedented domestic terrorism, the security services created the impression that the group was a much greater threat to American security than they actually were. Although 1969 saw some ninety-three explosions in New York City and sixty-three in San Francisco alone, these explosions came from a variety of sources. Nixon referred to the Weathermen as the 'most violent, persistent, and pernicious of the revolutionary groups'. In April 1970 Attorney General John Mitchell launched indictments against twelve Weather Underground leaders, with the FBI launching what they stated was one of the greatest manhunts in American history. Although the leaders of the radical groups did not want to admit to the reality, the wider public was turning against the student movement. When four innocent bystanders were shot dead at Kent State University in May 1970, following the student unrest generated by Nixon's belated admission that he had taken the war into Cambodia, the public reaction was muted. The public supported the president's attempts to end the war with his approval rating increasing (Morris & Carter, 1996, p. 216). On 8 May some seventy student protesters were beaten up near Wall Street, showing the general public were now increasingly tired of the protest movements.

One of the main leaders of the Weather Underground was Bernardine Dohrn, a twenty-seven-year-old law graduate, dubbed 'La Passionaria of the Lunatic Left', with Daniel Flynn commenting that her knee-high boots, mini skirt, leather jacket and shades certainly attracted recruits (Flynn, 2008, p. 312) and clearly did not reflect the image that most people before, or since, would have of a terrorist. Todd Gitlin has stated that Dohrn was a mix of 'sex queen and street fighter', and proved more successful in recruiting women to the cause than any other radical group (Gitlin, 1993, p. 386). Dohrn's most controversial statement came in Flint at the end of 1969, when she told supporters of the movement that it was time for violence and chaos to avenge the death of Fred Hampton. Commenting on the sadistic killings of the pregnant Sharon Tate and others at the home she shared with movie director husband Roman Polanski, Dohrn stated 'Dig it! First they killed those pigs, then they ate dinner in the same room with them. They even shoved a fork into the victim's stomach! Wild!' Dohrn has stated that the comments were ironic, prompted by the amount of attention that the mass murders were receiving, Unsurprisingly, such comments brought a huge amount of negative publicity for both her and the groups she supported.

Dohrn's voice could be heard on a tape recording of 21 May 1970 when the Weather Underground issued a Declaration of a State of War against the American government, with the text also being printed in the *New York Times* four days later. They stated that they would employ revolutionary violence and guerrilla tactics in aiding their fellow African American revolutionaries. Bill Ayres would later describe the message as one of defiance and hyperbole (Ayres, 2009, p. 227). The group warned a new campaign would begin with an attack on an American symbol of justice within the following two weeks; that target turned out to be the New York Police Headquarters. In a demonstration of how common threats were during that time, police ignored the group's bomb warning. Although damage was modest, eight people sustained slight injuries. The message was clear, American security services were unable to protect themselves (Burrough, 2015, p. 130). Following this attack greater security was brought in. ID checks were made at public buildings, bathrooms were locked as a precaution. The group aided the escape of Timothy Leary[29] from prison, gaining them column inches. On 24 August a large bomb attack on the Army Mathematics Research Centre, housed at the University of Wisconsin's Sterling Hall, caused the unplanned death of Dr Robert Fassnacht, who was working late. Richard Nixon would condemn the 'vicious bombing', as he increasingly moved to push Americans to stop accepting the use of violence as an acceptable tactic.

Despite there being over 500 people to feature on the FBI's Ten Most Wanted Fugitives list, first established in 1950, only ten of these (up to 2016) have been women. Dohrn would be the fourth woman to appear on the list when she was added in October 1970, following a series of explosions at various locations across America.

The group would make headlines again when they attacked the US Capitol on 1 March 1971. A bomb in the first-floor men's room caused around $300,000 of damage, the first attack on the Capitol since the British burning of 1814. In 1972 the group, now down to a rump of hardcore supporters, launched only one attack,

29 Timothy Francis Leary (1920-1996) was a psychologist most famous for his experiments with the the drug LSD.

although this was conducted against the highly symbolic target of the Pentagon. The bomb, planted in a women's restroom on the outer ring of the building, would cause damage but no casualties and a note again claimed the attack to be in response to ongoing bombing against the Vietnamese.

Their final hurrah would be a manifesto they entitled *Prairie Fire*, in which they took credit for nineteen acts of terrorism, and promised future actions. However, after the mid-1970s the movement faded away as the Vietnam War had finally drawn to a close, and the potential pardon offered by President Carter to draft resisters brought many former members out of the shadows. Many came forth to authorities, who were increasingly uninterested in the previous activities of the group members anyway. By 1980 both Bernadine Dohrn and Bill Ayres had given themselves up to the authorities. But the charges against Ayres had already been dropped, and the FBI were not that interested anymore in Dohrn. She eventually faced court in Chicago for her previous actions, but received a fine of just $1500 and three years' probation. Dohrn has remained a controversial character, and has long stressed her emphasis was always to attack property and not people. In 1995 she and Ayers met Barack Obama, then in the process of preparing for his senate campaign. Her support of Barack Obama during the 2008 presidential campaign caused some media interest and anti-Obama posters of the time directly linked the future president to the pair.

Another important female figure of the late 1960s was Jane Alpert. She was part of the New York City Collective, seen as only slightly less of a threat than the Weathermen. Joining with her lover Sam Melville[30] she played a role in a series of bomb attacks in 1969. Alpert would take part in attacks on the Chase

---

30 Samuel Melville, whose original name was Samuel Grossman, was killed in a prison riot in September 1971.

Manhattan Bank, Standard Oil and General Motors, as well as an attack on the Criminal Court building, often carrying the bombs in her purse (Eager, 2008, p. 47). Not only did their bomb attacks increase the level of fear and unease in the city, but their actions generated the potential for copycat actions and saw the police having to deal with hundreds of additional false bomb threats, or false alerts.

Alpert would place a bomb on the fortieth floor of a New York federal building that housed the US military. As the bomb went off at 2 am Alpert watched and noted that she felt the explosion 'brought the revolution a step or two closer' (Alpert, 1981, p. 214). The reality was that their campaign would not last long; the FBI were soon onto Melville, and he was caught and sent to Attica Correctional Facility. Alpert was also rounded up, but skipped her $20,000 bail on the urging of Weathermen Mark Rudd and poet Robin Morgan, who encouraged her to go underground. She remained so until 1974, meeting up with other underground luminaries such as Dohrn. She eventually pleaded guilty and would be sentenced to twenty-seven months in prison for conspiracy to bomb buildings and skipping bail, although she served slightly less time for good behaviour. In 1981, once the statute of limitations on any crime had expired, she wrote her memoirs, *Growing up Underground*, where she portrayed herself as a weak figure, dominated by Melville, overcome by the excitement of her involvement with the revolutionary cause.

The Black Panther Party for Self-Defense was formed in Oakland, California in 1966 by Bobby Searle and Huey Newton. They argued that white police forces constituted an 'occupying force' in the ghetto (Gitlin, 1993, p. 348). The group were inspired by Che Guevara as well as figures such as Franz Fanon, whose critique of colonial control *The Wretched of the Earth* emphasised that decolonisation was always a violent process designed to break the spirit, and that the process of liberation through violence could be uniting and restore notions of self-respect (Simmons, 2010, p. 47). Many members of the Party were increasingly disenchanted with the ghettoization, poverty and lack of progress for African Americans. The group were opposed to the existing political and economic system and sought the overthrow of both. The group did not initially form as a terrorist organisation but became more radical, with shoot-outs and bombing attacks encouraged by figures such as Eldridge Cleaver, who advocated armed resistance in the form of kidnappings, hijackings, and bombings. Black Power radicals would also adopt the tactic of hijacking in order to fly to Cuba to gain asylum (Hyams, 1975, p. 177). Indeed Cuba became the location of choice for many hunted African American militants, including for a time Huey Newton, with entire houses set aside for those seeking political asylum (Kurlansky, 2005, p. 174).

Some, such as Assata Shakur, a former member of the Black Liberation Army who escaped from prison in 1979 (having been convicted of murder), remain there to this day, although in 2017 President Trump indicated he wanted to see the return of fugitives in exchange for better relations. The movement would have been stronger had it worked in full cooperation with groups such as the Weathermen, with whom it did collaborate for a limited period. Richard Nixon argued that the Panthers were closely affiliated with North Korean groups and even radical Arab terrorists.

In 1969, the year that the group engaged in gun battles with the police in both Chicago and Los Angeles, J. Edgar Hoover declared that the Black Panthers were the most dangerous internal threat that America faced (Crenshaw, 2011, p. 198). The organisation was bigger than the Weathermen but still had only a few thousand members, although these were organised into local inner city chapters, which proved harder to penetrate. The movement had its own newspaper. In addition the movement ran soup kitchens and literacy programmes. President Nixon was alarmed to note in 1970 that upper class whites, including Mrs Leonard Bernstein, had engaged in fundraising for the group (Ambrose, 1989, p. 332). For a short time in the early 1970s the group even received official recognition from the Algerian government, complete with their own embassy where Eldridge Cleaver held court. The group were not afraid to take on the police in gun battles, which so perturbed Richard Nixon that in November 1970 he gave a statement regarding the shootings and bombings. Having consulted with FBI boss J. Edgar Hoover, Nixon issued a Presidential Directive that more federal help would now become available to help combat the growing problem. He ordered that the investigative resources of the Department of Justice would be available to state or even local police if requested, in dealing with any crime perpetrated against a police officer (Nixon, 1970, p. 1064).

A major crackdown was thus implemented, which saw Black Panther leaders targeted for arrest, the police being incentivised in the work as they were being directly targeted by the group. In 1968–69 there were thirty-one raids against Panther offices in eleven states. President Nixon boasted that in 1969 some 348 Panthers had been arrested for serious crimes. Founder Huey Newton declared in 1972 that the campaign of militancy was over, but by that time, the FBI's campaign had significantly reduced the ability of the group to conduct attacks, leaving a divided and weakened group to limp on. The Black Power movement would also lose ground in part due to assimilation policies pursued by President Johnson and indeed later presidents.

Nixon's Huston Plan, named after Tom Charles Huston, was a programme designed to counter revolutionary violence by using wiretaps, mail opening and surveillance, which gained the support of the president, but ironically not J. Edgar Hoover, by now weary of being criticised for violations of civil liberties. Hoover demanded the programme be stopped, but Nixon ordered it continue without

Hoover's knowledge. Finally however, the president refused to directly sign the order and the plan quickly died. In justification, Nixon would point out that domestic terrorism rose at the same time that J. Edgar Hoover cut back on controversial surveillance operations, such as the planting of bugs and use of informants, indicating his belief that such tactics had proved effective in reducing terrorism (Nixon, 1979, p. 472).

Just as the white radical groups would splinter into even more radical divisions, so did those organised by the African Americans, with the Black Liberation Army (BLA) breaking away from the Black Panther Party in May 1971. The group first attacked two policemen on 19 May, the birthday of Malcolm X, before the killing of two police officers two days later signalled the arrival of a new and violent group who were unafraid to target and kill police officers of both races. By far the most important chapter of the group was located in New York, led by Nathaniel Burns (later to be become known as Sekou Odinga) and Anthony Coston (who became known as Lumumba Shakur). Both were former members of the Black Panthers. Although the group issued communiqués following some attacks, information about the group remains sparse, but Burrough outlines that the group was a black underground urban guerrilla movement. Lacking a centralised leadership, its decentralised structure made it harder for the police to track down members initially. Once it had been accepted that this was a new radical group, intent on attacking police officers, President Nixon soon ordered J. Edgar Hoover to use all available means to destroy it, and a squad was set up in order to specifically achieve that (Burrough, 2015, p. 197). Seven police officers had been killed in less than a year in four different states by people claiming to be part of the BLA, although authorities were not keen on advertising the possibility that there was a rogue group within America targeting police officers. Richard

Daley would push the idea of a nationwide threat by the group, first in the *New York* magazine, and then in the book *Target Blue* (1971). Here, Daley's actions has echoes of those of Allan Pinkerton, with the Molly Maguires and Michael Schaack with the Haymarket plotters, by stressing the threat posed by the group, he was able to increase his own profile and sales.

Whilst the group lacked formal leadership, the group would also have a key female member, who, like Dohrn, would achieve significant notoriety, potentially well beyond any threat she genuinely represented or actions that she took, indeed both these aspects are heavily debated. JoAnne Chesimard, who become known as Assata Shakur, having survived being shot during a robbery in Manhattan in March 1971 would go on to receive considerable press attention, as 'a machine-gun-toting, grenade-tossing, spitting-mad Bonnie Parker' who seemed to be the blueprint for the badass heroines of the popular blaxploitation movies of that time (Burrough, 2015, p. 239). Such an image may help to explain why she became the most wanted female in New York's history. She even remains on the FBI's most wanted terrorist list to this day in connection with the murder of a New Jersey state trooper, having escaped from prison in 1979 with the help of associates who smuggled a gun into the prison. The gunning down of the last main active player in the movement, Twymon Meyers, heralded the effective end of a group that has not left a large imprint on the American psyche.

To add to the outbreaks of terrorism that were becoming increasingly common within America came a resurgence of the Puerto Rican separatist movement. Those supporting the independence of the island raised money via illegal activities at home and used this to finance attacks both in Puerto Rico itself and on the American mainland (Lutz & Lutz, 2007, p. 106). The focus altered from choosing symbolic or strategic targets to targeting civilians, which would make them a significant terrorist group in modern American history.

By 1969 a new movement appeared, the Armed Revolutionary Independence Movement (MIRA) and they began a series of small bombing attacks around New York. In the end over a hundred small bombs would be linked to the group, some attacks causing minor injuries. The attacks came to an end in 1971 following various arrests. J. Bowyer Bell and Ted Robert Gurr note that part of the reason for the resurgence of their campaign was deep frustration over what was actually very limited support for independence on the island itself. Although support in 1952 had stood at around 19 per cent, only 6.5 per cent of the population voted for independence in 1976 and this had fallen further to 4.4 per cent by 1993 (Hewitt, 2003, p. 34), showing that the violent campaigns proved hugely unsuccessful in terms of galvanising support for their cause. *Fuerzas Armadas de Liberacion National* (FALN) started a new terror campaign in August 1974 with a series of bomb attacks that again targeted New York. The bombing attacks grew in intensity in October and in December a bomb packed with nails severely injured a policeman, Angel Poggi, who ironically was one of the 600 Puerto Ricans who worked for the police force.

The biggest attack by the group brought terror back to the heart of New York, when on 24 January 1975 they detonated a bomb at the historic Fraunces Tavern, which would kill four people and injure fifty-five. The fact that the bomb went off at 1.22 pm during the busy lunchtime period demonstrated that the bombers intended to maximise the number of victims. Indeed, in terms of fatalities, this was the biggest attack on New York City since the Wall Street Bombing of 1920. The tavern was popular with bankers and stock brokers, being situated very close to Wall Street. The bombers would also have been aware of the history of the venue. Founded in 1762, the Chamber of Commerce had been founded there in 1768 and the Tavern played a role in hosting both sides during the War of Independence. On 25 November 1783, as the last British troops left New York, the last city to be occupied, George Washington dined there and invited his officers of the Continental Army to re-join him there nine days later to bid the British farewell. A note by the bombers in a nearby phone booth stated that they had targeted the Tavern as they wanted to target bankers and stock brokers, as these were not working class or 'innocent' Americans. 'We ... take full responsibility for the especially detornated (sic) bomb that exploded today at Fraunces Tavern, with reactionary corporate executives inside.'

This attack was part of a larger series of bombings over the spring and summer, the attacks being targeted largely at financial institutions that the group believed in some way were involved in exploiting Puerto Rico. By September 1975, Cuba's leader Fidel Castro was organising a Puerto Rican solidarity conference, much to America's annoyance (Mount, 2006, pp. 41–42), but this did little to spur the cause of independence and the attacks continued. On 27 October came an attack on the State building as part of ten pipe bomb attacks in three cities, Washington D.C., New York and Chicago. Over a twelve-month period FALN planted twenty-five bombs, with the police having little success in tracing the culprits. Law enforcement agencies believed that the group were responsible for forty-nine bombs attacks from 31 August 1974 to 18 February 1977. Some of the later attacks corresponded with legal hearings against prospective members of the group. The problem of Puerto Rican terrorist attacks was deemed so significant that a conference was called to address the problem, to be held on the island, but this had to be cancelled when those who were planning to attend were threatened by the group.

FALN even attacked the FBI offices in New York in 1977 as well as Department of Defense facilities. It is likely that the group were aided in their actions by the moribund Weather Underground movement (Burrough, 2015, p. 390). On 3 August 1977 a series of attacks struck across New York, with one person killed in the Mobil Oil headquarters. Warnings phoned in to the *Eyewitness News* station stated that there were bombs placed at the World Trade Center, causing the first evacuation of the two towers (Burrough, 2015, p. 401). Bombings continued, although the main bomb maker, Willie Morales, would be seriously injured whilst preparing bombs in his New York apartment. Morales was arrested and imprisoned, although bizarrely, despite losing nine fingers in the explosion still managed to get out of his third-storey prison cell and climb down to waiting accomplices and freedom. In 1979 the group threatened to blow up New York's Indian Point nuclear facility and papers uncovered in 1980 suggested the group would attempt to kidnap high profile politicians such as Ronald Reagan (Hoffman, 1986, p. 12).

In May 1981 came an attack at JFK airport where a bomb was placed in a men's room and its detonation would kill twenty-year-old Alex McMillan; two other bombs would also be discovered at the airport. As Pam Griset and Sue Mahan note, the FALN were the last left-wing group to conduct a terrorist campaign within the US. Another group *Los Macheteros*, would attack American planes at a base in Puerto Rico and kill an American soldier and injure three others in San Juan. Eleven FALN members were arrested in Illinois in 1980, and seventeen more arrests of FALN and *Los Macheteros* members in 1985 seriously depleted the groups, although occasional terrorist attacks in the name of independence have continued on Puerto Rico itself.

The Symbionese Liberation Army, which began at Berkeley, has been described as one of the most incompetent and bizarre urban terrorist groups ever. The group attracted some student members but actively recruited criminals, which clearly facilitated the movement in engaging in both murder and robbery. Their ideology would prove somewhat hazy, but their 1973 manifesto, in an echo of the anarchist rationale, declared 'revolutionary war against the

Fascist Capitalist Class, and all their agents of murder, oppression and exploitation' (Nacos, 210, p. 66). Despite stressing that the organisation was multiracial, their first act was to be the killing of African American Dr Marcus Foster at the Oakland public school. Foster's 'crime' had been to propose that the police become involved in curbing school violence and supporting the use of identity cards. The brutal murder of Foster alienated many potential members and was openly denounced by the Black Panthers. The group only ever contained a handful of members and was led by escaped convict Donald DeFreeze. DeFreeze was influenced by the writings of prison activist George Lester Jackson (1941–1971), whose book *Soledad Brother* proved to be a bestseller. Defreeze had escaped from Soledad Prison.

Easily their most notorious action came in February 1974 with the kidnapping of newspaper heiress Patricia Hearst, then aged nineteen, demanding that her family give millions of dollars of food aid to the poor, something the family set about attempting to carry out. The events surrounding Hearst's kidnapping attracted the greatest amount of media attention after Watergate. Headlines about the kidnapping grew more hysterical when she was identified robbing a bank in San Francisco two months later, having been won over to the kidnapper's cause after being kept for eight weeks in a closet and threatened with execution. From this switch of allegiance to the terrorist group, the phrase 'Stockholm Syndrome' became a widely known expression to describe a situation where over time hostages and hostage takers form an emotional attachment (Crenshaw, 2011, p. 133). Defreeze died along with four other members of the group in a shoot-out in Los Angeles in May 1974. Despite his death, Hearst remained with the few other active members of the group, who now announced that the group would be called the New World Liberation Front and who called for more bombing attacks in America. The group, or indeed groups operating under that name would continue a bombing campaign that lasted until 1978, confined largely to California.[31] Eventually the group would carry out more bombings than any other underground group, and these only ended when the main perpetrator of the bombings, Ronald Huffman, was arrested after killing his partner at the farm on which they produced copious amounts of marijuana.

Patricia Hearst was finally arrested in San Francisco in September 1975. Her court case brought into focus the question of whether Hearst was a victim or a terrorist, although she did not help swing feelings towards the former when she gave her occupation as 'urban guerrilla'. Her trial on robbery charges would inevitably be high profile and brought a wave of terrorism, including an attack on the Hearst family home at San Simeon, as well an attack at another Hearst property at Wynton, California, by the New World Liberation Front. With the jury unsympathetic to her plight, she was sentenced to seven years in prison, although she was eventually freed by Jimmy Carter in 1979.[32]

In 1975 President Ford would face two assassination attempts within just a few days. The first attempt was by Lynette Alice ('Squeaky') Fromme, who was a devotee of mass murderer Charles Manson.[33] Ford himself states that he went to shake her hand before noticing the .45 calibre pistol in it, from which he quickly ducked, whilst Fromme shouted 'This man is not your president'

---

31 1973 and 1974 were especially violent years in California with a series of murders and violent attacks on whites by four Black Muslims. These were the so called 'Zebra Killings' and the perpetrators were sentenced to life imprisonment in March 1976 for the killing of fourteen people. The killings were random, taking place at night and were racially motivated, but there was no discernible political motive.

32 She was pardoned by President Clinton in 2001. The final prison sentences for former members of the group were not passed until 2003 for the deaths of two people killed in a bank robbery in 1975, the year the movement effectively ended.

33 Fromme was born in Santa Monica in 1948 and had joined Manson's circle in 1967. Manson, who died in 2017, and his followers were found guilty of several brutal murders including that of actress Sharon Tate. Fromme was sentenced to life imprisonment and was finally released in 2009.

(Ford, 1979, p. 310). There are question marks over her intention, and even whether she intended to kill the president, given that the chamber in the gun was empty, although the gun did contain four bullets. Remarkably the president gave videotaped evidence to state he did not hear the click of a gun, but Fromme was still found guilty of the assassination attempt. Just seventeen days after what Ford believed to be 'an aberration', a more serious attempt to kill him was made when Sara Jane Moore fired at the president when he was leaving the Saint Francis hotel in San Francisco. The bullet passed between Ford and Defense Secretary Donald Rumsfeld before hitting the wall of the hotel (Rumsfeld, 2012, p. 190). Her attempt to get off a second shot was thwarted by former marine Oliver Sipple. Moore was a 45-year-old who held radical political views and was connected to radical groups in the area. Earlier that day Moore had been arrested on an illegal gun charge, but was quickly released. Moore at the time was unrepentant, stating that she had intended to kill the president and cause chaos. Moore would be found guilty of attempting to assassinate the president and was sentenced to life imprisonment. Like Fromme, she would not be released until after Ford's death.[34] Dominic Sandbrook has commented that despite the seriousness of the attempts, there was no anguished national debate and no rush of support for the president, as such actions were no longer seen as exceptional or shocking (Sandbrook, 2012, p. 43). Given the deaths of John F. Kennedy, Malcolm X, Martin Luther King, Robert Kennedy and the attempted assassination of George Wallace during the previous decade, such a point certainly rings true.

The year ended with another massive explosion, this time at the TWA terminal at La Guardia airport. The bomb, which was the equivalent of twenty-five sticks of dynamite, had been placed

34 Moore would be released in 2007, by which time she stated in interviews that she had altered her views and that she regretted trying to kill Ford.

in the bagging area and generated deadly shrapnel from baggage carousels and coin lockers when it exploded at 6.33 pm. Only half an hour earlier two flights had landed, creating a potentially much higher death toll. As it was, the explosion killed eleven people and injured seventy-five. The attack was the worst on New York since the Wall Street attack in 1920. FBI Director Clarence Kelley argued that terrorism was the ultimate evil in society, and that no one could consider themselves immune from terrorist acts. This bombing was in fact one of eighty-nine that were attributed to terrorism in 1975 (Perlstein, 2014, p xiv).

There remains some debate about who planted the bomb. Whilst suspicion fell on Puerto Rican separatists, the case remains one of the most puzzling chapters in the history of American terrorism, yet like so many incidents of this kind it has faded from public consciousness. Curiously, given that an act of terrorism is intended to publicise or create support for a cause, no group has ever claimed responsibility for the bombing. There were to be no prosecutions and even today the attack remains an unsolved case.

The most plausible theory behind the attack revolves around Croatian nationalists campaigning for the liberation of their country from the control of Dictator General Tito, who had ruled over Yugoslavia since World War Two. New York police suspected the attack may be the work of Zvonko Busic, who was imprisoned for planting a bomb at Grand Central Terminal in September 1976, which would kill one of the police officers attempting to defuse it. The La Guardia bombing reinforced the idea that New York was the stage for groups seeking attention for international causes, coming so soon after the Puerto Rican attacks. Busic also used fake explosives in the 1976 hijack of T.W.A. Flight 355 plane at La Guardia airport. Busic committed suicide in September 2013 at the age of 67, having always protested his innocence over the T.W.A. bombing.

The violent campaign of those fighting to free Croatia should not be underestimated; Brenda and James Lutz state that there were 128 worldwide terrorist attacks connected to this movement between 1962 and 1982, some of which were conducted in the US. For example, in August 1978 Croatians would seize control of the West German consulate in Chicago. Other émigré groups also utilised targets in the US to bring attention to the situation in their home country to the international community or to their own peoples, including the Jewish Defense League, as well as groups linked to Cubans, Armenians, Haitians, Sikhs and Taiwanese.

Other groups actively engaging in violent acts on American soil included Omega 7, M-17 and *El Condor*, who opposed the leadership of Fidel Castro and who committed bombing campaigns at various locations including fifty bombings in Miami and attacks in New York. The groups were determined to prevent any accommodation that America may have been considering with the Castro regime (Zebich-Knos & Nicol, 2005, p. 168) although more worrying was their attack on a Soviet ship in New Jersey. Cuban extremists were responsible for ten murders and 168 terrorist incidents from 1968 (Hewitt, 2003, p. 18). The group faded after its leader Eduardo Arocena was jailed for the killing of a Cuban diplomat in 1983.

Complicating definitions of terrorism in America during this period, there was the formation of the right-wing Jewish Defense League (JDL) which was formed in New York in 1968 by Rabbi Meir Kahane. Kahane had been forced to leave Israel due to his extreme stance against Palestinians. Unusually, the acts of terrorism conducted by the group within the US were aimed at raising the profile of the oppression of Jews by the Soviet Union. The group killed five people in a total of 115 terrorist incidents ascribed to the group (Hewitt, 2003, p. 18). The activities of the group included both murders and bombings, with thirty convictions for members of the groups for violent offences. Kahane's murder in 1990 by Islamic terrorists will be considered in chapter seven.

As the 1970s came to an end, the radicalism of the early part of the decade faded quickly. There remained the final revolutionary stragglers. An explosion in Boston in April 1976 at the Suffolk County Courthouse injured twenty-two people and was carried out by the Sam Melville Jonathan Jackson Unit, who turned out to be a small group led by Ray Levasseur. After spending some time in Vietnam he had discovered the works of Che Guevara and grew even more enraged about the colour divides in the US. His intermittent bombing campaigns (often funded by bank robberies) would carry on into the 1980s (under the name United Freedom Front in the latter years) until he was finally caught following the allocation of huge police resources in November 1984. The communiqués from the group focussed on the need for prison reform, but as time went on the group increasingly supported the Puerto Rican independence movement, one attack even being stated to be in commemoration of the Puerto Rican attack on the House of Representatives in 1954. Levasseur and a group called the 'Armed Resistance Unit' led by former Weatherman member Laura Whitehorn, who carried out eight bombings between 1983 and 1985, were essentially the last active groups of the radical era that had dogged America since the late 1960s to be captured.

As left-wing terrorism's embers in the United States finally died in the early 1980s, there would be a rise in violent actions by right-wing militia. In September 1983, The Order, an adjunct of the Aryan Nations, founded by Robert Matthews and inspired by the book *The Turner Diaries*, not only engaged in a series of robberies but bombed a Jewish synagogue and most notably murdered Jewish radio talk-show presenter Alan Berg outside his home in June 1984 (Wright, 2007, pp. 88–9). In November 1984 an eight-page 'Declaration of War' was issued by thirteen members of The Order vowing to kill all politicians, judges, bankers, soldiers and police offers who got in their way. The Covenant, Sword and Arm of the Lord group also targeted the Jewish community, and the group were guilty of murder as well attempting to carry out acts of sabotage and planning the assassination of various law enforcement officials. There would follow a major targeting of Patriot groups during the period from 1986–88, with around thirty Patriot leaders arrested. One member, Richard Wayne Snell, would be convicted of the killing of an African American police officer and was executed on 19 April 1995. As will be seen in chapter seven, this would be the same date on which Timothy McVeigh would carry out his truck bomb attack on the Alfred P. Murrah Federal Building. The Covenant, Sword and Arm of the Lord group had planned a truck bomb attack against the same building in 1983.

Despite the fact that the end of the 1960s and the early 1970s represents the apogee of terrorism within America in terms of frequency, the issue did not dominate American headlines. This can be explained by the sheer number of attacks, coupled with the fact that less than 1 per cent of them during this era led to a fatality (Burrough, 2015, p. 5). In addition, terrorism had to compete with a myriad other high-profile issues facing America during this period, from the protracted and humiliating end of the Vietnam War to détente, Watergate, the Presidential Pardon, oil price shocks and the growing problems of lower economic growth, high inflation and rising unemployment.

President Carter would seek to explain the fall in terrorist attacks by pointing out that during his presidency he attempted to protect the rights of the Palestinians, America did not have bases in Saudi Arabia, or what he termed sensitive Arab States, NATO forces were not dispatched to fight in Arab countries and finally, America was adopting a tougher position with Libya and other states that supported terrorism (Carter, 210, p. 121).

Although there would be a brief resurgence in underground radicalism in the mid-1970s, caused by public distrust and anger over Watergate, FBI scandals and also the resurgent Puerto Rican independence movement, in reality many of the driving forces of internal terrorism were already beginning to fade ahead of Carter's election in 1976. Although Nixon had heightened tensions with the extension of his bombing campaigns into Laos and Cambodia, he soon began a pull-out from South East Asia. By 1972 US troops numbers had declined to less than 100,000 and at the end of the year Nixon famously declared 'peace was at hand'. American troops finally left Vietnam in April 1975, removing the last vestige of an issue that had so galvanised internal terrorism. Many of the leading figures of the radical movements moved into hiding or gave themselves up.

Also dwindling in intensity were the radical civil rights groups. The Black Panthers faded during the 1970s as police surveillance and internal disagreements took their toll. Puerto Rican separatists had also all but ended their violent struggle by the late 1970s. Carolyn Gallaher notes that by 1977 recorded terrorist attacks within the US had declined to no more than one hundred and the number was continuing to fall. Even when considering the number of such attacks, the reality was that these groups never posed a threat to the American system. The groups only ever contained modest numbers, and internal disagreements over violent tactics often led to their fragmentation. The groups cooperated with each other only on a limited scale and never succeeded in getting anything but token assistance from forces outside of the US. The campaigns in America, whilst violent and causing deaths, injuries and the destruction of property, never reached the level of violence seen in other countries or regions during the 1970s (such as Italy, Germany or Northern Ireland). Whilst the worst of internal terrorism was over, American would now begin to face other terrorist threats. Whereas much of the terrorism of the 1970s had been from left-wing causes, increasingly, internal terrorist attacks would be conducted by right-wing extremists. In reality the biggest terrorist threats that America would face came internationally from states that supported terrorism; America would dub such countries 'rogue states' and their importance and impact will be discussed in the following chapters.

6

THE US AND INTERNATIONAL
TERRORISM, 1968–1989

America emerged from World War Two as the world's preeminent economic and military power and it soon set about expanding its global presence. The long history of isolationism in American foreign policy was dead. As American power and influence grew, the country increasingly saw a rise in attacks on its businesses, officials and citizens overseas. Although, as we have seen, there have been notable exceptions such as the Puerto Rican separatists, and many of the anarchist leaders did import their ideas of 'propaganda by deed' into the US, until the 1960s America was largely unaffected by international terrorism. Before that time, it was highly unusual to hear a president refer to terrorism, helping to foster the belief that the concept was new. President Johnson did begin to use the term during the Vietnam War to describe violent acts undertaken by North Vietnamese forces, with the American response being couched in terms of counterterrorism (Winkler, 2006, p. 35). 1968 brought a significant upsurge in international terrorism, brought about by the rise of international media coverage and mass air travel. While much high-profile terrorism took place during the 1970s, including the multiple hijacking of passenger planes at Dawson's Field in Jordan, and the Munich

Olympic attack by Black September forces, America stood on the outside of such events, although often involved behind the scenes, and altering policy as a result. Such detachment ended when the Iranian Embassy in Tehran was stormed and fifty-two Americans would be held hostage for over a year. The Reagan years from 1981 therefore began in the shadow of international terrorism, the threat of which became so elevated that by 1985 he had declared the first 'war on terror'.

The large increase in international terrorism was personified by the sharp rise in aircraft hijackings, which would soon take on far more serious dimensions than simple detours to Havana. There were twenty-two hijackings to Cuba in 1968, rising to forty in 1969. Plane hijackings to Cuba were becoming so common that some pilots took to keeping a map of Havana's Jose Marti airport on hand; a travel writer jokingly advised his readers to carry a hijack bag in the case of an unplanned visit to Havana (Hyams, 1975, p. 177). There was even a new kind of rule of the road established, whereby those unwillingly flown to Cuba would be treated well. They would be photographed, led through the airport to buy tourist souvenirs, such as Cuban cigars, which would then be confiscated upon their arrival back in the US. Despite a lack of formal diplomatic relations between America and the regime of Fidel Castro, a treaty was concluded between the two nations which helped in greatly reducing such hijackings. If the flights to Cuba were an annoyance for both countries, this only represented a distraction and those on board the aircraft suffered little more than frayed nerves and a considerable delay to their journey. The Federal Aviation Administration gave advice to hijacked passengers to remain passive when in a hijacking situation.

The majority of aircraft hijackings in the years 1969–72 occurred in flights originating in the US, with some fifty-eight incidents, although most of these were not politically motivated. The prevalence of hijacking led to the secret service advising President

Nixon not to allow members of his family to use commercial airlines (Thomas, 2016. p. 285). Terrorists would now begin to utilise aircraft in a way that was considerably more than an annoyance.

The year 1968 would see a huge upsurge in international terrorism, and whilst much of this would be focussed on the Middle East, inevitably America would become increasingly embroiled in these terrorist events. There was a large rise in high-profile international terrorist hijackings by groups connected to Palestinian causes. Three members of the Popular Front for the Liberation of Palestine, led by Georges Habash, hijacked a plane flying to Rome on 23 July 1968. Maximising the publicity that their actions brought, the hijacking would not come to an end for another forty days, leading the hijackers to deem their actions a great success.

Hijacking took on an even more serious dimension when four planes were simultaneously hijacked, three of them flown to Dawson's Field in Jordan on 6 September 1970. The events took place despite an Interpol alert that terrorists were planning hijacks (Raab, 2007, p. 25). The hijackers found themselves with around three hundred hostages and with a major international incident on their hands. Multiple hijackings were not actually a new phenomenon, the first example taking place when three pilots working for Czechoslovak States Airlines took control of three aircraft and flew to West Germany to seek political asylum. However, in that case the passengers were in no danger and either opted for asylum or returned home. In Jordan, the situation was volatile and dangerous and passengers were at real risk. At the conclusion of events on 28 September, Nixon met some of the returning American hostages, taking time to explain and justify the quiet, behind-the-scenes diplomacy he had adopted.

Eventually a deal was done (controversially) to free the remaining prisoners on the aircraft in exchange for Palestinian prisoners including Leila Khalid. The Palestinians were inspired by the success of the Vietminh against America. The hijackers made clear that they wanted to target US interests because of her foreign policies. This was an immediate 'victory' for the Palestinians and their cause was centre stage; but the spotlight faded and Egypt and Jordan would distance themselves from the movement.

A splinter group, 'Black September', was formed, supported by Arafat. The plan was to overturn King Hussein's regime. Wasfi Tal (Jordan's Prime Minister) would be assassinated by the group in Cairo in November 1970. For the Black September group, however, their most notorious act was yet to come.

Richard Nixon in an address to Kansas State University stated that the events in Jordan marked the 250th takeover of a plane since the skyjacking era had begun in 1961 and that the events had sent shockwaves of alarm across the world; he condemned holding passengers under the potential threat of death, and referred to the rising use of violence and terror as akin to a disease that was spreading (Nixon, 1970, p. 758). As part of his response Nixon created a Federal Air Marshal programme and declared that any country where planes landed would be held accountable for protecting the lives of Americans and the property of US companies.

A curious aside, the most unusual hijack of this era came on 24 November 1971 when a passenger listed as D. B. Cooper took control of a flight from Portland to Seattle, claiming to have a bomb in his bag. In exchange for the release of the other passengers and crew, he was provided with $200,000 (equivalent to about $1,250,000 today), four parachutes and the plane was refuelled. He then ordered the pilot to fly to Mexico City, but at a height of only 10,000 feet. Soon into the flight, having selected one of the parachutes, he made his escape, jumping out of the plane via the back airstair, taking the money with him. Cooper was never to be seen again, despite letters sent to newspapers claiming to be from the hijacker. The case remains the only unresolved hijacking in the US, despite a forty-five year manhunt.

In November 1972 Nixon signed the Instrument of Ratification of the Convention for the Suppression of Unlawful Acts against the Safety of Civil Aviation, a multilateral treaty. He pledged to back what became known as the Montreal Convention or Sabotage Convention and work with the United Nations and International Civil Aviation Organisation in order to deal with 'despicable acts of terrorism' (Nixon, 1974, p. 1081).

Crucial to the countermeasures to the change in terrorist activity was the introduction of boarding gate security checks, made a legal requirement in 1973. These new measures proved to be a considerable success, with attempted hijackings falling to just three in the year after the measure was introduced, compared to thirty-one the year previously. Amazingly, and alarmingly, the searches revealed some 3,500 pounds of high explosives and 2000 guns (Wilkinson, 2006, p. 128).

Driving terrorist activity against America would be the country's role in supporting Israel. Ever since the 1940s, America's relationship with Islamic countries has been complicated by its support of Israel. Any attempt by the US to play a more neutral role or assume the role of honest broker in the Middle East would be destroyed by the Six-Day War in 1967. During this war Israel would gain control of West Bank and the Golan Heights, as well as parts of the Sinai. America had tried to prevent the war and relations with Israel had the potential to be damaged by the latter's attack on the American surveillance ship the USS *Liberty* on 8 June, which killed thirty-four Americans and led to a multimillion dollar payout. Nevertheless, America still stepped in with arms and support that helped keep Israel strong, to the fury of the surrounding Arab nations. Paul Wilkinson draws attention to the impact of the 1967 war and notes that from 1968–72 there was a huge upsurge of actual or potential hijackings, bombings, shootings and other terrorist attacks against Israel and American personnel (Freedman, 1986, p. 43).

Six years later in the Yom Kippur War America again would step into protect a key ally, with many seeing America as saving Israel from defeat, further antagonising the neighbouring countries and creating a festering resentment against the US. This was the time when America greatly expanded its arms supply to Israel (Clarke, 2003, p. 43). Not all authors argue that America's interventions in the region have a negative outcome; Barry and Judith Rubin paint a benevolent picture of American involvement in the Middle East in *Anti-American Terrorism and the Middle East*. However, perceptions are key, and increasingly those opposed to Israel's existence began to turn their anger and resentment towards the US. Perhaps the most important figure to be galvanised by these events would be Osama bin Laden, who directly linked his radicalization to the 1973 war, as shown in chapter eight.

Resentment against America for its support of Israel was the reason cited by Sirhan Bishara Sirhan, a Palestinian refugee who had settled in the US in 1956 and who was not known to the security services, for assassinating Robert Kennedy at the Ambassador Hotel in Los Angeles just after he had been declared the winner of the Californian presidential primary on 4 June. Just over a week previously at a speech at Temple Neveh Shalom in Portland, Kennedy had argued for the sale of fifty Phantom jets to Israel. Sirhan even possessed a newspaper article which discussed Kennedy's support for Israel when he was arrested.

Guided through the crowded kitchen space close to the stage, Kennedy was shot three times at close range, including a fatal head shot. Five others were shot in the melee before the gunman was subdued. At this time there was no official protection for presidential candidates, although this was immediately changed by President Johnson and very shortly after by Congress. Perhaps inevitably, not least because of the Kennedy name, there has been much speculation about the events, the motives of the gunman and indeed whether Sirhan was the true or only gunman.

Dan Moldea, after extensive research and interviews with relevant witnesses, including hours of interviews with the alleged assassin, would change his initial view and concluded that Sirhan was the sole gunman. He concluded that claims Sirhan could not remember either picking up his gun, entering the kitchen area or shooting the president, leading to the theory that he was somehow 'mind controlled' by an outside agency, were simply falsehoods to disguise the truth (Moldea, 1995, p. 300). Curiously, Moldea does not argue that there was a political motive for this killing, since he did not find anything connected to the Palestinian cause in Sirhan's notebooks, but he did find a passage that advocated the overthrow of the president. Authors continue to dispute the events and Sirhan's role in them. However, Moldea, whose work was reprinted for the fiftieth anniversary of Kennedy's passing in 2018, placed the assailant in the same category as other assassins who had killed merely to prove themselves or compensate for failed personal circumstances.

In 1972 the Black September group would strike again on the biggest media stage there is, the Olympic Games. The Munich Games were watched by around 13 per cent of the world's population (Jackson, 2011, p. 53). Eight Black September members targeted Israeli athletes, two of which were killed with another nine initially taken hostage. Germany, hosting the games for the first time since 1936 and anxious to show a positive image to the world, downplayed the security shortcomings (the hostage takers, dressed in tracksuits, were even helped over the fence into the Olympic Village at 4am by American athletes returning from a night of drinking). The kidnappers demanded the swapping of the hostages in exchange for 236 Palestinian prisoners held by Israel. Acting in front of such a large global audience reduced the German's government's room for manoeuvre. The hostage takers were even able to watch the events live on TV and could view any attempt to storm their location. The influence of the media had never been so fully utilised by terrorists and this created a powerful lesson for future terrorists. The conclusion for the German authorities was disastrous since it ended in a gun battle which left all eleven Israeli athletes dead, along with five terrorists and a German policeman.

Three of the attackers were arrested but later released when terrorists managed to gain control of a Lufthansa jet. Abu Daoud would later confess to his role in an autobiography. He claimed no injury was ever intended towards the athletes.

Whilst not directly involved with events, President Nixon could hardly avoid commenting on the ongoing situation. On 5 September whilst in San Francisco Nixon addressed reporters. He stated the events involved international outlaws 'who will stoop to anything in order to achieve their goals'. Just twenty days later Nixon announced the establishment of a 'Cabinet Committee to Combat Terrorism' due to the 'importance and urgency [of] the worldwide problem of terrorism'. This Committee, chaired by the Secretary of State, included the treasury, defence, and transport secretaries, as well as the Attorney General and Director of Central Intelligence. Their aim was to look for the most effective ways of preventing terrorism both within the US and abroad. The Committee was to coordinate the various agencies, look at the best ways to implement programs, assess the potential of swift reaction to terrorist events, consider budgeting needs and report back directly to the president. Two days after his memorandum Nixon argued it was necessary as terror 'threatens the very principles upon which nations are founded' and argued that all states would be united by the common danger of terrorism, a position far removed from that taken by Reagan less than a decade later.

As Joseph Campos states, Nixon was the first president for whom terrorism entered presidential rhetoric. Nixon, Campos argues, was the first to frame terrorists as criminals who employ indiscriminate violence and therefore retribution should be the basis on which US policy should rest. Nixon established a policy of no concessions, no negotiation and no escape from justice. In October 1972 Nixon had already signed a bill making it a federal offence to harass, assault, kidnap or murder a foreign official, their family or an official guest of the US whilst that person was in America.

Although a low-key approach to hostage crises in the Congo in 1964 and 1967 worked out for President Johnson, Nixon began to take a harder line with a 'no negotiation with terrorists' strategy. This of course would have consequences. In March 1973 seven Black September terrorists stormed the Saudi Arabian Embassy in Khartoum, Sudan, during a farewell event for the American chargé d'affaires George Curtis Moore. Among their demands was the freeing of hundreds of prisoners including Robert Kennedy's assassin Sirhan Sirhan. After three tense days the group did surrender, but hearing the president's words, they simply saw no value in keeping their hostages alive. Moore, the American Ambassador Cleo A. Noel Jr, and a Belgian official were all killed. This incident did not receive a mention in Nixon's voluminous memoirs published in 1978.

Despite the deaths in Munich and negative media coverage, the large number of high-profile terrorist events conducted to highlight the cause of Palestine succeeded in placing their campaign high up the political agenda, and much to Israel's objections the PLO were awarded observer status at the United Nations in November 1974.

In July 1978 President Carter wrote to Libya's controversial leader Muammar Gaddafi informing him that if he welcomed hijacked commercial planes into his country instead of agreeing to return the hijackers to the place of the original hijack, all flights to and from Libya would cease. Gaddafi, perhaps noting that the president was informing him in a private letter, duly ended any Libyan policy of admitting such planes (Carter, 210, p. 206). This was to prove important as the unwillingness of governments to welcome hijackers, coupled with heightened security measures, made the practice largely fall into abeyance, until it was dramatically resurrected on 9/11.

Whilst Americans were increasingly targeted by terrorists after 1968, it was the taking hostage of (initially) sixty-six staff at the American Embassy in Tehran in November 1979 that brought home to many Americans the ways in which terrorism, in this case state-sponsored terrorism, could expose American weakness in a country still reeling from the failure of the Vietnam War. In 1953 a coup d'état against elected Prime Minister Mohammad Mussadegh, was organised by the US and British governments, and Iran became a military dictatorship under Shah Mohammad Pahlavi. The Shah bought up a third of all American arms sold abroad and received a visit from President Carter at the end of 1978, where the President described Iran in flattering terms as an 'island of stability in one of the more troubled areas of the world' (Carter, 1982, p. 437). Resentment over Western influence mounted over time and would culminate in the Iranian Revolution. As the Shah left Iran to seek medical treatment for cancer, Ayatollah Khomeini seized the opportunity to return from exile in Paris to take control of the country in January 1979.

Carter's decision, despite his own reservations, to allow the ailing Shah to enter the US for medical treatment proved to be fateful. It was this action in particular that drove radicals into a state of fury, as Iranians feared that America would again try to re-impose their will upon Iran (Kinzer, 2003, pp. 202–3) The attack on the American embassy took place on a Sunday when no marines were even stationed at the front gate to protect the embassy from being stormed by students led by Ibrahim Asgarzadeh. The students wished to make their criticisms of American policy heard by seizing the embassy for two or three days. However, a day after the events Ayatollah Khomeini saw a perfect opportunity to seize full political control, as well as an opportunity to embarrass and humiliate the US, 'the Great Satan'. Whilst Islamist movements had been developing in the 1970s, the events in Iran in 1979 gave them a huge stimulus and groups loyal to the revolutionary cause took root throughout the Middle East. Kinzer argued that America's actions in 1953 directly led to the events of 1979, and brought about a new radical leadership in Iran, which set about propagating terrorism against the West via support for movements such as Hamas and Hezbollah (Kinzer, 2003, p. 203).

Lesser known is the fact that Khomeini deliberately stirred up more hatred against America. In November 1979 he called the crisis a war between 'Islam and the Pagans' and pushed Muslims to move against American imperialism and attack their embassies abroad (Winkler, 2006, p. 56).

Such language would echo messages later given out by Osama bin Laden when he claimed that there was a battle between the people of Islam and the 'global crusaders' (Lawrence, 2005, p. 108). Khomeini announced that the Americans were behind the takeover of the Grand Mosque in Mecca, the holiest site in the Islamic world. In reality religious zealots from within Saudi Arabia had stormed Mecca and there was no American involvement, but in the highly charged atmosphere, the American Embassy in Islamabad was stormed and set on fire, forcing the occupants to hole up in a safe room in crowded conditions. When the siege subsided the occupants were able to escape, but two Americans and two Pakistani staff were dead and America's prestige further undermined by a group of Islamic extremists, Jamaat-e-Islami.

Although Carter himself would portray the actions of Iran as international terrorism, he initially attempted to avoid this description, rarely mentioning the term in the first eight weeks of the crisis. Indeed, when Carter eventually moved towards labelling Iran's action as terrorism, this provoked an angry response from the Ayatollah Khomeini, who appeared on CBS-TV news to defend the Iranian position and try to portray America as the instigator of terrorist acts (Winkler, 2006, p. 39). Remarkably, Iran took out paid advertising space in American newspapers, and even allowed NBC to interview the hostages in their attempts to maximise publicity and defend their actions. Iran was able to exploit American vulnerability and after releasing fourteen hostages still held some fifty-two Americans for a total of 444 days, releasing them only after interminable diplomatic wrangling minutes after Ronald Reagan had been inaugurated in January 1981. The hostages were held in harsh conditions, threatened with execution, they were blindfolded and paraded on TV in the knowledge that such images would be shown around the world. President Carter was aghast at the unprecedented Iranian actions, but he proved powerless to free the hostages during his term of office, notably failing in both his diplomatic and military efforts to free those held. In April 1980 Operation *Eagle Claw*, an attempt to rescue the hostages, resulted in eight Delta Force operatives being killed when a helicopter collided with a C-130 transport plane. The eight dead Americans would be left behind and their bodies were displayed on the streets of the Iranian capital. The botched attempt contrasted markedly with successful raids at Entebbe, Uganda, when Israeli forces rescued 102 passengers, and the rescue of all eighty-six passengers by West German military at Mogadishu, Somalia, in 1977, both planes having been hijacked by factions of the Popular Front for the Liberation of Palestine. America had failed to deal successfully with the actions of a rogue state, and the botched rescue mission further eroded American prestige. The American people were reminded daily of the ongoing crisis when CBS news anchor Walter Cronkite ended his nightly updates by stating how many nights the hostages had been held captive.

Carter's handling of the hostage situation showed patience and he exhausted all diplomatic channels. Carter, and the presidents that followed him, were anxious not to alienate the Muslim population, and he demanded the media not portray the events as a battle between America and the Islamic world. As will be seen, Ronald Reagan would avoid pushing for an American invasion of Libya because of fears of alienating Muslim countries, and George H. W. Bush went out of his way to include Muslim partners in his coalition against Iraq in 1991. George W. Bush drew a distinction between the Muslim world and those seized by radicalism, as well as quickly stressing the need to protect Muslims in the US soon after the 9/11 attacks, even visiting a mosque soon after the attacks (2005, p. 142).

The inauguration of Ronald Reagan in January 1981 was overshadowed by the spectre of terrorism that would increasingly dominate his political agenda. The Iranian hostage crisis may have ended on his first day in office, but Reagan made it clear that the battle against international terrorism would be high on his priorities and that he would have more effective answers to the issue of international terrorism and the growing problem of rogue states. During the course of his presidency, especially when dealing with his own hostage situations in the Middle East, just as President Carter had done, Reagan increasingly became emotionally engaged with the issue (Wills, 2003, p. 47), which may go some way to explaining Reagan's mistakes during the Iran–Contra affair. Welcoming the hostages back home on his first full day in office he stated 'Let terrorists beware that when the rules of international behaviour are violated, our policy will be one of swift and effective retribution.' That same month Reagan's Secretary of State Alexander Haig in his first news conference said that terrorism would take priority over notions of human rights, as it was argued that terrorism was the ultimate abuse of such rights.

However, in reality, Reagan had few answers to the rising problems of terrorism. Carol Winkler notes that 550 Americans lost their lives to terrorism during the Reagan presidency (Winkler, 2006, p. 65) and David Wills states that there were

636 terrorist incidents against American targets during the Reagan years (Wills, 2003, p. 6). James Patterson believes that part of the reason for attacks against America lay not in the fact that American wealth and power brought envy and resentment, but that many people were angry at America's imposition of certain regimes upon them, such as American interventions which removed leaders in Chile in 1973[35] or Iran in 1953, and replaced them with military dictatorships. These factors help to explain the proliferation of terrorist attacks upon the US during the 1980s. American diplomats would find themselves targeted in many locations across the globe, with military personnel or government officials being killed in Mexico, Greece, Pakistan and Lebanon. Bombs also exploded outside American embassies or military bases in Italy, West Germany, Portugal, Peru, Bolivia and Kuwait City, a prelude to the far more devastating attacks in the 1990s (see chapter seven).

Reagan would view the struggle against terrorism very much through the prism of the Cold War, with terrorist attacks being ultimately orchestrated by the USSR. Whilst terrorism was an international issue, which impacted on the Middle East and Europe to a far greater extent than the US, the idea was that the secret hand of the Kremlin was the connecting force behind terrorist attacks. Alexander Haig was one of the first to encourage a receptive president to draw a clear link between terrorism and communism. Haig was quick to announce such a link at his first news conference just eight days after Reagan's inauguration. The fact that the Cold

---

35 The Chilean coup organised by the US replaced democratically elected socialist president Salvador Allende with a military junta under General Pinochet. The date of the coup, September 11 (9/11), gave the Chilean people their own reason to remember this particular day of the year. Pinochet remained in office for seventeen years, with a poor human rights record that saw the deaths of well over 3000 citizens. 'Behind the other 9/11' draws on declassified documents to prove that Washington backed Pinochet's reign of terror (*Newsweek*, Latin American edition).

War was entering a period of increased friction following the Soviet invasion of Afghanistan in 1979 only added to the tensions. The arguments which underpinned the president's understanding of terrorism being connected to communism were simple, appealing and easy to relate to. Haig was not alone in allowing this fallacy to ferment in the president's mind, as William Casey, the veteran head of the CIA, also encouraged Reagan to think in these terms. In Reagan's Address to the Nation on Events in Lebanon and Grenada in October 1983, he declared that, despite their distance apart, Moscow was behind the violence, providing 'direct support through a network of surrogates and terrorists' (Reagan, 2004, p. 194).

Another person pushing such an explanation was Republican House Minority Whip Newt Gingrich, who blamed the USSR for all international violence. In effect, the Soviet Union and its client states could be the scapegoat for all acts of terrorism that took place in the world. Much of the philosophy behind this thinking came from the book *The Terror Network* by Claire Sterling in 1981, having previously set out her case in the *New York Times* and *Washington Post*. Sterling claimed that terrorist groups around the world were growing in number, connected by training camps and arms suppliers, all linked to the Soviet Union whose intention was to demoralise the West. Unsurprisingly, reviewers such as John Cooley invited her to check her facts and look more deeply at what breeds terrorism.

By April 1981 a new Subcommittee on Security and Terrorism had started to meet and its hearings would only serve to provide more ammunition to this bogus theory. As Randall Law has stated, the irony was that the CIA had actually supplied some of the arguments for the book based on 'black propaganda' and when William Casey said he had learned much from the book, it was clear that the misinformation had come full circle and the CIA were now believing their own propaganda (Law, 2009, p. 276).

A second edition of the book in 1982 even praised Haig's comments, but the reality was that much of the material it contained was self-perpetuating myth. This is not to suggest that the Soviet Union was totally innocent of the charge that they were involved in supporting some terrorist groups or terrorist states. Laqueur notes that there was clear cooperation between the Soviet Union and North Korea and Cuba, with looser affiliation to Libya and Algeria (2012, p. 201).

These states, along with Iran, increasingly appeared on the State Department's annual report of countries that sponsored terrorism. Such countries were to be officially designated as terrorist supporters under the Export Administration Act of 1979. Before that time America referred to states that conducted appalling abuses against their own citizens, such as Pol Pot's Cambodia, South Africa under Apartheid, or Idi Amin's Uganda, as 'pariah states'. However, the focus would transfer to states that supported external actions against America or its interests. Indeed, America offered support to Pol Pot, the genocidal leader of the Khmer Rouge, and to a segregated South Africa, as a bolster against communism.

As part of the effort to combat communism Reagan signed National Security Directive 166, which stepped up aid to groups fighting against Soviet forces in Afghanistan. The policy of supporting or covertly supporting Islamic rebels had begun in the summer of 1979, when National Security Advisor Zbigniew Brzezinski, who was something of a 'hawk' when it came to the influence of the Soviet Union, persuaded President Carter to provide covert aid for the nascent *mujahideen* against the pro-Soviet government. Aid to the rebels was increased in 1980, and Carter even moved to work with the Chinese on supplying the rebels as part of a package of measures designed to opposed Soviet actions, which George Herring has argued was part of an overreaction to Moscow's attempt to shore up a regime in Kabul, which they considered part of their own sphere of influence (Herring, 2011, p. 853). There was also a push by Brzezinski to refer to those opposing the USSR as 'freedom fighters'. Reagan's policy was to support the advancement of Wahhabism, a stricter and more fundamentalist form of Islam, which they saw as acting as a bulwark against communism. In October 1986 Deputy Director of the CIA and future Defence Secretary Robert Gates even visited a *mujahideen* training camp to see how American support was being utilised. Gates notes in his memoirs that Pakistan chose which warlords to supply the American equipment to, which proved to be groups supporting Islamic fundamentalism (Gates, 2014, p. 335–6). One of the several downsides to this strategy was that it failed to give America any contacts on the ground in Afghanistan when they came to search for bin Laden (Clarke, 2003, p. 52).

The one-dimensional thinking on foreign policy that was almost exclusively designed to tackle the perceived rise of the threat to America's interests from the spread of communism gave little thought as to what would be the longer term impact of supporting such a strict form of religious orthodoxy. In their attempt to create a unified fighting force to take on the Soviets, America would end up training and equipping some of the world's most radical extremists. Saull and Colas state that America took an active role in creating a reactionary political movement, the blowback from which was directly connected to 9/11 (2006, p. 79). Some of the Afghan fighters were well trained in deadly skills. Once the war in Afghanistan was over, these skills would be increasingly utilised against the US, creating perhaps the most dramatic incidence ever of 'blowback', a CIA term denoting serious unintended consequences from covert operations. Whilst figures are difficult to fully ascertain, by the late 1980s America was linking its funding to that supplied by Saudi Arabia, meaning that funding of over $3 billion was given over to the *mujahideen* (Heymann, 2000, p. xxiv).

One event in 1982 would have a significant impact on the future of terrorism. A lack of clear understanding and approach in the Middle East between Washington and Tel Aviv saw Israel invade Lebanon on 6 June. Refugee camps housing thousands of Palestinians were shelled by Phalange forces at Sabra and Shatilla whilst Israeli forces stood back, causing the deaths of 700 people. The horrifying pictures of the attack created intense pressure for the US to condemn the actions of its ally. Some 18,000 people lost their lives in the invasion. These events would be cited by Osama bin Laden as the main motivation behind his attacks on 9/11, as will be seen in chapter eight. International intervention saw PLO forces move into Jordan as Israel marched into Beirut. To add to the confusion president-elect Bachir Gemayel was assassinated on 14 September. Reagan was shocked and outraged at these events, and in August – against the wishes of Defense Secretary Casper Weinberger – agreed to send 1500 peacekeeping troops to Beirut as part of a multinational force with French, British and Italian forces, to be deployed around the airport area. The move was questioned by such figures as future Vice President Dick Cheney. A Commission led by Admiral Robert Long would later conclude the marines in Beirut lacked the necessary training and support to deal with the situation (Wills, 2003, p. 79).

Anger rose against the US, as America was seen to favour Amine Gemayel as president, brother of the slain president-elect. His Maronite Christian beliefs, coupled with his closeness to Israel, antagonised Muslim groups who could not envisage America as a neutral figure in the ongoing war. The smallness of the military presence made it impossible to make any positive difference to the chaos on the ground. Soon the Americans themselves would become the central target for reprisal attacks. On 18 April 1983 a major suicide attack against the American embassy in Beirut killed sixty-three people, seventeen of whom were American, among them Robert Ames, the CIA's leading expert on the Middle East.

This was only the prelude to an even bigger truck bomb attack at the US Marine Barracks on October 23. It was later estimated that the explosives used were the equivalent of 9,500 kg of TNT. The bomb killed 220 marines and twenty-one navy medical personnel; this was the largest tally of casualties lost in a single day since the Battle for Iwo Jima during World War Two. That same day a suicide bomb attack killed fifty-nine people at the French barracks.[36]

Reagan would record in his diaries (2007, p. 189) his belief that Iran was behind the attack. American investigations would later add some weight to Reagan's belief, concluding that Shia radicals directed by Iran and Syria had conducted the attack. The events led to the State Department adding Iran to its official list of states that sponsor terrorism in January 1984. Reagan would insist that there no need 'to cut and to run', stating that America would never by forced out by terrorism, as this would only encourage terrorists further (Wills, 2003, p. 67). In reality, pressured by Congress, the Pentagon and adverse public opinion, Reagan agreed to remove Americans from the area by the following year, creating a no-go area for westerners for many years to come and helping to lay the groundwork for Reagan's future hostage crises. As George Schultz would argue, the withdrawal of American troops from the country left the very clear message that terrorism works (1993, p. 644). Philip Jenkins has argued that the withdrawal from the Lebanon, now judged to be no longer part of American strategic interests, gave Islamic militants the twin messages that unconventional forces could overwhelm a much more powerful adversary and crucially that America had a low tolerance for casualties (Jenkins, 2006, p. 284). Similar messages had been sent during the Vietnam War and indeed would be sent again following America's withdrawal from Somalia (see following chapter). Back in America, these

---

36 December 1983 brought a similar attack on the US Embassy in Kuwait City by the al Dawa group as part of a larger series of attacks. There were five casualties, but none of these were American.

devastating truck bombs led to additional security measures that included blocking traffic from in front of the White House, lest there be a copycat attack.

David Dodge would be the first of seventeen hostages kidnapped as he left his office in Lebanon in July 1982 and whilst Dodge would eventually be released the following year, this was not to be the case for all of the others. William Buckley, the CIA Chief who was a personal friend of CIA Director William Casey, was kidnapped in Beirut, tortured and died in captivity in 1985.

Remarkably, the taking of American hostages outside of the country only became a crime in US law in 1984, and the assaulting, maiming or murdering of American citizens two years later. Reagan was acutely aware of the political dangers of having American hostages paraded on news reports across the world, and had to tread a line between acknowledging the events and not getting so close to the hostage issue, as Carter had. Reagan was publicly accosted by the family of hostage Father Lawrence Jenco, ironically at an event to meet with the families of the soon-to-be released hostages from flight TWA 847, which made his advisors even keener to keep him away from the issue of American captives. But the meeting left a deep impression on the president, who strove to find ways to free the hostages. In an echo of the letters sent from captives of the Barbary pirates nearly two centuries before, Reagan would receive copious correspondence from the families of those held captive. Some high-profile politicians were supportive of the president. The governor of New York, Mario Cuomo, wrote to Reagan in June 1985 commending Reagan's firmness and reflecting on the difficulty of the president's position in trying to achieve 'the safe return of our Americans without creating invitations to further terrorism' (Reagan, 2004, p. 461). At that time seven Americans were being held captive in Lebanon.

Reagan's public position had to be that America could never give way to terrorist demands and there could be no deals.

In reality his attempt to deal with the issue through back door channels resulted in what was easily the biggest scandal of his presidency and brought him close to impeachment. The details of the Iran–Contra affair would not break until Reagan's second term, and involved a complex arrangement whereby Israel acted as America's intermediary in supplying weapons to Iran, a country which since 1980 had been at war with its neighbour, Iraq. That America was supplying such weapons in breach of an arms embargo was damaging enough, but when it was revealed that monies from the arms sales were diverted to the Contra Rebels in Nicaragua, an action effectively been banned by the Boland Amendments passed in Congress (Byrne, 2014, p. 55), something approaching a constitutional crisis was created. Since the Contra Rebels had engaged in terrorist methods, some of which, it was revealed, were taken from what was dubbed a 'CIA Murder Manual', the American public began to question whether or not America itself had become a state sponsor of terrorism (Winkler, 2009, pp. 72–73).

The whole murky affair was being run by staff in the White House basement, and the extent of Reagan's direct knowledge of events has never been fully ascertained, despite the setting up of a blue-ribbon commission to investigate the affair led by Republican John Tower, who would conclude that the president was well intentioned but unaware of the facts. His portrayal as remote from or ignorant of the events (despite testimony of key figures such as Oliver North and later former National Security advisor John Poindexter, who both claimed otherwise) protected Reagan from impeachment. However, the Tower Report of February 1987 did conclude that the president's actions 'ran directly counter' to his promise to deal harshly with terrorism (Schaller, 1992, p. 166). Reagan's rhetoric was clearly not matched in practice.

Although in reality weapons sales to Iran has secretly begun in 1981, in 1985 the idea was put forward that providing military equipment to Iran would move the country away from the need for Russian military assistance. This was rejected by Defence Secretary Casper Weinberger, who blamed much of the damaging initiatives on Bud McFarlane. Weinberger was especially damning about McFarlane supplying Iran with military intelligence to better attack Iraq, whom America were supporting at the time. Another explanation offered to the American people about these arms sales was that they were an attempt by the Reagan administration to free the hostages held in the Middle East, since Iran had potential influence over groups who were holding the hostages. Although he specifically denied knowingly trading arms for hostages, Reagan sought to portray the trade as a necessary evil for the greater good of freeing American hostages without treating directly with terrorist groups. Reagan also made it clear that he hoped it was possible to achieve some kind of rapprochement with moderates within Iran.

Reagan's strategy did result in the release of three hostages, but other hostages were taken to replace them and the potential hostage price increased. Rossinow argues that Reagan simply did not have a clear approach on how to deal with this difficult and complex issue. For example, an attempt at a military response via the unsuccessful targeting of Hizbollah leader Mohammed Fadlallah in Beirut in 1985 resulted in the bombing of a crowded market killing eighty people (Rossinow, 2014, p. 187).

With terrorism maintaining a high profile during Reagan's first term, a new National Security Directive was signed in April 1984. NSDD-138 listed terrorism as a threat to national security and committed America to using force, including the potential use of pre-emptive or retaliatory strikes, to combat the threat of terrorism. The Directive stressed that America had a right to defend itself against states that support terrorism. David Wills has argued that NSDD-138 was a seminal shift in policy which amounted to a 'declaration of war on terrorism' (Wills, 2003, p. 19). So in theory terrorism could not go unpunished, but this was not always easy to enforce in practice. Key to Reagan's terrorist strategy was George Schultz, a very different figure to Haig. Schultz was especially concerned about terrorism and became one of the most outspoken hawks on the issue.

In October 1984 he stated that the USA might have to take preventative or even 'pre-emptive' action against states that perpetuated terrorist attacks. Such a pre-emptive strategy would be controversially outlined by George W. Bush in his West Point speech of June 2002 (see chapter eight). Schultz's hawkish position set him aside from others in the cabinet, notably Defense Secretary Casper Weinberger, and the antipathy of the two towards each other can clearly be seen in their respective memoirs.[37] Schultz argued for both 'pre-emption and retaliation' since terrorism represented a threat to civilised life and that passive defence did not provide enough of a deterrent. He argued that 'terrorism is being used by our adversaries as a modern tool of warfare' and that America could 'expect more terrorism directed at our strategic interests in the years ahead'. In the October speech he stated that America should be prepared to move forward quickly and not always with evidence that would stand up legally – yet he also argued that America would always be governed by the rule of law. He called for international cooperation on the issue.[38] In such statements

---

37 Casper Weinberger's *Fighting for Peace* was published in 1990 (London: Michael Joseph), George Schultz's *Turmoil and Triumph*, nearly three times longer, was published in 1993 (New York: Charles Scribner's Sons).

38 Schultz contributed to the book *Terrorism: How the West Can Win* in 1986, edited by Benjamin Netanyahu, future Prime Minister of Israel. There is an interesting contribution in the book by British historian and journalist Paul Johnson: 'Let us debate privately among ourselves when, and if so how, we will be prepared to discard the obstacle of sovereignty and national frontiers, which shelter the state terrorists. Let us calmly and discreetly amass and train the forces which will be necessary for such police action and discuss how we will deal with the political and international consequences. Let us decide in good time the limits beyond which terrorist states will not be allowed to pass, and let us perfect a military instrument of fearful retribution when and if those limits are crossed.'

Schultz seemed to be moving ahead of the position taken by the president. Given his advocacy of pre-emptive action prior to 9/11, he is considered the father of the Bush Doctrine (Starr-Deelen, 2014, p. 47). It was unsurprising that Reagan would be tackled on the subject during the 1984 presidential debates with Walter Mondale. A somewhat testy Reagan had to respond to criticisms that warnings about American safety had been ignored prior to the Beirut attacks.

By July 1985 the issue of terrorism had moved to the top of the Reagan administration's agenda. One of the main reasons for this was the hijack of TWA flight 847, which had departed from Athens on 14 June, by radical Shi'ite Muslim group, Hezbollah. The aircraft was carrying 135 American citizens, which made up the bulk of the passengers. Reagan's claim in the presidential debates that the issue of skyjacking had been effectively dealt with was given the lie. The hijackers shouted 'New Jersey' and 'Marines' at the distressed passengers, who were unaware this was a reference to the American battleship that had shelled targets in the Lebanon. The hijackers attacked the Americans on the plane and would murder American navy serviceman Robert Stethem, dumping his body outside the plane, in full view of the media.[39] The hijackers sought to maximise the international coverage of the hijack by flying the plane back and forth between Beirut and Algiers, an action that also made any potential rescue by Delta Force very difficult to achieve.

The hostage releases, which included Greek music star Demis Roussos,[40] were facilitated by the leaders of Syria and Iran (Rossinow, p. 187) and would come in stages as the events played

---

39 Reagan would greet Stethem's body as it arrived in the US, stressing America would make no concessions to terrorists.

40 Demis Roussos (1946-2015) was an Egyptian born singer. He spent his thirty-ninth birthday on the hijacked plane, thanking his captors at a press conference for his good treatment, which included a birthday cake.

Right: America would experience its first 'arms for hostages' deal during wars with the Barbary pirates. (Courtesy of the Rijksmuseum)

Below: John Brown's actions in the 1850s were of course judged differently in the northern and southern states, creating an early debate between the difference between a 'terrorist' and a 'freedom fighter'. (Courtesy of the Library of Congress)

Tafiletta the Greate Xeriffe, or Emperor of Barbary. etc.

HARPER'S FERRY INSURRECTION—INTERIOR OF THE ENGINE-HOUSE, JUST BEFORE THE GATE IS BROKEN DOWN BY THE STORMING PARTY—COL. WASHINGTON AND HIS ASSOCIATES AS CAPTIVES, HELD BY BROWN AS HOSTAGES.

Left: Lynching was common following the Civil War, peaking in the 1890s. However, the practice continued on long into the twentieth century. Unusually, and somehow adding to the horror, the caption to this ghastly image identifies the surnames of the three men: 'Lynching of Redmond, Robertson and Addison, 1892'.

Below: The Molly Maguires were first mentioned in newspapers in the 1850s and represented what Laqueur has referred to as 'working-class terrorism'.

James McParland infiltrated the Molly Maguires and his testimony led to the executions of over twenty members, but debates about the very existence of the group continue. (Courtesy of the Library of Congress)

Some anarchists believed that their liberation would come with the invention of dynamite. However, as with the Molly Maguires, the terrorist threat was overplayed by authorities who used the events at Haymarket to crack down on perceived radicals.

The anarchist trials and executions that followed the Haymarket bombing resulted in an international outcry. (Courtesy of the Library of Congress)

Leon Czolgosz was a self-proclaimed anarchist, whose assassination of President McKinley caused serious harm to the movement. (Courtesy of the Library of Congress)

Emma Goldman was dubbed 'Red Emma' and 'The Anarchist Queen' and became the most prominent anarchist figure in the US. (Courtesy of the Library of Congress)

Bombing attacks in the US would become all too frequent during the early twentieth century. (Courtesy of the Library of Congress)

The 1910 *Los Angeles Times* building bombing was dubbed the 'crime of the century' and killed twenty-one people. (Courtesy of the University of Southern California Libraries)

Alexander Berkman described himself as a 'terrorist by conviction' and spent twenty-two years in jail for his attack on Henry Frick, the chairman of the Carnegie Steel Company. (Courtesy of the Library of Congress)

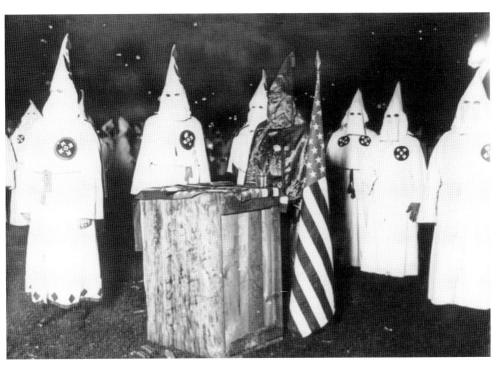

In 1915, a new Ku Klux Klan was formed. This Klan would expand their influence into the Northern states and also focussed their actions against Jewish and Catholic communities. (Courtesy of the Library of Congress)

Above: The second Klan peaked in popularity in the first half of the 1920s, as the First World War, the Red Scare, the League of Nations debates, and mass migration both within, and into, the US, stoked nativist fears. (Courtesy of the Library of Congress)

Left: The Vietnam War would be instrumental in provoking direct actions against American foreign policy, at home and abroad.

The Weather Underground movement issued a 'declaration of war' against the American government. Key figures such as Bill Ayres, Bernadine Dohrn and Mark Rudd wanted to bring the horrors of the Vietnam War home to America. (Courtesy of the FBI)

The Kent State University shootings, in which four student bystanders were killed by the National Guard, failed to generate great sympathy for the protest groups, showing that America was becoming tired of the radical movements. (Courtesy of the US National Archives and Records Administration)

Left: The Black Panthers, formed in 1966, were dubbed by J. Edgar Hoover the greatest threat to American internal security. This image was taken at the Black Panther convention in 1970. (Courtesy of the Library of Congress)

Below: The Demilitarized Zone looking toward North Korea. 'Rogue states' played a major role in attacking American interests from the 1970s, although this has declined since the end of the Cold War. (Courtesy of Filzstift under Creative Commons)

The Great Leader and the Dear Leader., Kim Il-sung and Kim Jong-il. President George W. Bush first identified North Korea as one-third of the 'axis of evil' in his State of the Union address on 29 January 2002. (Courtesy Roy Calley, from *Look with your Eyes and Tell the World: The Unreported North Korea*)

Iranian rebels at makeshift barricades during the Iranian Revolution of 1979. The Iranian hostage crisis demonstrated that there were limits to American power.

Above and left: The attacks in
Lebanon against the American
barracks and embassy in
1983 ushered in a new era of
suicide bombing designed to
maximise casualties. (Courtesy
of the US National Archives
and Records Administration)

The *Achille Lauro* hijacking of 1985 by the Palestine Liberation Front was one of a number of high-profile terrorist actions in the decade. The group killed disabled Jewish passenger Leon Klinghoffer, leading to President Reagan's unsuccessful attempt to arrest the hijackers on Italian soil. (Courtesy of the US National Archives and Records Administration)

The Lockerbie bombing of December 1988 killed 270 people. Unusually for a terrorist incident, no one claimed responsibility and there remains disagreement as to who was behind the attack. (Crown Copyright)

The 1993 World Trade Center bombing killed six and injured over 1,000, but the attack was designed to kill 250,000 people. The connections of the bombers to wider radical international terrorism were not fully understood at the time. (Courtesy of Eric Ascalon under Creative Commons)

The Twin Towers, completed in 1973 and briefly the world's tallest buildings, were seen as the epitome of American capitalism and were therefore selected as a key targets by Al Qaeda. (Courtesy of Wally Gobetz)

The memorial to the 2002 Bali bombing. Seven Americans died in the attack, but the bombers intended to kill far more American tourists. The attack on such a 'soft' target shows the problems involved in America protecting its citizens abroad.

Bernadine Dohrn and Bill Ayres remain controversial figures in the US, with opponents quick to pick up on their support for Barack Obama. (Courtesy of Joe Lustri under Creative Commons)

The wreckage left by the US bombing of Abu Musab al-Zarqawi's safe house in June 2006. The US government distributed photographs of Zarqawi's corpse afterwards to prove that he was dead. (Courtesy of the US Government)

The 2013 Boston Marathon bombing killed five people and demonstrated the continuing threats America faces from terrorism. (Courtesy of Aaron Tang under Creative Commons)

out over a sixteen-day period. America played down any suggestion of involvement, yet encouraged the Israelis to release Palestinian detainees and thereby give way to the terrorist's demands. Israel did indeed agree to a prisoner release of 756 Shiite prisoners, and this, coupled with the fact that America would make a commitment to the territorial integrity of the Lebanon, clearly cast serious doubts on western governments' attempts to assure the world that they had not given into terrorist demands. Terrorism had once again brought concessions by America (and Israel) and had therefore proved to be successful.

As a direct result of these events there would be a reassessment of counterterrorism policy via the Vice Presidential Task Force on Combating Terrorism, chaired by George H. W. Bush. Despite a recommendation that America respond militarily to the actions of the hijackers, this did not take place due to the threats posed to American hostages in the region. As a small compensation, one hijacker Mohammed Hammedei was caught, tried and imprisoned by West Germany (refusing American extradition requests); America's own capture of one of the terrorists, Fawaz Younis in late 1987, providing another small crumb of consolation.

Set against such a background of high-profile terrorist actions came Ronald Reagan's Speech to the American Bar Association. Reagan departed from the narrative that the Soviet Union was the linking thread to all these terrorist events, something that the American people were increasingly sceptical of. He outlined a 'steady and escalating pattern of terrorist acts against the United States and our allies'. The speech would identify states that America considered to be the chief sponsors of international terrorism, noting the closeness of the state to the USSR. He stated that the CIA had linked Iran to fifty-seven terrorist attacks and had been behind a plot to attack the US Embassy in Italy. Reagan then outlined the threat from Libya, North Korea, Cuba and Nicaragua, who he said were training, financing and controlling terrorists to attack American targets and citizens. He referred to this collection of states as 'an international version of Murder Incorporated' intent on disrupting American foreign policy and removing American influence from areas of the world. Towards the end of the speech he gave a memorable warning: 'The American people are not going to tolerate intimidation, terror, and outright acts of war against this nation and its people. And we're especially not going to tolerate these attacks from outlaw states run by the strangest collection of misfits, loony tunes, and squalid criminals since the advent of the Third Reich.' Whilst the words would be different, many of the same statements and the same tone would appear again in Bush's 'Axis of Evil' speech in 2002.

Iran would be seen as central to the sponsorship of international terrorism. Indeed, even the more moderate Bill Clinton called the country 'the most dangerous state sponsor of terrorism'. The State Department accused Iran of training and supporting extreme Islamist movements throughout the Middle East. The US claimed that Iran took part in five major terrorist attacks in 1987 alone. Germany, France, Britain and even Switzerland accused Iran of being behind terrorist actions. Much to America's frustration, Iran worked against Middle East peace agreements.

Given the prevailing atmosphere of the time it is not surprising that the Reagan administration would elect to increase support for the Afghan *mujahideen*. America saw this as an area where they could put the most military pressure on the USSR and push them to further drain their already faltering economy. Under President Carter aid had been modest, and the covert action programme was still only worth $35 million in 1982, but this had risen to $600 million by 1987 (Clarke, 2003, p. 50). In 1986 the CIA increased shipments of weapons including Stinger missiles, which proved to be highly effective in shooting down Soviet helicopters. Steve Coll indicates that the missiles were sent via Pakistan, around the same time that bin Laden moved his family to Peshawar and at the same time that America was looking at the most effective way to defeat the Soviets. This raises the obvious question of whether there developed any direct relationship between America and the man who would soon become their most wanted terrorist. Coll's answer to this intriguing question is that although the Arab volunteers who moved into the battlefield were welcomed by the Afghans, Assistant Undersecretary of Defence Michael Pillsbury discovered that the Afghan fighters did not want weapons shipments to go to anyone else other than directly to them. An attempt by Salem bin Laden to use America's help in supplying his brother with portable missiles failed to generate an American response. There is therefore no evidence that the American government moved to directly supply the Arab volunteers, and private means had to be used to directly supply Osama bin Laden with weapons (Coll, 2009, pp. 286–7).

The terror attacks continued, further demonstrating America's vulnerability as well as the limitations of their foreign policy. On 7 October 1985, six days into her journey, the Palestine Liberation Front (PLF) took control of a luxury cruise-liner, the *Achille Lauro* off the coast of Egypt. Although most passengers had disembarked for a day trip to view the pyramids at Giza, ninety-seven passengers stayed on board, twelve of whom were American, and around 300 crew (Wills, 2003, p. 40). The terrorist's demands included the release of fifty Palestinians being held by Israel. The terrorists singled out a Jewish disabled passenger, Leon Klinghoffer, whom they shot and killed, before throwing his body overboard; later his body would wash up on the Syrian shore and was returned by the Syrian government. Once this became known the American government immediately set out to arrest the hijackers, despite a previous deal that had been agreed which had allowed them to surrender to the PLO in Tunis.

The resolution would prove to be deeply unsatisfactory for the Reagan administration. Reagan attempted to organise a deal with

Egyptian leader Hosni Mubarak to get the hijackers turned over
to him. In fact, the hijackers were joined by Abu Abbas and Hani
Al-Hassan, who boarded their plane at Cairo. When Reagan failed
to secure the handing over of the terrorists, once their plane had
departed from Egypt bound for Tunisia, American planes were
scrambled and moved to intercept, forcing it to land at the Sigonella
NATO base in Sicily. However, much to the frustration of Reagan
his statement to the terrorists, 'you can run but you can't hide'
would soon prove to be premature. Following a tense stand-off, the
Italian authorities, who had not been fully informed of America's
plans and who enjoyed good relations with both Egypt and the
PLO, refused to let the fifty heavily armed American troops board
the plane and arrest the hijackers and their additional 'envoys',
Abu Abbas and Hani Al-Hassan. Reagan's personal call to Italian
Prime Minister Benedetto Craxi, defused the situation, but only
by agreeing to order American forces to stand down. Whilst the
American actions showed the kind of tough line America wanted
to pursue after Reagan's speech, and whilst the American public
broadly supported his actions, the outcome powerfully exposed
the limitations of American power. The Italian government refused
to allow the terrorists to be sent to the US, although they did arrest
four of them and charge them with murder, three receiving long
prison sentences. However, Abbas and Hassan refused to leave the
safety of the plane, which effectively enjoyed Egyptian protection,
and were allowed to depart to Yugoslavia, much to the anger and
deep frustration of Reagan. Abbas later made his way to Iraq,
where America finally caught up with him in April 2003 following
the US invasion and he died in custody the following year.

Despite all the tough rhetoric of Reagan from 1981 onwards,
the attempt to arrest the terrorists would be one of only two
occasions where America would attempt direct military action.
The second occasion would provide some limited success for
Reagan in tackling the most outspoken supporter of terrorism,

Colonel Gaddafi of Libya. Having labelled the country a base for communist subversion, in 1981 America banned the import of Libyan oil and set about increasing support for surrounding states which opposed Gaddafi. When it was announced that the country was planning to assassinate President Reagan, that hit squads were converging on Washington D.C. in December 1981, it was clear that Libya was taking over as their new bête noire, even if these reports of assassination squads would prove to be false (Wills, 2003, p. 167). Gaddafi's open support of terrorism, for example in his statement in September 1985 where he claimed that Libya had the right to export terrorism to America, made him an obvious target. By 1985, America were giving consideration to Operation *Tulip* and Operation *Rose*, the first utilising Libyan exiles, the second an invasion from Egypt, in order to remove Gaddafi from power. Operation *Tulip* began but had to be cancelled when information leaked out to the *Washington Post* (Stanik, 2003, p. 103). Simultaneous grenade and shooting attacks took place at the El Al counters at Rome and Vienna airports on 27 December 1985, killing eighteen people, including an eleven-year-old girl who was one of five American victims, with over a hundred people injured. Although the attack was linked to Abu Nidal, America argued that Libya had aided the terrorists and the attacks led to them severing all economic ties with the country on 7 January 1986. It also ordered its citizens to leave the country in advance of what looked likely to be an American military attack under the name Operation *Prairie Fire*,[41] although this was opposed by Casper Weinberger, and did not go ahead (Wills, 2003, p181). The situation became increasingly bizarre when the two leaders began trading public insults. Reagan referring to Gaddafi as a barbarian and the 'mad dog of the Middle East', with a goal

41 Curiously, Prairie Fire had been the name of the 1974 manifesto published by the remnants of the Weather Underground (see chapter five).

of a worldwide fundamentalist Muslim Revolution. On 28 March Gaddafi was calling on all Arab people to attack any target connected to America and stated that a state of war now existed between the US and Libya (Weinberger, 1990, p. 132).

It was to be the attack on La Belle Discotheque in West Berlin which finally spurred America to military reprisals. The nightclub was known to be a frequent hang-out for American military servicemen. A huge bomb ripped through the club on 5 April 1986, which killed Sergeant Kenneth Ford and injured seventy-eight Americans, a Turkish woman would also be killed and in total 229 people would be injured. The following day President Reagan would address the American people informing them that American intelligence had decrypted communications that provided the smoking gun: Tripoli had contacted its People's Bureau in East Berlin on 25 March and 4 April concerning an attack designed to cause maximum injury. For the State Department this was yet another example of Libya orchestrating terrorist attacks, their having already identified fifty instances between 1979 and 1985 (Winkler, 2006, p. 68).

America responded with a direct military attack on April 15, an operation which they dubbed *El Dorado Canyon*. Despite an Executive Order (12333) forbidding the US from engaging in assassination, American planes attacked Gaddafi's headquarters in the capital, terrorist training facilities in Benghazi, as well as the Murat Sidi Bilal training camp. The Americans claimed the raids killed thirty-six people, although the Libyans would put the figure at over 100 dead, which Gaddafi claimed included his 18-month-old adopted daughter Hana.[42] Two American servicemen would die in the military actions that night. The fact that France and Spain refused to allow their airspace to be utilised also showed divisions within the allies over the attack.

---

42 Her death was unconfirmed, with some sources suggesting this was in fact Libyan propaganda.

Although there would be immediate reprisal attacks against state department personnel in Sudan and Yemen as well as the execution of Peter Kilburn and two other British hostages who were being held captive in the Lebanon, the number of Libyan-supported terrorist attacks fell from nineteen in 1986 to five in 1988 (Haun, 2015, p. 142), There was a clear reduction in the belligerent Libyan rhetoric against the US. (This apparent success for US policy has been challenged by Bruce Hoffman, who has argued that Libya, after a short gap, actually increased its terrorist activity, 2006, p. 263). The bombing of Libya did not lead on to future military action against states seen to be sponsoring terrorism and the issue began to slide down Reagan's list of priorities towards the end of his term. One final aspect that is of note here is that although Reagan did eventually agree to strike at Libya, his actions were slight compared to notions of regime change that were initially considered. One of the reasons behind the decision not to proceed with the removal of Gaddafi's regime was concern within the US over America's relationship with the other Islamic States, Such concerns would not stop direct attacks on Iraq by all three of Reagan's successors.

There were many problems that faced America in dealing with rogue states. America's fostering of relations with nations that potentially shared their common interests led them to remove Iraq from their list of states that sponsored terrorism in 1982. Former Defence Secretary Donald Rumsfeld would visit the country in 1983 and 1984 as Ronald Reagan's 'Personal Representative of the President of the United States in the Middle East'. This was the highest level of contact between the two countries in twenty-five years, despite the fact that America both knew about, and had indeed publicly condemned, Saddam Hussein's use of chemical weapons in the war against Iran. Rumsfeld, keenly aware of the easy availability of the footage of the meeting, opens up his memoirs *Known and Unknown* with a discussion of it, noting Hussein's use of chemical toxins, but stressing that other nations in the region were even less 'appetising' to do business with (Rumsfeld, 2012, p. 4). By November 1984 full diplomatic relations had been re-established, despite the fact that Iraq still clearly sponsored terrorism and used chemical weapons once again in August 1988 against the Kurdish population (Berman & Gentleson, 1991, p. 120). America provided military support to prevent Iraq from losing its long-running war with its neighbour Iran, and the country would not re-emerge as one of America's terrorist-supporting nations until its invasion of Kuwait in 1990.

A direct attack on Iran was complicated by its relationship with the Soviet Union, a factor that was even truer for another state on America's terrorism radar, Syria. This did not prevent a disastrous strike on Syrian anti-aircraft guns housed in East Beirut in December 1983, in retaliation for these guns targeting an American reconnaissance plane. The incident saw two planes shot down, one pilot was killed and a navigator, Robert O. Goodman, held captive amidst much international attention, until the Reverend Jesse Jackson went to Damascus to secure his release.

Reagan's term of office would end as it began, with terrorism taking centre stage. On 21 December 1988, Pan Am Flight 103 was blown out of the sky over Scotland. The explosion killed all 259 passengers on board, but as the plane had been delayed, it was not over the Atlantic as the bombers had planned, and the death toll rose higher as the engines from the disintegrating airliner ploughed into the village of Lockerbie, killing another eleven people. The 189 Americans on board the aircraft included intelligence agents. A warning about a possible terrorist attack had been received at the American embassy in Helsinki. The warnings were not followed up at Frankfurt airport, the plane's departure point. The plane would land at Heathrow before setting off for J.F.K. Airport in New York. Curiously for a terrorist incident, no one before or since has convincingly claimed responsibility for the attack, creating intense speculation as to the reasons behind the bombing, as well as the culprits, although some Reagan officials suggested that the attack could have been retaliation for the 1986 bombing of Libya (Winkler, 2006, p. 68).

The United Nations Security Council imposed economic and diplomatic sanctions against Libya for the failure to turn over the bomber of Pan Am 103, which represented the first time that such international action had been agreed in response to a terrorist incident.

In August 2003 Libya acknowledged responsibility and agreed to pay $2.7 billion in compensation, although debate still rages over who actually conducted the attack and why.[43] Abdelbaset Ali Mohmed Al Megrahi was eventually found guilty of murder in connection to the bombing and sentenced to life imprisonment, although he was released due to failing health in 2009 and died in 2012. Whilst not directly implicated in the bombing, speculation has included the idea that the bombing was revenge by Iran for the shooting down of an Iranian plane (Iran Air 655) which was travelling in Iranian airspace and was shot down by the USS *Vincennes* in July 1988. This disastrous mistake by an American navy crew resulted in the deaths of all 290 people on board. America would eventually agree to pay damages to Iran in 1996 of $131.8 million, although this did not stop Iran offering a $10 million reward for anyone who helped avenge the destruction of their airliner.

Rogue states abandoned or reduced their support for international terrorism for a number of reasons after 1989. The years 1989–91 saw the collapse of communist regimes in Europe, and indeed the collapse of the USSR itself, splintering into

---

43 Libya also accepted responsibility for the destruction of UTA Flight 772 in September 1989 over the Sahara Desert, seven Americans were among the 170 dead.

fifteen separate countries. With the Cold War at an end, the rationale for state support of some terrorist groups was removed and former Soviet allies found themselves losing a powerful ally who had provided both military and often economic support (this was especially true for states such as Cuba, who ended their support for any movements that could be seen as terrorists). North Korea's economic plight also forced it to reduce attempts to foster its Juche (self reliance) philosophy on the world.

The Reagan years began at a time when Cold War tensions had been rising. Reagan's hawkish stance against communism translated into the simplistic assumption that the Kremlin was behind the increase in terrorist attacks against Americans (and other western powers) during the 1980s. Figures such as Alexander Haig, who would be Reagan's first Secretary of State, sold a president highly receptive to such notions the fiction that terrorism was part of a broader campaign conducted by the communists to undermine America's influence in the world. In this reheated Cold War during which Reagan sought to reverse the perceived decline in America's strategic position, his thinking was understandable. By linking terrorism to communism, he gave the issue of terrorism a high priority from the outset of his presidency and indeed made the issue of terrorism something of a national obsession. By 1984–5 the issue vied to be at the top of the administration's priorities, and Reagan sought to set out a strong position against both terrorists and the rogue nations that offered support to them. In reality, Reagan's strong rhetoric was backed up with only very limited direct military intervention. Reagan's emphasis on tackling communism led to his support for administrations that would later be branded as rogue nations by future Republican leaderships, as in the case of Iraq. More significantly, America did not question the spreading of Wahhabism in Afghanistan. This strict form of Sunni fundamentalism was encouraged by the Saudi Arabians, who saw themselves as the true custodians of the Islamic faith, and were keen to counter the Shia theology being spread by Iran, a rival state in their quest for regional dominance.[44] The invasion of Lebanon by Israel in 1982 provided a spark for future Al Qaeda retribution, and also brought America reluctantly and halfheartedly into the region, where they would face devastating bomb attacks that undermined their confidence and willingness to remain. The two bombing attacks followed by American withdrawal from the region encouraged militant Islamic movements to see America as vulnerable to unconventional warfare that sought to maximise casualties.

Whilst this era represented a high water mark for state support of terrorism, fear of the closeness that some rogue nations had to Moscow meant that only Libya, by far the most open state supporter of terrorist groups, would suffer a direct military attack by American forces, (notwithstanding the American attack on Syrian forces in Lebanon), after which Libya at least desisted from verbal support of terrorism. The issue of terrorism took a back seat during the last two years of Reagan's term of office, overshadowed by the president's rapprochement with the Soviet Union, only to dramatically reappear with the downing of Pan Am Flight 103 over Lockerbie, an incident which still remains surrounded in some mystery in terms of its perpetrator and motive. Although Reagan had signed NSDD-138, which opened the potential for more direct and proactive strikes against terrorist forces and rogue nations, a line pushed by Secretary of State George Schultz, in truth Reagan never really adopted an aggressive foreign policy against such states, fearful of inflaming Islamic opinion, as well as reprisals against America hostages in the Middle East. Indeed the central themes of NSDD-138 would be much closer to the stance adopted by George W. Bush from 2001. As shown in the previous

---

44 The vast majority of Muslims in the world identity with the Sunni tradition; divides between Sunni and Shiites stem from disagreements over the succession to the Prophet Mohammad upon his death in 632.

chapter, internally America faced far fewer internal terrorist threats than had been the case during the 1970s; Reagan did not have to have to worry about the left-wing terrorism movements that had been so prevalent a decade prior to his election. His terrorist focus was very much on events abroad. The end of his terms of office coincided with the terminal decline of the 'evil empire' of the Soviet Union. Whilst this meant left-wing terrorist movements declined even further across the world, it would see the 1990s burdened with twin threats, from right-wing terrorists and radical Islamic movements, now freed from Cold War struggles, and it is these elements that will be focussed upon in the next chapter.

7

A BIGGER BANG:
US TERRORISM IN THE 1990s

The end of the Cold War brought significant changes in terms of the threats posed by terrorism to the US. In some ways the threats had been easier to identify and address before, especially if dealing with rogue states. By 1991 the US still listed six countries as such: Libya, North Korea, Syria, Iran, Cuba – and Iraq, who were returned to the list after their invasion of Kuwait in 1990. However, individual countries were far easier to deal with than terrorist groups, as economic or political pressure could be applied and agreements made. Indeed, the start of the 1990s saw an end to the holding of western hostages in the Middle East, with all American hostages (or their remains) finally released in 1991. They included Terry Anderson, who had spent nearly seven years in captivity, the longest spell of any of the American hostages held in the Middle East. This was not without some controversy as not only did Israel agree to release some Arab prisoners, but the US released some $278 million to Iran as compensation for previously seized military equipment, meaning that the hostage taking had yet again resulted in substantial concessions from the West.

Although Reagan's successor, George H. W. Bush, was highly experienced in foreign affairs, the collapse of the USSR in

1991 spelled the end of the bi-polar world and left America as the world's sole superpower, now having to deal with a myriad of potential terrorist threats. Despite Reagan's breakthrough in relations with Soviet Leader Mikhail Gorbachev, America still thought in Cold War terms and with the collapse of the Soviet Union, they stopped funding research into terrorism. This was a disastrous decision as terrorist cells, without the focus of the Cold War, now proliferated. James Patterson has noted, for example, that terrorist cells had spread across more than sixty countries by the year 2000 (2007, p. 386). Bush's experience also extended to knowledge of threats posed by terrorism, as Vice President he had chaired the president's task force on combating it. He recognised the need to remain vigilant, stating that 'Terrorism, hostage taking, renegade regimes, and unpredictable rulers, new sources of instability – all require a strong and an engaged America' (cited in Wilentz, p. 294–5). One of those sources of instability proved to be Afghanistan, from where the last Soviet troops departed a month after Bush's inauguration leaving behind the puppet regime of President Najibullah, which collapsed in April 1992.[45] During the Bush presidency 1989–93, the president made the issue of terrorism more low-key than during the Reagan years, aided by the fact that there were fewer high-profile terrorist events; the rise of terrorism as a direct threat to America as a result of the end of the Cold War took a few years to manifest itself. In 1990 the number of international terrorism incidents declined to 455, from 856 two years earlier (Simon, 2001, p. 25).

And there was another negative outcome to what seemed at the time to be a major foreign policy achievement, the successful liberation of Kuwait in 1991 following its invasion by Saddam Hussein's Iraq the previous summer. This would prove to be a pivotal event in turning

---

45 Najibullah would be taken from the barely guarded UN compound in Kabul and savagely executed by the incoming Taliban regime in September 1996.

the forces of terrorism against America. Such a possibility looked remote when Bush utilised an international coalition that liberated Kuwait in just one hundred hours. However, Bush had to deal with a situation where Saddam Hussein was threatening not to allow thousands of foreigners, including hundreds of Americans, out of Iraq or Kuwait, creating potentially the biggest use of hostages as human shields in history, far outweighing the hostage crises faced by Eisenhower in the 1950s. Eventually, Hussein would slowly release the hostages, attempting to seek maximum propaganda value, but this failed to prevent war.

A far more significant legacy of the Iraq conflict came with Osama bin Laden's outrage at seeing American forces move into the Gulf. Eventually some 500,000 American troops moved into the Gulf area (Bush and Scowcroft, 1996, p. 479). Bin Laden had in fact been so infuriated by Saddam Hussein's attack on a fellow Arab state that he offered to organise and lead a military force of militants against Iraq, but such an offer was quickly dismissed as impractical (Burke, 2007, p. 136). Had American forces left the Middle East following the end of the war, Bin Laden's ire may have subsided, but having western forces remain so close to the holiest of cities, Mecca, left him plotting revenge against America (Lawrence, 2005, p. 16). American forces, albeit scaled down, remained in Saudi Arabia, and America would negotiate basing agreements with four more Islamic states in the Gulf: Kuwait, Qatar, Bahrain and Oman (Clarke, 2003, p. 70). There would also be various consequences after Bush's decision to stay firmly within the UN Mandate to liberate Kuwait and not continue onto Baghdad. Had Bush marched into the Iraqi capital, he quickly recognised it would end the international coalition that he so painstakingly put together, which included troops from Syria, Pakistan, Oman, Qatar, Bahrain and the United Arab Emirates, amongst the twenty-four military participants who liberated Kuwait. In *A World Transformed* George Bush and Brent

Scowcroft note presciently, 'Had we gone the invasion route, the United States could conceivably still be an occupying power in a bitterly hostile land. It would have been a dramatically different – and perhaps barren – outcome' (Bush & Scowcroft, 1996, p. 489). Ironically, Bush's decision to stay within international agreements left Saddam Hussein in power. Hussein would not only plot his revenge against Bush, but would go on to offer support to various terrorists, factors which would lead Bush's son to engage in an invasion of Iraq in 2003, which indeed had an outcome somewhat similar to that predicted in *A World Transformed*.

It would be Bush's successor, Bill Clinton, who would have to deal with these increased dangers. He warned of them and commented that post-Cold War the lids had been lifted from 'many cauldrons of ethnic, religious and territorial animosity'. Clinton would face the dual threats of the rise of right-wing terrorism in the US and the threat of Islamic terrorism, both at home and abroad. The former threat was growing, although it represented a much smaller threat than that of left-wing terrorism during the previous decades in terms of the number of attacks. The number of overseas attacks on American targets on average declined during the Clinton years, compared to the Reagan and Bush eras (Winkler, 2006, p. 127). However, the attacks that now took place were often far more deadly, seeking to maximise casualties, with around a third of all terrorist assaults being aimed at American targets (Griset & Mahan, 2003, p. 278).

Clinton in turn would make terrorism a top-level national security policy during his time in office. Carol Winkler notes that a significant amount of presidential discourse was given over to the dangers of terrorism, demonstrating Clinton's recognition of the growing dangers. Donna Starr-Deelen points out that threats from rogue states were fading, replaced by new dangers arising from more religiously inspired non-state terrorist networks (Starr-Declen, p. 101). Madeleine Albright, who was the first ever female

Secretary of State, appointed under Clinton, stated that Clinton used the 'bully pulpit' of the White House to 'heighten awareness of the terrorist threat and rouse global support for defeating it' (Albright, 2003, p. 371).

Clinton had been in office for less than a week when Mir Amal Kansi opened fire on a line of slow-moving traffic with an AK-47 assault rifle outside the CIA headquarters at Langley, Virginia. Two CIA workers were killed and three others injured. After he had finished shooting Kansi drove off and made his way out of the country, sparking an international manhunt. He was eventually traced to the Pakistan/Afghanistan border in 1997, and brought back to America via an agreement with Pakistan. Kansi stated his aim was to kill the CIA director in retaliation for America's policies towards Muslim countries. Kansi was charged with murder, and given a death sentence in a Virginia court, as at the time of his actions Federal law had no death penalty for acts of terrorism.

A frightening foretaste of future events came within six weeks of Clinton's inauguration when, at lunchtime on 26 February 1993 the World Trade Center was attacked via a massive truck bomb planted in an illegally parked yellow Ryder truck van in the basement. The World Trade Center, completed in 1973 and with the twin towers at the time being the world's highest buildings,[46] symbolised America's corporate heart, in many ways the ultimate encapsulation of capitalism. The twin towers were described by Donald Rumsfeld as 'symbols of America's economic strength' (2012, p. 335). Some 50,000 people worked in the towers, with around 200,000 visitors a day. The towers had office space for banks, airline companies as well as the secret service and FBI.

---

46 The North Tower at 1368 feet, was 6 feet higher than the South Tower; they would quickly lose their status as the world's tallest buildings.

The bomb contained some 1200lbs of explosives and probably cost no more than a few hundred dollars to make. Indeed, the operation was so strapped for cash that one of those involved in the operation, Mohammad Salameh, returned to the van hire company in New Jersey to collect a deposit of $200. He claimed the van had been stolen the night before the attack. The explosion made a crater 200 foot wide and five storeys deep that created the potential for the foundations that kept out the waters of the Hudson River to be breached. Some were overcome by the fumes from hundreds of burning cars which were pushed upwards through the lift shafts and ventilation systems. Six people died and over a thousand were injured. Trial Judge Kevin Duffy stated that the event had caused more hospital casualties than any event in America since the Civil War.

Despite the long history of terrorist attacks that had plagued New York City there was still an initial reluctance to accept the fact that the city had been the target for a major international bomb attack. *Newsweek* stated the events had 'rattled the country's confidence, dispelling the snug illusion that Americans were immune, somehow, to the plague of terrorism that torments so many foreign countries' (cited in Hewitt, 2003, p.12). A few days after the attack the *New York Times* published a letter from 'the fifth battalion in the Liberation Army' penned by Yousef, who took credit for the bombing, stating that the rationale for the attack was American 'political, economical and military support to Israel'.

As some kind of grudging recompense for all the suffering, Barton points out that the bombing generated around $200 million in economic activity in an area still recovering from the financial slump of the late 1980s, as the authorities rushed to reopen the World Trade Center by May (Barton, 1999, p. 92). With horrible irony, after the reopening Guy Tozzoil, former chief of the Port Authority's World Trade Center Department, who was in the building at the time of the attack, bragged that he knew the towers would not fall down.

The main culprit was soon identified as Ramzi Yousef, described by Simon Reeve as 'a master of explosives' able to create bombs with increasing destructive capacity (1999, p. 75). Shortly after planting the bomb, he simply took a flight to Karachi and then flew on to Quetta to join his family. Yousef left the US on a passport bearing his real name, Abdul Basit Karim, and the US quickly began an investigation into his activities, which would place Yousef on the FBI's Ten Most Wanted list. Yousef's background revealed that he had been trained in the war against the Russians in Afghanistan. Yousef had arrived in New York the previous year, permitted entry despite the concerns of a border official after claiming that he faced persecution in his native Iraq. During an interview at the airport he unsurprisingly denied being a terrorist when asked the question by a customs official.

Prior to entering the US at the end of the 1980s Yousef apparently studied a Higher National Diploma in computer-aided electrical engineering at the West Glamorgan Institute of Higher Education at Swansea in the late 1980s.[47] This fact was reported in Simon Reeve's book *The New Jackals: Ramzi Yousef, Osama Bin Laden and the Future of Terrorism* in 1999, which was the first full-length study of the rise of bin Laden to explore his links to other terrorist incidents and groups. Reeve took much of his information from Neil Herman, who led the FBI Joint Terrorist Task Force in 1993, and it has been accepted by many sources since. This information has been questioned as Yousef used many aliases and may well have taken his identity from a student who did study in the UK but was killed during the Iraqi

---

47 This was renamed the Swansea Institute of Higher Education in 1992 and in 2008 Swansea Metropolitan University, which has created some confusion in news sources, leading some incorrectly to report that Yousef studied at Swansea University.

invasion of Kuwait in 1990[48] although Swansea library textbooks were located at places Yousef had stayed.

Although Reeve states that Yousef's father was a key influence in bringing him to the militant cause, he argues that Yousef was actually radicalised in Swansea, having become friendly with members of the Muslim Brotherhood there. In reality, Yousef's transformation into most wanted terrorist started at the terrorist training camps in 1991, where he met Afghan veterans who had fought against the Soviet Union. Yousef himself had visited Afghanistan in 1988, a time when the Soviets were already in the process of withdrawing their troops. The Soviet Union's withdrawal agreement was on condition the West, along with Pakistan, withdraw their backing of *mujahideen* forces, but Reagan ill-advisedly continued to supply them even once the Soviet withdrawal was complete.

One of the most intriguing aspects is Yousef's links to bin Laden, which Reeve admits were 'shrouded in secrecy and confusion'. Bin Laden himself claimed not to know Yousef and that he had no role in the 1993 World Trade Center bombing. The investigation into Yousef's activities soon revealed other cells and groups both in the US and overseas. For the first time the US began to fully recognise the fact that former *mujahideen* soldiers who had fought the Soviets in Afghanistan were now turning their deadly skills against the US. It was also the first time that intelligence agencies would find the name Osama bin Laden, albeit as one of a great many leads that the extended investigation would gather.[49]

There had previously been an even earlier potential link to bin Laden, following the killing of Rabbi Meir Kahane on 5 November 1990. Whilst his assailant El Sayyid Nosair would astonishingly

---

48 Karim's identity (with a potential alternative spelling) was questioned by Professor Ken Reid, who had worked at the Institute. Reeve does draw attention to the possibility that Yousef had stolen his identity (p. 251).

49 Reeve would also raise the possibility that Saddam Hussein was involved in the first World Trade Center plot.

escape conviction for this crime, he would be found guilty of two other non-fatal shootings in making his escape. His trial funds seem to have been paid for by bin Laden, and Nosair's accomplices would later be involved in the 1993 World Trade Center plot. Documents found at Nosair's home, linking him to an 'Afghan Services Bureau' were taken away, but the files were in Arabic and not translated at the time by the FBI, depriving the police of potential early leads in the 1993 World Trade Center bombing.

Yousef would also be a leading player in 'Operation Bojinka',[50] which was discovered by accident in January 1995 following a fire at the Dona Josefa apartment in the Philippines where Yousef and his accomplice Abdul Murad were busy making bombs. As the occupants fled, police discovered a computer and discs which outlined the plot. It would involve targeting eleven airliners simultaneously flying over the Pacific, making recovery of the wreckage and victims extremely difficult. Bombs would be planted under seats[51] by recruits, who would then depart from the aircraft during a stopover, meaning that the planners had not yet decided to engage in a suicide mission. Richard Clarke states in his memoirs that when the events were reported to them, they took the initial threat so seriously that they grounded incoming flights into the US from the Pacific region (Clarke, 2003, p. 94). In addition, there had been plans to assassinate President Clinton during a trip to the Philippines, as well as the President of the country, Fidel Ramos. By January 1995 they were working on a plan to assassinate Pope John Paul II, with bombs or the use of snipers, during the Pope's visit that month. There were also plans to attack the US Embassy in the Philippines, along with

---

50 Bojinka is a Serbo-Croat word meaning explosion.

51 Indeed this had happened in a practice run when a bomb was placed under seat 26K on a Philippines aircraft in December 1994, killing a Japanese passenger and injuring eleven others before the plane made an emergency landing.

the International School, Catholic churches and government installations (Fouda & Fielding, 2003, p. 99).

Yosri Fouda and Nick Fielding claim in their book that there was also evidence of an alternative plan for hijacked planes to fly into the World Trade Center, the White House, the Pentagon, the John Hancock Tower in Boston, the Sears Tower and the Transamerica Pyramid in San Francisco. If correct, American officials had the blueprint for the future 9/11 attack, as the computer discs were handed over to US intelligence agencies who would use them in the prosecution of Yousef. Having fled the Philippines he would eventually be located in Islamabad, Pakistan, via the help of an informant Ishtiaque Parker, who was increasingly concerned by Yousef's actions; although he was also aware of the $2 million dollar reward for his capture. During his trial he would explain that the intent of the truck bomb was to topple one tower onto the other with the plan of killing some 250,000 people. Such a statement showed the direction of a terrible new form of terrorism which sought to maximise casualties. Yousef stated in court that he was proud to be a terrorist, although both Jason Burke and Simon Reeve have argued that his actions often reflected those of a cold-blooded killer, rather than a religious fundamentalist. Yousef would end up at a maximum security prison in Florence, Colorado, where he remains to this day. Having won the right not to have to face total solitary confinement, he would find himself enjoying his limited out of cell time with Unabomber Ted Kaczynski, and prior to his execution Oklahoma bomber Timothy McVeigh.[52]

The attack on the World Trade Center was actually part of a wider terrorist campaign that involved targeting the United Nations headquarters and the Lincoln and Holland tunnels. This section of the plot would be foiled. These events brought to trial the highly

---

52 Ray Levasseur would also spend time at this prison after his conviction on conspiracy charges in 1986 (see chapter five).

prominent figure of Omar Abdel Rahman, a blind Egyptian Sheik, whose sermons of hate encouraged others to violence. Rahman's radicalisation increased following the 1967 Six-Day War and he had been jailed in Egypt in 1970, but was rehabilitated and became a professor of theology as Assiut University, interpreting the writings of Sayyid Qutb (Cooley, 2002, p. 30). Rahman moved to the US from the Sudan in 1990, encouraged by members of the *mujahideen*. Despite being on a 'lookout list' a series of what were effectively termed administrative errors allowed him both a visa and then a green card in 1991. Rahman would exploit the free speech that was guaranteed in the US and gave sermons that looked to incite violence, often citing the works of Sayyid Qutb. Eventually, Rahman and nine other defendants were convicted in 1995 of conspiracy to wage 'a war of urban terrorism' in the US. The trial that would take seven months and involve some 200 witnesses. He would die in prison in North Carolina in 2017.[53]

The idea of attacking high profile buildings was certainly not new. London Bridge, billed by the *New York Times* as the 'most thronged thoroughfare in the world', was targeted by bombers in December 1884 although no one was killed and damage was slight. The Greenwich Observatory, or possibly the Greenwich Mean Time Gate Clock, seems likely to have been the target of a French anarchist who died when his bomb exploded prematurely in 1894 close to the Observatory. Joseph Conrad would use the events in his novel *The Secret Agent*. Perhaps the most famous attempt of all to blow up a famous landmark was Guy Fawkes's failure to blow up the Houses of Parliament in 1605.

Back in February 1974, Samuel Joseph Byck, depressed at his failure to hold down a job, and the fact that five months previously his wife had divorced him and taken custody of their four children,

---

53 In late 2005 another plot to detonate explosives in railway tunnels under the Hudson River was foiled. *New York Times*, 7 July 2006.

began to associate his problems with the political corruption that was daily being displayed by the Watergate scandal, which would eventually bring down the presidency of Richard Nixon. Stating a need for citizens to 'take back their government', Byck, after making one final tape recording to explain his actions, rushed through security at Baltimore International Airport, shooting dead a police officer with his Smith and Wesson, boarded a plane and threatened the pilots. His plan was to hijack the Delta plane and have it flown into the Whitehouse in the hope of killing the president. James Clarke considers the plot the most 'bizarre assassination ever attempted' and it quite literally never got off the ground as the pilots refused to accede to Byck's wishes. Both were shot and the co-pilot killed by Byck, who eventually shot himself.

In September 1994 a stolen Cessna 150 private aircraft, piloted by Frank Eugene Corder and unchallenged by any defence forces, crashed onto the south lawn of the White House, having collided with the branches of a magnolia tree that had been planted by President Jackson, and came to rest under President Clinton's bedroom. Clinton had been staying at Blair House that night due to repairs at the White House, so was never in any danger, but even this almost farcical event raised questions about the potential use of aircraft to attack symbolic targets.

On 24 December 1994 an Air France flight was hijacked in Algiers after a two-day standoff and the shooting of three passengers. The plane was flown to Marseille, from where the hijackers demanded the plane be refuelled with three times the required amount of fuel to get to Paris, arousing deep concerns from security services. The hijackers, from the Armed Islamic Group of Algeria, intended to blow the plane up over the Eiffel Tower, the extra fuel to add to the destruction. Having received intelligence indicating this course of action, French security services successfully stormed the plane, killing all four hijackers. So crashing planes into political or high-profile targets had been attempted long before 9/11.

In December 1992 outgoing president George H. W. Bush, in response to a humanitarian crisis that was threatening to engulf Somalia, moved in 28,000 US troops during Operation *Restore Hope* in order to provide and distribute aid to millions who were on the edge of starvation. With no Cold War considerations, America's sole rationale to be in the country was to deliver humanitarian aid. But American involvement in another Islamic country provided further fuel to radical Islamists. America would soon become involved in a brutal and bitter civil war and found its own forces under attack by Somali warlords, notably Mohamed Aideed. When two Black Hawk helicopters were shot down with hand-held, rocket-powered grenades over the capital Mogadishu on 3 October 1993, eighteen American servicemen were killed and eighty-four injured. The body of one of the dead soldiers was dragged across the streets of the capital. Footage of these events soon flooded the world's media. The events were enough to hasten the departure of US Secretary of Defense Lee Aspin. The losses yet again highlighted the limitations of American power and President Clinton, under pressure from Congress, made the decision to withdraw American forces, although not until March 1994. Although the US remained for months after the October attacks, and still remained as part of the UN forces, the perception – as with Beirut – was that American forces were vulnerable to both unconventional attack and to public pressure to avoid casualties, and that such attacks would potentially force the US to alter her political course. This was not a lesson lost on Osama bin Laden, who since being expelled from Saudi Arabia (even having his citizenship revoked in 1994), had been resident in the Sudan since 1992, not so far from the events in Somalia. In fact, bin Laden would seem to have been in league with Aideed forces, sending military advisors to the country, although this information was not known at the time (Clarke, 2003, p. 88). This is disputed, given that some of Aideed's own forces stated that the first they had heard of bin Laden was when he boasted of his links to the attacks (Burke, 2007, p. 149).

President Clinton became increasingly concerned about terrorist groups getting hold of chemical, biological or even nuclear weapons (9/11 Report, 2004, p. 174). Such fears were prompted in part by a sarin gas attack in March 1995 on the crowded Tokyo subway by the doomsday cult Aum Shinrikyo led by Shoko Asahara. Sarin is a chemical weapon far more deadly that cyanide and the attack killed twelve people. This tally could easily have been far greater, indeed there were five thousand affected by what was ultimately a fairly crude attack involving sharpened umbrellas and plastic bags. There were also later reports that the group had attempted wider biological attacks, including attacks against American bases, where thousands of US troops and their families lived. Given these terrifying possibilities and the group's stated intention to conduct attacks in America, President Clinton drew attention to the threat of a chemical, biological or even nuclear attack on American soil, signing Presidential Decision Directive 39 giving responsibility across government agencies to deal with such attacks against America. Clinton moved to vaccinate the entire US military against anthrax, as well as tightening up security in American laboratories and working closer with the Russians to prevent possible bio-weapons falling into terrorist hands. Additional Clinton Directives (62 and 63) aimed to better apprehend terrorists, disrupt networks, protect Americans overseas, look at ways to better secure cyber systems and infrastructure, and prevent terrorists getting hold of weapons of mass destruction. In December 1998 Osama bin Laden stated that it was the duty of Muslims to acquire such weapons.

The year 1995 would bring the biggest terrorist attack in America's history. Timothy McVeigh was a twenty-seven-year-old Gulf War veteran, who believed that American was in decline and that federal control and state intervention were the main cause. Hoffman notes that McVeigh had come to believe that the government was attempting to ban privately held firearms, with surveys in 1993 starting to show a majority of Americans were beginning to support restrictions. The passing of the Brady Bill (1993) and the Federal Crime Bill (1994) fed fears that the state was steadily removing citizens' rights to bear arms, which were enshrined in the Second Amendment.

McVeigh was outraged by the actions of federal government at Ruby Ridge, Idaho, where the wife and son of Randy Weaver, who was accused of firearms-related offences, were killed in a shootout with US officials during their attempt to arrest him, and the events at Waco where members of the Branch Davidian cult led by David Koresh[54] held out for fifty days against the FBI. Four officials already lay dead when the FBI made the decision to storm the compound. This resulted in an inferno, with Koresh having soaked the compound with gasoline. Seventy-six people died, twenty-four of them children. The events succeeded in enraging right-wing 'Patriots' who saw them as an attack on the American right to liberty and to bear arms. As Stuart Wright notes, mistakes were made by government authorities and the Patriots were able to portray the events as an illegal federal siege (2007, p. 154).

Although militia forces had been growing in some states after World War Two, fed by communist fears, starting in Montana a number of new militias began to surface and grow across the US. It is possible that some fifteen million Americans were or are members of such groups (Heymann, 2000, p. xxvii), an extraordinary number. Wilentz estmates that some 800 armed militias were now spread across some twenty-three states (2008, p. 352).

McVeigh had also been highly influenced by Andrew Macdonald's anti-Semitic book *The Turner Diaries*, first published

---

54 Koresh, whose real name was Vernon Wayne Howell, had been born in Houston, Texas in 1959.

in 1998, which portrayed white supremacists blowing up the FBI headquarters in Washington with a truck bomb, later crashing a nuclear weapon into the Pentagon. The book was seen as prophetic by members of the Patriot groups (Wright, 2007, p. 113). The book's lead protagonist aimed to provoke an uprising based on ideas of 'propaganda by deed'. Sections of the book were located in McVeigh's car following his arrest. McVeigh attempted to visit the Waco site; he was even photographed there by the FBI, staying for days in his car as close as the police allowed, distributing anti-government literature whilst events unfolded.

McVeigh would pack the Ryder truck with 5000lbs of ammonium nitrate and nitromethane. The explosive was made from fertiliser and ingredients that were readily accessible and designed, in McVeigh's words, to create a 'body count'. McVeigh parked outside the Alfred P. Murrah Federal Building on 19 April, exactly two years to the day of the end of the Waco siege. Just after 9 am the truck bomb exploded, killing 168 people, including nineteen children attending an office worker's child care facility. Following this attack day care centres were to be banned from federal buildings. The attack injured nearly 700 people in an explosion so large that it measured 6.0 on the Richter Scale (Davis, 2007, p. 146). McVeigh would be stopped by state trooper Charles Hanger as he headed out of the area as he lacked a license plate. Having discovered a loaded weapon in the vehicle Hanger arrested McVeigh, who was therefore already in custody when it was discovered he matched the descriptions given of the bombing suspect.

McVeigh, like John Brown, had wanted to spark a violent counter insurgency via his actions, and like John Brown moved to embrace martyrdom and ended his legal appeals in late 2000. He revelled in the fact that his execution was international news; he suggested that his execution should be televised. Such a suggestion echoed the wishes of Giuseppe Zangara, who had also wished for photographers at his execution in 1933, as explored in chapter four. McVeigh's death, whilst un-televised, was witnessed by 232 survivors and members of victims' families. McVeigh was keen to make sure his motivations for the devastating attack were known and stated that he wished to die a martyr. He was finally executed in June 2001, making this the first federal execution since 1963, with his co-conspirator Terry Nichols given life imprisonment. He would attract supporters and defenders. Gore Vidal, the veteran political commentator, who corresponded with McVeigh during the last three years of his life, argued that McVeigh might not have been responsible for planting the bomb, and that the FBI knew of a wider plot. Vidal, who would be one of five people McVeigh invited to attend his execution, stated that McVeigh saw himself as a John Brown figure and compared McVeigh to Paul Revere.

Simon Reeve would explore the idea that Terry Nichols, McVeigh's co-conspirator, met with Yousef in the Philippines ahead of the Oklahoma bombing to learn about how to cause the greatest amount of destruction. The possibility that white supremacists and Islamic terrorists may have collaborated intrigued Richard Clarke, although he could find no conclusive proof (2003, p. 127). The Defence attorney Steven Jones argued that McVeigh was part of a wider international conspiracy involving bin Laden, Iraq and white supremacists, but such connections were dismissed by the judge (Winkler, 2006, p. 128). Such themes are also explored in *The Oklahoma City Bombing and the Politics of Terror* by David Hoffman, which draws frequent parallels between McVeigh and alleged J. F. Kennedy assassin Lee Harvey Oswald, and sees the bombing as part of a major international conspiracy that the government sought to cover up. He argues that the level of destruction to the Alfred P. Murrah building could not have been achieved via the fertiliser bomb that McVeigh was alleged to have used and that a weapon of mass destruction, such as a small nuclear device supplied by overseas agents was really to blame for the huge impact of the explosion. (The idea that any nuclear device could be detonated anywhere in the world, let alone in a city, without a trace, is difficult to credit.) Stuart Wright in his excellent study *Patriots, Politics and the Oklahoma City Bombing* linked McVeigh to the wider Patriot movement within the US, but does not uncover any links to overseas terrorist groups.

Given these events it was not surprising that Bill Clinton would state that terrorism had 'assumed new and quite dangerous dimensions' and that new thinking was required on how to deal with the threat. Clinton was keen to portray terrorism as simply an act of murder in an attempt to delegitimize the acts, they were simply the 'wilful killing of innocent civilians'.

Under Clinton the world became increasingly familiar with the term 'weapons of mass destruction' and Clinton was keen, as others had before him, to see terrorism in simple terms, as good versus evil. He would follow Reagan's example with Libya early in his presidency with a show of force against Iraq, launching twenty-three Cruise missiles in June 1993. This, it was stated, was in retaliation for Saddam Hussein's support of terrorism, not least a plot to kill George H. W. Bush during his visit to Kuwait in April 1993, which was linked to Hussein's intelligence services (Starr-Deelen, 2014, p. 90). As with Gaddafi, this attack did seem to help rein in the actions of Hussein. Hussein had further antagonised America by offering rewards to the families of suicide bombers who attacked the US.

With the threat from large-scale terrorist plots rising, Clinton became increasingly concerned about attacks on targets such as nuclear power stations, as well as the growing possibilities of cyber attacks. He was wary of arranging public drills for such events as a biological, chemical or even nuclear attack by a terrorist group in order to avoid provoking fear or alarm among the American populace. Clinton's Presidential Directive 39 made the prevention and management of the consequences of a terrorist attack with a weapon of mass destruction the highest priority and Directive 62 set up the Office of the National Coordinator for Security, Infrastructure Protection and Counter-Terrorism – including a brief to plan for the use of a WMD against the US (Clinton, 2004, p. 789). *The Washington Post* of 10 September 1996 noted that an extra $1.1bn was going to be allocated to combat terrorism – including stricter airport controls.

At least one ongoing terrorist saga would come to an end at this time. Since 1978 a lone wolf terrorist had been at large in the US with a campaign that lasted about as long as that of George Metesky. A mail bomb sent to Northwestern University in Illinois that injured a campus police officer, began a sporadic but increasingly deadly terrorist campaign. A bomb planted on an American Airlines flight from Chicago in November 1979 failed to explode, but passengers suffered from smoke inhalation, and this had the potential to be fatal. Bombs tended to target university staff at prestigious institutions including Vanderbilt University and the University of California, Berkeley, although the first fatality would be a computer store owner in 1985. After another attack on a computer store owner in 1987 the bomber went quiet, only to re-emerge in 1993, claiming another two fatalities by 1985. After seventeen years, police were still no closer to finding the culprit until, as was the case with Metesky, there was an agreement to let the bomber publish his grievances, on this occasion a 35,000-word document entitled *Industrial Society and its Future*, which railed against modern industrialisation and was a rallying call to protect the environment. The bomber even gave an undertaking that if published, he would cease his bombing campaign. It was published in both the *Washington Post* and the *New York Times* on 19 September 1995. As hoped, the contents of the text sparked a lead and on the suspicions of his brother David, Theodore Kaczynski, a former assistant professor in mathematics from the University of California's complex at Berkeley would be arrested in a remote cabin in Montana. Kaczynski would plead guilty to the charges and would eventually be sentenced to life imprisonment in 1998, serving his time at the supermax prison in Florence, Colorado. Kaczynski was effectively an eco-terrorist, who Nancy Gibbs argues was radicalised in the movements of the 1960s, although he always remained something of a loner (Gibbs & Allis, 1996). The text itself has achieved significant sales of more than 15,000 copies, although any royalties or income from the brief production of Unabomber T-shirts and posters went to the victims of the attacks.

Ramon Spaaij states that 'lone wolf terrorism' is a small, but notable, aspect of terrorism that began to increase across the world in the 1990s. Although extreme in his actions, Kaczynski has not been alone in taking violent actions for environmental reasons. In 1993 nine small bombs were placed in department stores by animal rights activists. Supporters of the Earth Liberation Front (ELF) and the Animal Liberation Front (ALF) were behind around 600 eco-terrorism attacks causing some $43 million of damage between the years 1996–2002 according to the FBI (Nacos, 2010, p. 69). Indeed in 2005 the FBI stated that violent animal rights extremists and eco-terrorists posed one of the most serious threats to America. Eleven people were indicted in 2006 on sixty-five charges, which included arson, sabotage and conspiracy against government facilities as well as research centres and private companies. The ELF destroyed five luxury homes in Washington State in 2009, which were built on wetlands.

Under pressure to take a firmer stance against terrorists, Clinton moved to pass the Antiterrorism and Effective Death Penalty Act, which was designed to speed up the process of conviction and trial for terrorist offences. Just as with laws passed in 1798, 1917 and 1918, the act helped remove those considered terrorists and also brought restrictions on immigrants from abroad who were suspected of terrorist activities. The Act allowed officials to designate any foreign organisation as one that engages in terrorist activity. The Act also looked to prevent assistance to any country that supported terrorism, including stopping the export of any defence-related materials to those not in accordance with America's anti-terrorism strategy. The act would also begin to restrict the financial affairs of suspected terrorist groups and expand provisions against aid and money laundering. The impact of this aspect of the act was always going to be limited, since many terrorist attacks are relatively inexpensive. The official 9/11 Commission Report concluded that the total cost of the 9/11 operation was thought to be between $400,000 and $500,000.

In reality, the death penalty was hardly going to deter those who were prepared to be killed. Despite the fact that the Oklahoma bombing was home-grown terrorism, Clinton also introduced the Illegal Immigration Reform and Immigrant Responsibility Act in 1996, which aimed to clamp down harder on illegal immigration, and indeed, illegal aliens were deported in greater numbers after the Oklahoma bombing. During the last five years of his presidency, Clinton steadily increased funding for counterterrorism measures, from $5.7 billion in 1995 to $11.1 billion in 2000 (Clarke, 2003, p. 97).

In the 1990s there was the growing threat of what can be termed 'moralist terrorism'; those wishing to prevent abortions would engage in violent measures including the firebombing of abortion clinics, kidnapping of medical officials as well as the killing of doctors. Roe v Wade had legalised abortions in 1973, but it was 20 years later that anti-abortion groups turned especially violent. Seven doctors would be slain by extremists, including Dr David Gunn in 1993, John B. Britton in 1994 and Dr Barnett Slepian in 1998, who was shot and killed in his own kitchen by anti-abortionist James Kopp. Inevitably, the rise in violence and harassment of officials in the practices connected to abortions led some medics to end their involvement in such procedures, providing another example of terrorism achieving a particular, if incredibly limited, aim.

The Army of God, an extreme, loose association of fundamentalist Christians declared war 'on the child-killing industry' and attacked not only abortion clinics but also nightclubs with gay and lesbian clientele. The movement's loose structure is conducive to lone wolf terrorists such as Eric Robert Rudolph, who was responsible for the attack on the 1996 Atlanta Olympic Games. During the Games Rudolph placed a shrapnel bomb in the Centennial Olympic Park where thousands had gathered for a late-night concert on 27 July. He placed the device near the sound tower and quietly made his way out of the venue. The bomb had already been spotted ahead of a telephone warning, but the evacuation was incomplete when it exploded, killing Alice Hawthorne and injuring 111 others. A Turkish cameraman also died of a heart attack whilst rushing to the scene. Despite the high-profile nature of the attack the perpetrator remained at large. A letter sent to the press linked the attack to the Army of God. Rudolph was finally tracked down in May 2003 in North Carolina, eventually being sentenced to life imprisonment without parole, having pleaded guilty to the Atlanta attack as well as the bombing of two abortion clinics and a gay nightclub in Atlanta in 1997.

Whilst terror attacks came from both internal and external sources in the US, such attacks increasingly showed the growing danger from right-wing internal forces. From 1980–89, 170 people had been indicted for domestic terrorist offences, 103 attached to right-wing groups – these were mostly white and male.

Terrorism returned to New York in February 1997 when Ali Hassan Abu Kamal, an English teacher from Palestine, having purchased a semi-automatic pistol in Florida the same day he obtained a state residence card, opened fire on the Observation Deck of the Empire State Building. The gunman would injure seven sightseers and killed a Danish tourist before turning the gun on himself. The Mayor of New York, Rudolph Giuliani, raged against the supply of a 'murder weapon' to Kamal, calling the supply of the weapon 'totally insane' and demanding tighter gun laws, causing a rift with the Florida governor Lawton Giles. Whilst the gunman seemed to have recently lost his savings in a poor business venture, there was a note found on him which expressed anger at the way in which America supported Israel against the Palestinians. As a result of this attack the Empire State Building installed metal detectors, which remain in place to this day.

Five years before 9/11 the FBI concluded that Islamic radicalism represented the greatest threat to the US, noting that groups had the ability to attack the nation's infrastructure. In 1995 Benazir Bhutto, the leader of Pakistan, would tell journalists ahead of a visit to the US that the Afghan terrorist camps were undermining the entire state of Pakistan, and that Ramzi Yousef had planted bombs in an attempt to assassinate her (Cooley, 2002, p. 212).[55]

A new factor to note at this time is the setting up of Al-Jazeera, a news broadcaster located in Qatar that began broadcasting in November 1996, providing twenty four-hour output by 1999. The news channel has proved controversial both within and outside of the Arab world. The channel would supply Osama bin Laden with an outlet for his video messages. He made his debut on the channel on Christmas Day 1998, his message exhorting Muslims to kill Americans, British and Jews in retaliation for the attacks in Iraq. An exclusive ninety-minute interview with bin Laden was soon screened to millions of viewers, just days after America had added him to the FBI's Ten Most Wanted list. The programme was to be repeated after 9/11. President Clinton had largely avoided talking directly about bin Laden or Al Qaeda, to avoid enhancing his reputation in the Arab world.

---

55 Bhutto would be assassinated in 2007, although there is some debate about who organised her killing.

It was not just the West that had cause to fear bin Laden's increased ability to get his message across. Most countries in the Middle East opposed the screening and soon the channel would be in conflict with Saudi Arabia, a schism that has only widened in recent years. Bin Laden would use the channel as his mouthpiece to the outside world. Whereas other Arab news channels had ignored his messages, Al Jazeera would always play the video or audio tapes. Jason Burke has stressed the importance of bin Laden being able to get his messages out to the wider Arab world via television and later the internet (Burke, 2007, p. 39). Controversially, the American leadership pushed the Emir of Qatar, Sheikh Hamad bin Khalifa al Thani, to reduce the amount of coverage being given to bin Laden but the Emir refused, citing the fact that this was an independent news channel over which he had no control (Miles, 2005, p. 122). This did not prevent American cooperation with Qatar, as the Al-Udeid airbase is on Qatari soil, from where the Americans would launch the invasion of Iraq. In reality some of bin Laden's taped messages were not always shown in their entirety by the channel. The attempts to control any footage connected to Al Qaeda by both the Bush and Blair administrations were ridiculed by bin Laden (Lawrence, 2005, p. 112).

For the remainder of the 1990s most attacks happened outside the US. In November 1995 a car bomb outside the National Guard building in Riyadh killed five Americans. This was a prelude to an attack on the Khobar Towers that housed the American forces at the Dharhan military base, which killed nineteen US servicemen and injured 372, in June 1996. It showed how difficult it was to protect Americans overseas, even in a country like Saudi Arabia. The FBI investigation into these attacks (and the later African Embassy attacks), created friction with the Saudi Arabian authorities, who were seen as not fully cooperating with the investigation; they refused to allow potential suspects to be questioned. It was not until 2006 that an

American district court officially laid the blame for the attack at the door of the Iranian government (Wilentz, 2009, p. 375).

In August 1996, Osama bin Laden publicly issued a jihad to expel polytheists from the Arabian peninsula. A second jihad was declared in February 1998 by the World Islamic Front, of which bin Laden was one of four signatories, against 'Jews and Crusaders' stating that it was the duty of true Muslims to kill 'the American and their allies – civilians and military' in order to liberate the Islamic territory. This fatwa passed unnoticed by most Americans as most news agencies did not report it. Bin Laden's name was little known outside of intelligence services and prior to the fatwa his name had featured in the *New York Times* on only fifteen occasions, most of which were fleeting mentions (Zuckoff, 2019, p. 4).

Lax security at American embassies in Africa, along with the relative lack of local security services, made the continent an inviting place for Al Qaeda to make good on the fatwa bin Laden had announced against America. In August of that year there were attacks on the American embassies in Nairobi, Kenya, and Dar es Salaam in Tanzania. The attacks comprised easily the most devastating assault upon American civilians overseas. The attack in Tanzania killed eleven people and injured around eighty, but the Kenyan attack killed 213 (twelve of whom were American) and over 4000 people were injured. It is possible that the attacks were intended to be part of a bigger effort, as Reeve has suggested that attacks on US targets in Uganda were also being planned. If embassies in general ceased to be secure zones then the perpetrators of the attacks would have undermined the diplomatic world order.

During the summer of 1998, 'the ignominy of the Monica Lewinsky affair unravelled like an overwrought witch hunt' (Ambrose & Brinkley, 2011 p. 447), fascinating and repelling Americans, but also obscuring the growing threat posed by radical movements to American interests. There was no warning of the attacks. Acting on intelligence, Clinton agreed to Operation *Infinite Reach*, which launched seventy-nine Cruise missiles at targets in Afghanistan and the Sudan, including directly targeting bin Laden. Bin Laden survived, although around twenty people died in the strikes. The Al-Shifa pharmaceutical factory was hit, which America later admitted produced much needed medicines for a poverty-stricken nation. This failed attempt would inevitably come into sharper focus after 9/11 when three-quarters of Americans after 9/11 stated that Clinton had not done enough to stop bin Laden (Winkler, 2006, p. 151).

Indeed, the failed attempts to eliminate bin Laden only made the problem worse by increasing bin Laden's profile and sending the message that America had been foiled again. Jason Burke has noted that the attacks gave bin Laden cult status, as the man who stood up to the super power of America (2007, p. 181). The attacks solidified the relationship between bin Laden and the Taliban, removing any chance of them possibly abandoning bin Laden in exchange for international support. Anti-US feeling increased; an attack on the Planet Hollywood restaurant in Cape Town killed two people in January 1999. Whilst Clinton tried to avoid language that suggested terrorism could be defeated, he did raise expectations by his attacks on Al Qaeda. As the Clinton administration launched a military strike against Al Qaeda targets only three days after the president admitted his dalliance with Lewinsky, the US Secretary of Defence William Cohen was accused by the press of using military action to deflect media attention. Another important and unfortunate by-product of the Lewinsky affair was that Clinton and FBI Director Louis Freeh became alienated. The focus of the FBI would be more upon the investigation of the president rather than the sharing of what would turn out to be crucial intelligence information regarding the growing terrorist threat. As Clinton was being formally investigated, he was in no position to replace Freeh.

The African Embassy attacks certainly succeeded in bringing Osama bin Laden to prominence. On the FBI's Ten Most Wanted Fugitives poster, there was a $25 million reward for his capture, bin Laden listed as being wanted in connection to the African Embassy bombings. In 1999 President Clinton would sign an executive order declaring Al Qaeda a terrorism organisation, which allowed the US to impose sanctions against the group.

Despite Clinton's stress on the importance and dangers of terrorism, there was always the accusation that Clinton could have done more. Unsurprisingly, right-wing politicians such as Donald Rumsfeld stated that Clinton acted indecisively. However, even friendly biographers such as Joe Klein state that Clinton could have taken further actions to deal with the rising terrorist threat (Klein, 2002, p. 72), but Clinton was still dealing with an American public who saw terrorism as remote and would not have accepted any of the major changes in policy at home or abroad that Bush was able to introduce after 9/11. Even Clinton's most implacable political foe, Newt Gingrich, despite heavy criticism of Clinton after 9/11, never pushed the president to take any stronger measures on the issue of terrorism (Gillon, 2008, p. 271). In fact, Clinton pushed strongly, and was successful in getting Congress to sanction an additional $10 billion in funding towards combating terrorism in 2000. Sensitive to the criticism of those who felt he did not do enough to deal with terrorism during his presidency, Clinton has dedicated a section of his presidential library to showing how he attempted to combat terrorism, stressing that he made the issue a top-level national security policy.

Clinton did at least enjoy some success with the foiling of the Millennium Plot in 1999. The discovery of this plot was accidental and down to a highly diligent customs official. Ahmed Ressam was caught driving some 130 pounds of explosive material in from Canada. Canadian officials were aware of his contacts with Al Qaeda and that he was an illegal alien, but did not share this information, demonstrating how poor the sharing of relevant terrorist information was prior to 9/11. Over time, Ressam's plans became known and he later shared information about his contacts with Al Qaeda, allowing the authorities to make a number of arrests. His plans would have seen two bombs detonated at Los Angeles International Airport, an attack on the USS *The Sullivans*, as well as attacks in Yemen and Jordan.

The National Commission on Terrorism informed Congress in 2000 in their report, 'Countering the Changing Threat of International Terrorism', that America, as the world's sole superpower, would likely face increased threats from groups and individuals who would no longer look towards state sponsorship, but instead would be loose entities linked by a religious affinity or a common hatred of the US. The report called for cooperation by the intelligence agencies and directly noted the threat from bin Laden and his network. (See appendix.)

In 1997 a National Security Council memo had been sent to the Pentagon warning of the rising likelihood of attacks on US ships in foreign ports, specifically identifying Yemen as a stronghold for terrorists (Wilentz, 2008, p. 406). Yemen was the site of a hotel bombing as early as December 1992 by Al Qaeda operatives against American forces, but based on intelligence of an attack, they had already moved out. Despite the dangers within the region, in December 1998 the US and Yemeni governments signed an agreement to allow refuelling in the port of Aden. Although in January 2000 an attempt to attack USS *The Sullivans* failed when a boat loaded with explosives sank in the harbour, on 12 October 2000 a small vessel loaded with explosives made up to look like a service boat and piloted by two Al Qaeda suicide bombers in white overalls moved up to the USS *Cole* being refuelled en route to Iraq to support the United Nations embargo against the country. Security lapses on board the USS *Cole* were compounded by restrictions on opening fire at an Arab port and the terrorists were able to detonate their cargo towards the mid-section of the ship, causing the death of seventeen crewmen and injuring thirty-five others. The crew of the *Cole* struggled to keep the ship from sinking. The fact that these events took place in Yemen, the ancestral home of the bin Laden family, again threw the spotlight onto Al Qaeda, but any hopes for a joint investigation by American and Yemeni officials soon foundered (Shay, 2007, p. 128). The events did prompt the United Nations to take action, by now grown weary of the Taliban's links to terrorism. They demanded that the Taliban give up bin Laden, and when this demand was refused the Taliban's financial assets were frozen. In a postscript to the events, one of the suspected key figures in the attack, Jamal-Al Badawi, who had escaped from prison twice, was killed by an American strike in Yemen in January 2019.

Although the George H. W. Bush years largely escaped serious acts of terrorism, the Clinton era was bookended by them. Clinton's term began with the attack on the World Trade Center, and ended with the attack on the USS *Cole*. Clinton did take more action against terrorism than many of his critics give him credit for and has been defended in his actions by Richard Clarke, his counter-terrorism Tsar. Whilst the direct links between bin Laden and events such as the Somalia attacks and any direct relationship to Ramzi Yousef may have been missed, it is possible such evidence simply did not exist, and we may never know the true extent of such connections. Even if Yousef offers to give further evidence, as briefly seemed the case in recent years, his veracity will always be in doubt. Clinton directly targeted bin Laden in a failed raid in August 1998, which some detractors unfairly saw as an attempt to deflect attention from his own internal problems. Clinton was especially concerned about the threat from weapons of mass destruction and made a special point of briefing the incoming Bush regime on the rising threat from Al Qaeda. However, it is fair to say that partly because of the Lewinsky affair, and partly due to the increased polarity of American politics, Clinton did not, and to an extent could not, devote as much of his energies to dealing with the growing threat as he would have liked. It has also been noted in this chapter that there was no appetite either in Congress, or within the country, for the large-scale security measures that were so readily accepted after 9/11. There was a clampdown on some of the right-wing groups within America after the Oklahoma bombing and the number of active Patriot groups fell from 858 to less than 200 (Wright, 2007, p. 18).

Despite the increase in intelligence about militant Islamism, which included knowledge about the threat posed by Osama bin Laden, the attacks on the World Trade Center, on the American embassies in Tanzania and Kenya, as well as the very high-profile attacks in Oklahoma and at the Atlanta Olympics and Empire State Building, the American public remained largely apathetic about the prospects of a major terrorist incident taking place on the American mainland. The last Gallup poll taken ahead of the 9/11 attacks revealed that less than a quarter of Americans listed themselves as 'very worried' or 'somewhat worried' about the threat from terrorism. Terrorism still remained an abstract concept to most Americans, and neither Congress nor the Republican Party placed emphasis during the 2000 campaign on issues related to terrorism.

Aside from some coverage of trials linked to the 1998 embassy bombings, there was little media attention related to any terrorism matters in the five months leading up to the attacks of 9/11. With the rising tide of the terrorist threat essentially missed, with the Bush administration taking its focus elsewhere, with media interest low, and finally, with the mistaken belief that external terrorist groups did not have the ability to successfully target the US, the opportunities to prevent the future events were missed and the stage was set for the most devastating terrorist outrage of them all.

8

9/11 AND BEYOND

The events of the morning of 9/11 are etched onto the mind of everyone who viewed them. They took place over just 102 minutes. In this chapter we consider the attack and look at the reaction of the Bush administration and the changes it brought about in both internal and external policy. Internally, legal changes have been dominated by the PATRIOT Act and the setting up of the Office of Homeland Security, and externally the response has been marked by a second 'war on terror', and the American invasions of Afghanistan and Iraq. In the final parts of this chapter there is a consideration of some of the other developments in the war on terror, including the anthrax attacks, the final capture of Osama bin Laden, and the Boston bombing. The incidences of terrorism on American soil have decreased to modest levels compared to the heyday of the 1970s, but terrorist threats are very much present both at home and abroad. Ironically, given the stress Bush placed on rogue states after 9/11, during the 2000 election campaign his focus had been neither on terrorism or even on foreign policy. After 9/11 the Bush regime made the war on terror its central tenet.

Despite the inevitable changes in personnel brought about by a new regime, the Bush administration chose to retain the services of Richard Clarke, Clinton's counter-terrorism coordinator, who stressed to the incoming administration the importance of staying focussed on the rising threats posed by Al Qaeda. Later, Clarke suggested Bush had not taken the threat seriously and quickly moved his focus to confronting China and pulling out of the ABM Treaty, suggesting that Bush had ignored repeated warnings and had not done enough to protect the country from impending attack (Clarke, 2004, p. xxix).

Outgoing Defence Secretary Bill Cohen also made a point of discussing with incoming Defence Secretary Donald Rumsfeld the threats from Al Qaeda in the light of the attack on the USS *Cole*. On 6 August 2001 President George W. Bush's Presidential Daily Brief came with the headline 'Bin Laden Determined to Strike in US' (9/11 Report, 2004, p. 261). However, the report lacked specifics and President Bush would later argue that the predicted attack was likely to be overseas (2010, p. 134). It certainly did not help the intelligence situation that Louis Freeh stepped down as head of the FBI in June 2001 and there no replacement until Robert Mueller was appointed just a week prior to the attacks.[56]

One key piece of intelligence was missed in July of 2001, when an FBI agent passed on what became known as the Phoenix memo, which informed the Bureau that bin Laden was potentially making a coordinated effort to send recruits to aviation schools, and that there were people of interest to the Bureau attending flights schools in Arizona (9/11 Report, 2004, p. 272). The memo had no real impact at the time and was not seen by senior officials.

A final chance to avoid the events of 9/11 came with the arrest of Zacarias Moussaoui, whose activities in a flight school in Minneapolis and background and beliefs prompted his arrest by the FBI, but only on charges of outstaying his visa. Whilst there was a suggestion that he intended to hijack a plane and

---

56 Robert Mueller would stay in the role until 2013, and would become more famous for his investigation and report into Russian interference in the US elections from 2017–2019.

even that the World Trade Center might be his target, there was little agreement between the security services and complex legalities prevented them from searching Moussaoui's apartment or computer. His links to Al Qaeda were discovered too late: the Americans actually had the twentieth hijacker, but could not join the dots in time. The failures to identify, respond and defeat the new threats to national security would be at the core of the 9/11 Commission Report.

The events of that fateful day would alter American security policy both internally and externally. Simply in money terms, insurance payouts amounted to around $20 billion, although this figure is less than that paid out for recent natural disasters; but it is thought that for a variety of reasons including cancelled business orders and a decline in tourism that America lost around $75 billion in gross domestic product by the end of 2001 (Law, 2009, p. 333). The American government would end up providing financial help to airlines in the wake of the attacks, as some airlines filed for bankruptcy. Over a million Americans lost their jobs in the three months after the attack, an astonishing figure. Bin Laden proudly boasted of the cost to the American economy; he claimed America had lost around $1 trillion overall in the attacks (Lawrence, 2005, p. 112).

We have seen that the methods used on 9/11 had been attempted before, but never with such dramatic consequences. Niall Ferguson considered that the novelty of 9/11 lay in the combination of different approaches with antecedents – air piracy and attacks against urban centres. Noam Chomsky has long been a critic of America's foreign policies and stated the new aspect of 9/11 was that the violence was directed at the US for the first time.

Before 9/11 many observers thought that hijackings were an outmoded tactic, placing much faith in the improved and increased security measures that now accompanied air travel. Trapped in Cold War thinking, people believed that the airborne threat was no longer viable and America had reduced the number of on-alert fighter jet sites from twenty-two to fourteen, with plans to cut this number to just four (Zuckoff, 2019, p. 21). Security was far more focussed on the idea that sabotage was the greatest threat to aircraft, despite the fact that only three cases of sabotage had been recorded during the five years leading up 9/11, whilst worldwide hijackings for the same period stood at sixty-four cases. There was no conception that an old terrorist tactic could be combined with suicide missions to create such a dramatic outcome (Crenshaw, 2011, p. 65).

The most infamous attack in the history of terrorism began with the departure of American Airlines Flight 11 from Logan International Airport, bound for Los Angeles at 7.59 am. On board were ninety-two passengers. Just fourteen minutes into the flight five men led by Egyptian Mohamed Atta hijacked the plane. At 8.46 amateur video footage would capture the Boeing 767 ploughing into the North Tower of the World Trade Center. At around the time the flight was being hijacked, United Airlines flight 175 left Logan International Airport, also bound for Los Angeles. On board were seventy-two passengers, and 26,000 gallons of kerosene. That amount of fuel was necessary for the flight; the hijackers deliberately targeted long-distance flights since they knew that the more fuel the plane was carrying, the greater the destructive power of the aircraft. This plane was also taken over by five hijackers. As the plane smashed into the South Tower of the World Trade Center at 9.03 am, the hijackers would have been keenly aware that by this point the assembling media would already be pointing their cameras at the burning North Tower. So the crash was seen live, with on-air news teams almost immediately able to deduce that they were witnessing an unprecedented terrorist attack.

The nightmare of the day was far from over, with American Airlines Flight 77, also on a long-distance flight from Dulles Airport to Los Angeles, crashing into the western side of the

Pentagon at 9.37 am killing all sixty-four passengers and crew. Finally, United Airlines Flight 93 out of Newark crashed into a field at Stoneycreek Township, Pennsylvania at 10.03 am, its passengers taking on the hijackers and bringing the aircraft down, having already discovered via the aircraft phone systems that they were part of a wider plan to crash the planes into symbolic targets and were possibly destined to crash into the White House (Tuman, 2003, p62).

With confusion reigning the various security agencies were simply unable to formulate a quick and effective response. By the time American airspace was closed, many federal buildings, including the White House,[57] Congress and various landmarks, as well as America's tallest buildings such as the Empire State Building, the Sears Tower in Chicago, John Hancock Tower in Boston, and even buildings as far distant as the Space Needle in Seattle and Transamerica Pyramid in San Francisco were all being evacuated. Although there have been many attempts to take control of aircraft, 9/11 represented the first occasions in which hijackers had taken full control of the flight deck and assumed control of commercial planes. By 10.28 am both towers had collapsed and there were close to 3000 dead from around eighty different nations.[58] America closed its airspace, ending all of the remaining 25,000 flights that took place daily in the US.

---

57 Whilst President Bush was visiting a school in Florida, Vice President Dick Cheney was moved to an underground bunker and other staff were quickly evacuated. David Frum described being sent out of the Whitehouse, asked to remove his ID and then being left out in the street (Frum, 2003, pp. 115–16).

58 The exact final death toll may never be known, but the tally does not include the additional deaths created by toxic exposure created by the events of the day, which would almost double the original death toll. Inevitably the events of this day gave rise to a vast number of conspiracy theories. For example, Michael Pardo has argued that the government knew of events beforehand and that Israel's secret service Mossad was behind the attack. Conspiracy theories are not addressed in this work; see *Political Conspiracies in America: A Reader* (2008) edited by Critchlow, D., Korasick, J., and Sherman, M.C. Bloomington, Indiana.

Intelligence agencies would inevitably fall under the spotlight. George W. Bush would argue that the events revealed that law enforcement agencies had failed to protect America (2010, p. 154). The reality was that information was not shared as a matter of course by these agencies. Historically, the FBI and the CIA had a fractious relationship and lacked coordination. In 1970 Hoover even stopped liaising with the CIA over a dispute regarding an FBI informant (Nixon, 1979, p. 473).

George W. Bush was informed that bin Laden was behind the 9/11 attacks just one day after they took place, although curiously bin Laden would only accept responsibility for the attacks a few days before the 2004 presidential election.[59] Bush would also note that only after the tragic events of 9/11 did the government fully understand that previous terrorist events both in the US and overseas had been a 'warm up', Bush going as far as to call all the events a 'master plan' (2010, p. 154).

All of the nineteen hijackers of 9/11, fifteen of whom came from Saudi Arabia, had entered the USA legally; as had Ramzi Yousef and Mohammad Salameh in 1992, Ali Hassan Kamal, Giuseppe Zangara, Oscar Collazo, Griselio Torresola, Sirhan Sirhan, as had the anarchists who attacked America a century or so previously.

There soon emerged a desire for revenge, which played into the hands of right-wing hawks, who would soon transform America foreign policy into a highly pro-active phase. The public did not turn against Bush, who enjoyed a 90 per cent approval rating after the attacks, but turned against previous president Bill Clinton. *The Washington Post* opined: 'One of the reasons there are enough terrorists out there capable and deadly enough to carry out the deadliest attack on the United States in its history is that, while they have declared war on us, we have in the past responded

---

59 The video tape was cited by Democratic candidate John Kerry as being an important reason why he lost the November election by thirty-five Electoral College votes. See Lawrence, 2004, p. 237.

(with the exception of a few useless Cruise missile attacks on empty tents in the desert) by issuing subpoenas.' (Krauthammer, 9 December 2001). A similar message came from the *The Chicago Tribune*'s John Kass, who declared: 'For the past decade we've sat dumb and stupid as the US military was transformed from a killing machine into a playpen for sociologists and political schemers.'

Many texts will tell you that Al Qaeda was set up at the end of the 1980s to further the aims of Wahabbism – a strict form of the Muslim faith practised in areas such as Saudi Arabia. The first recorded reference to any organisation called AQ appeared in a 1996 CIA report which suggested that Usama bin Laden[60] had organised AQ, an Islamic Salvation Front, in 1985 to fight alongside the *mujahideen* in Afghanistan. John Cooley also suggests that Al Qaeda was formed in 1985, establishing recruitment centres in Saudi Arabia, Egypt and Pakistan (2002, pp. 97–8). It was given a more interesting definition in 1998 in a State Department Report: AQ was 'an operational hub, predominately for like-minded Sunni Extremists'.

Bin Laden himself moved his operation to the Sudan during the period from 1991 to 1992, but whilst bin Laden and his funds were welcomed by the government there, the US increasingly pressured the country, listing the Sudan as a support state for international terrorism. This took a toll on the country's already dire economic status, and bin Laden and a modest band of supporters moved back to Afghanistan in 1996. Ironically, Sudan did surrender Illich Ramirez Sanchez, better known as Carlos the Jackal, who was wanted for a number of terrorist attacks, to French authorities in 1994, to demonstrate publicly that the country did not support terrorism; but the country continued to support Islamic terrorist groups (Shay, 2007, p. 46).

---

60 Variations on spelling from Arabic to English are common since there is no universally accepted transliteration. This spelling was used on the Most Wanted posters by the FBI, but the rest of this book uses the more common Osama.

Bin Laden's time in Afghanistan is as close, Jason Burke suggests, as Bin Laden ever got to having an important 'base' (2007, p. 5). Bin Laden enjoyed the support and protection of the Taliban regime led by Mullah Omar who controlled most of the country by the late 1990s.[61] There were a number of radical Islamic outfits in Afghanistan, many of whom had very different aims and objectives and bin Laden's attempt to unite these different groups failed as many had no interest in attacking the US.

Much has been written of bin Laden, and perhaps inevitably a lot of the early material that was published was of dubious accuracy. There are conflicting stories about bin Laden enjoying time in the West (a family shot of various bin Laden family members in Sweden in 1971 does not feature Osama). After 9/11 there were many false stories depicting bin Laden as everything from a man who had enjoyed a playboy lifestyle in the West, to a major heroin supplier. In reality no hard evidence exists that Bin Laden visited the West, unlike most of his many siblings. He was a pious individual who married at seventeen (Burke, 2007, p. 47). Lawrence Wright agrees with this background, although he believes bin Laden visited the West briefly to consult a doctor. In *The Looming Tower* (later a TV series) Wright traces bin Laden's path towards anti-Americanism and eventually terrorism. He argues Al Qaeda was formed in 1988, but that various people including Jamal Khashoggi, who was murdered in 2018, tried to get bin Laden to renounce terrorism.

It was certainly unfortunate that much of the FBI's early intelligence regarding Al Qaeda was given to them by the Sudanese militant Jamal al-Fadl. He left bin Laden's circle in 1995, having siphoned off some of bin Laden's money and looked to provide America with information in exchange for cash and protection. He is the source

---

61 Omar fled Kabul following the US invasion in October 2001. Never formally located, he has been reported dead on many occasions, but the Taliban seemed to confirm in 2015 that he had died two years previously.

for the formation of Al Qaeda being in 1989. During questioning by the FBI the claim was undermined by Al-Fadl himself. America was simply not used to a danger or threat that liked to hide. The lack of operational structure mean that the groups that have sprung up after the events of 2001 are more inspired by the ideas of Al Qaeda rather than taking any direct orders from it.

Some of the worst excesses of disinformation have at least been addressed. Steve Coll in his book *The Bin Ladens* looked in depth at the extended bin Laden family and pieces together his information from verifiable sources. Bin Laden was born in 1957 in Riyadh. The ancestral home of the family was in Yemen. He studied at the Management and Economics School at King Abd al-Aziz University in Jeddah. It was here that bin Laden began his political radicalisation. Some of the Islamic courses were taught by Muhammad Qutb, the brother of Sayyid Qutb, the latter's books *Signposts* and *In the Shade of the Koran* being read by bin Laden in 1976–77 (Coll, 2009, p. 204). Although bin Laden traced his own radicalisation to the 1973 Yom Kippur War, which he claimed had only been won with America weapons, aid and men.

Bin Laden's doctrines and beliefs did not come out of nowhere and there is a clear debt to the writings of Sayyid Qutb, an Egyptian born in 1906, who began working for the Ministry of Education in 1933, and who journeyed to the US in 1948 to look into education curriculum reforms (Toth, p. 13). Qutb would spend two years in the US, and even though Truman's America was a comparatively conservative place, Qutb still saw America as corrupt and decadent. Returning to Egypt, Qutb was shocked to see western encroachment upon his country. He wrote many works besides the eight-volume *In the Shade of the Quran*, although his writings are condensed into a single book, *Milestones*, which has been translated into English. His writings reflect his rejection of western influence. For example Qutb stated in *Milestones* that 'If Islam is again to play the role of the leader of mankind, then it is necessary that the Muslim community be restored to its original form.' These words would also reflect future statements by bin Laden. While such notions were consistent with the Quran, Qutb, and later bin Laden clearly had to find ways to explain why they ignored the Quran's teachings that there must no compulsion in religion and that the murder of one innocent represented the murder of mankind.

Qutb joined the Muslim Brotherhood, an organisation founded in 1928 by Hassan Al-Banna but which had been banned by President Nasser, and Qutb was placed in prison where he was tortured. Although he was released, by 1965 he was back in jail and the following year faced a three-month trial, which he used to call for a new Islamic movement. Qutb was sentenced to death, and although President Nasser, amidst major demonstrations in Cairo, attempted to rescind the death penalty, Qutb, like others before him, such as John Brown in 1859, knew that his death would give his words greater value and he was executed on 29 August 1966. By the time of his death Lawrence Wright notes that Qutb's followers were already growing in number.

America was seen as a malevolent influence, but the campaign for a jihad had to begin at home, in the Middle East. Qutb's writings provided a kind of Islamic manifesto in which he stated that a vanguard of leaders should help others to be steered back towards the pure values of the Quran. The battle for the resurgence of Islamic values was a 'cosmic struggle'. Qutb's legacy is a powerful one, not least in radicalising Osama bin Laden. Mohammed Qutb was able to get his brother's messages to new students and was supported by the Saudi government, keen to stop the spread of socialistic principles. The 9/11 Commission Report would also acknowledge Qutb's influence upon bin Laden (9/11 Report, 2004, p. 51).

Despite the huge resources allocated to the defeat of Al Qaeda and the capture of bin Laden, American forces found him so elusive that conspiracy theorists began to question whether he was still alive. Authors such as David Ray Griffin, for example, argued that bin Laden had died in December 2001.[62] Remarkably, bin Laden was still able to meet Western journalists after 9/11 and would continue to send in video and audio messages to Al Jazeera at irregular intervals. In addition, videos and DVDs would be distributed of executions and martyrdoms and soon the internet would also become a powerful tool to help terrorist groups to get out their messages and rally support.

Following the 9/11 attacks, bin Laden seemed initially reticent about accepting responsibility. He defended and supported the actions however, pointing to the target as being a financial one, rather than a school or housing complex (Lawrence, 2005, p. 119) and drew a distinction between attacking the US and a country such as Sweden.[63] Finally, in October 2004, bin Laden claimed responsibility and outlined the reasons behind the attack, specifically drawing attention to the 1982 invasion of Lebanon as the event which unleashed 'a strong determination to punish oppressors (Lawrence, 2005, p. 239).

Bin Laden was keen to issue public statements. From 1994 such statements were clearly aimed at wider audiences. The statements varied in length and addressed a variety of issues, but core themes were the plight of the Palestinians and western involvement in Muslim countries. Bin Laden wanted the wider world to know the motivations behind his jihad, and provide justification to the Arab world, often based on highly selective and misinterpreted

---

62 Griffin's book *Osama Bin Laden Dead or Alive* in 2009 considers the possibility that Bin Laden died of a lung condition in mid-December 2001 and that the later videos were forgeries of the West to keep alive the war on terror.

63 Sweden has not escaped terrorist attacks, as seen when an Uzbek national, Rakhmat Akilov, who supported extremist organisations, ploughed into pedestrians in central Stockholm in April 2017 killing four people. Akilov's application for asylum had been rejected.

sections of the Koran. He was not always fully consistent with his arguments, his statement that 'Many in the West are polite and good people' does not sit easily with his call to indiscriminate jihad. Whilst it would be fanciful to suggest bin Laden could have been negotiated with, in April 2004 he made an offer to end operations against states which promised not to attack Muslims or intervene in their affairs (Lawrence 2005, p. 235). Such an offer was in keeping with his key message of wanting the Islamic world to control its own affairs without intervention from the West. Bin Laden's messages, largely on audio tape, would continue until the end of his life.

As President Bush, unlike his father, had little foreign policy experience prior to standing in the 2000 presidential election, he surrounded himself with figures who had previously held senior roles, many of whom were hawks and had played key roles in setting out the 'Project for the New American Century' in 1997. Amongst those behind the neoconservative think tank were Jeb Bush, Dick Cheney, Donald Rumsfeld, and Paul Wolfowitz, and central to their core objectives was regime change in Iraq. Dick Cheney, who wielded immense power as a highly active Vice President, argued that in the face of terrorism, America had responded either 'weakly or not at all' (Cheney, 2011, p. 419, p. 438). Cheney argued this led to terrorists believing that all that they had to do was create sufficient American casualties in order to force the country to change course.

Such a position was taken by another key player in Bush's cabinet. Donald Rumsfeld who returned as Defence Secretary, having held the position under Gerald Ford, argued that America's previous stance against terrorists had not been strong enough and that 'weakness was provocative' to America's enemies. Cheney and Rumsfeld were determined not to repeat such inaction. Cheney saw the War on Terror as something likely to continue during his lifetime (2011, p. 332). The idea that terrorism was a perpetual war without borders had been argued by CIA Director William Casey in 1985. President Bush himself argued that since terrorists had declared war on America, he had little choice but to declare war on the terrorists (2010, p. 154).

On 24 September 2001 another right-wing figure within the administration, Attorney General John Ashcroft, stated that 'Terrorism is a clear and present danger to Americans today ... This new terrorist threat to Americans on our soil is a turning point in America's history' (cited in Croft, 2006, p. 52).

Despite the emphasis that Bush placed on rogue states, the reality was that terrorist threats from individual states had long since declined. Libya was removed from the State Department's list of states that sponsor terrorism, as was North Korea in 2008. Iran, which offered official condolences to America after 9/11 and whose people held candlelit vigils, had also moved away from such measures as hostage-taking, assassination and encouraging rebellion, although it continues to support Palestinian groups today and America still sees the country as the leading supporter of terrorism.

In his 2002 State of the Union Address Bush would discuss the threat posed by states that did not abide by international norms or treaty requirements and who posed a threat to the international order. Bush would use the word 'evil' five times to describe rogue states, noting that Iran, Iraq and North Korea 'and their terrorist allies, constitute an axis of evil, arming to threaten the peace of the world'. Bush's list was later expanded to include other long-standing foes of the US (notably Cuba). His speech bears a similarity to Reagan's terrorism speech of July 1985. One change in emphasis was the increasingly frequent modification of the word terrorism with the adjectives 'Islamic' or 'Middle Eastern'.

The major difference between the 1985 Reagan speech and the 2002 Bush speech was the amount of direct action that followed as a result. Except for the April 1986 bombing of Tripoli and the use of force following the *Achille Lauro* hijacking in Sicily (see chapter six), no other direct military action followed the 1985 speech. By contrast, Bush would respond to the events of 9/11 with not one, but two, military invasions, to remove the Taliban in Afghanistan in October 2001 and to remove Saddam Hussein's leadership in Iraq in March 2003.[64]

Some critics have pointed the finger of blame for the origin of 9/11 at the Reagan Administration. As discussed in chapter five, Reagan's foreign policy was very much Cold War-centred, which meant that he saw it in terms of defeating communism and Moscow as the driving force behind terrorism. Reagan's retreat from Lebanon and focus on hostages in the Middle East further emboldened those who wished to challenge the power of the US. Thus Reagan not only missed the growing threat from radical Islam but inadvertently aided its rise by supporting and supplying those who opposed the Soviet forces in Afghanistan.

As Professor Michael Howard stated: 'President Bush's declaration of a "war on terror" was generally seen abroad as a rhetorical device to alert American people to the dangers facing them, rather than as a statement to be taken seriously, or literally in terms of international law. But further statements and actions by the Bush Administration have made it clear that the president's words were intended to be taken literally' (cited in Hoffman, 2006, p. 19). David Frum states that Bush moved the war on terror from metaphor to fact (Frum, 2003, p. 142)

North Korea, Iran and Iraq had little in common and as Alexander Lennon and Camille Eiss note in their book *Reshaping Rogue States* there were greatly differing policies towards them by the Bush regime. The fact that all three states had in the past

---

64 Hussein was implicated in a plot to kill former president George H. W. Bush in April 1993 when he visited Kuwait as part of the follow-up victory celebrations. Eleven Iraqi nationals were arrested and explosives were recovered (Reeve, 1999, p. 248).

been linked to terrorist actions was enough to link them in the minds of many. 9/11 provided one of the biggest opportunities for rapprochement with Iran. It is interesting to note that Ramzi Yousef was behind an attack in Iran on 20 June 1994 when the Imam Reza shrine in Mashhad was bombed, killing twenty-six people and injuring 200 (Reeve, 1999, p. 66).

Bush declared a 'with us or against us' orthodoxy and the regime suddenly went headlong into a policy to defeat terrorism that reduced freedom at home and created much animosity against the US overseas. Authors such as Edward Lucas also see additional negative issues with the active war on terror: a weakening of the Atlantic alliance and with America now focusing elsewhere, allowing Russia to tighten the screw at home and bully neighbours abroad (Lucas, 2008, p. 3). Prior to 9/11 America disagreed with Russia's stance on Chechnya, which was attempting to become a separate nation, but after 9/11 Bush was ready to accept the idea that those battling Russia were Islamic terrorists.

Bush quickly moved to military action to remove the Taliban from power under Article 51 of the UN Charter, which allows for 'individual or collective self-defence'. This was accepted by the international community once the Taliban refused to give up bin Laden. American jets in conjunction with British forces began bombing Afghanistan and a little over a month later the Taliban were driven back towards the cave complex at Tora Bora. Both George W. Bush and Osama bin Laden would use self-defence as a justification for their actions.

The direction of American foreign policy was even more controversially spelled out in Bush's West Point speech of 1 June 2002. The speech indicated a new and far more pro-active stance in future American foreign policy. It was suggested by the Bush administration that America was now facing a fight for its very existence. Condoleezza Rice was not alone in arguing that after 9/11 America faced an existential threat to its security. Bush was now advocating a policy close to that outlined in NSDD-138. Eiss and Lennon have argued that the strategy of pre-emptive action is the policy that separates the Bush administration from those that had gone before it, although as we saw in chapter six, this approach had had an early advocate in George Schultz.

The lack of coordination between America's security agencies – exemplified by the Immigration and Naturalisation Service notifying a Florida flight school that it was granting student visas to Mohamed Atta and Marwan al Shehhi six months after the pair had been amongst those flying planes into the twin towers – led to the setting up of the Office of Homeland Security. This office consolidated twenty-two agencies and now employs around 200,000 people. The initial budget of more than $20 bn has grown to $51.7 bn for 2020. The US soon reported that 142 countries had acted to freeze suspected terrorist assets and some 153 organisations had had their funds either frozen or confiscated.

In addition the PATRIOT Act (Uniting and Strengthening America by Providing Appropriate Tools Required to Intercept and Obstruct Terrorism) was rushed into force, being signed by President Bush on 26 October, just six weeks after 9/11. The odd acronym of the act was actually coined by Congress, as the original title had been simply the Anti-Terrorism Act of 2001, a title Bush wanted to keep. In addition to removing legal obstructions to federal and state agencies sharing information, the legislation, far more controversially, expanded the ability to tap telephones, freeze assets, track internet usage and secretly compile intelligence files on individuals. Such powers had proved highly controversial in the late 1960s and 1970s.

Ishmael Reed has argued that the PATRIOT Act has precedents in the Alien and Sedition Acts of 1798. The Act gave substantial powers to detain suspected terrorists. Such wide powers seem to encroach on American freedoms and liberties but Bush stated upon signing the Bill, 'Today, we take an essential step in defeating terrorism while protecting the constitutional rights of all Americans.' The House of Representatives passed the bill by a vote of 357 to 66 and the Senate approved the measure 98 to 1, the sole opposing senator being Democrat Russ Feingold. Bush later justified the passing of the bill by stating that in the period from 9/11 to March 2003, the CIA reported some 400 specific threats every month. The Act was in fact just the most infamous of many new legal changes that were enacted following 9/11.

Amongst the legacies of this time is the prison at the American military facility at Guantanamo Bay, Cuba, though this was merely the most well known of a series of bases abroad in which America held detainees, some brought there by the process of rendition. Rendition took place before 9/11, with some seventy cases under Bill Clinton (Starr-Deelen, 2014, p. 101). Extraordinary Renditions, the full details of which are still undisclosed, involved the Bush Administration in facilitating the enforced removal of terrorist suspects to countries such as Egypt, Syria, Morocco, and Jordan. So worried were some members of Congress that John McCain pressured the government to accept a ban on torture in 2005.[65] This process proved so controversial that in 2005 Condoleezza Rice had to move to assure America's allies that she would not allow the use of cruel and degrading practices against any suspects, although the comments stopped short of a formal statement regarding the end of rendition practices (Wilkinson, 2006, p. 154). This allowed the US to capture and imprison potential terrorists, without having to abide by the legal safeguards that would prevail if those captives were brought to the US mainland. This point was openly acknowledged by President Bush, who took to defending conditions in the camp (2010, p. 166). Donald Rumsfeld justified

---

65 John McCain (1936-2018) was the Republican nominee in 2008. He had been tortured as a POW whilst serving in the Vietnam War.

the treatment of those held at the base by noting that the Geneva Convention did not apply to Al Qaeda terrorists, as they were not part of a nation-state (2012, p. 561).

Jeffrey Simon has drawn parallels between Al Qaeda and the Galleanists in terms of their operational structure, with a charismatic leader at the top and autonomous cells operating throughout the US taking advantage of a support base among the population who felt disadvantaged and alienated (Simon, 2008, p. 209).

At the start of October 2001, with America still reeling from the attacks in New York and Washington D.C., came another major terrorist incident. A number of parcels containing anthrax were sent initially to workers at America Media Inc. The first victim, Robert Stevens, was to be the first person in the US diagnosed with an anthrax infection since 1976. CBS and ABC News were soon targeted, as well as Democratic Senators Tom Daschle and Patrick Leahy. Discovery of the letters closed down the government mail system, causing significant disruption.

Some of the letters bore crude messages that suggested that they had come from Islamic sources, on whom suspicion quickly fell: 'Death to America'. The discovery of anthrax caused considerable panic in the US at a time when Americans felt highly vulnerable. The panic was also fuelled by various copycat actions, with some people sending various household white powders through the post. There was even a scare that both Dick Cheney and Condoleezza Rice had been exposed to deadly toxins. The post would no longer be sent to the White House but irradiated and opened offsite. Well over a thousand people were tested for contact with the infection and over thirty thousand people were given preventative treatment.

The anthrax attacks would eventually lead to the deaths of five people and eighteen more were infected. The type of anthrax used was of a highly refined nature, which limited its potential origins. Despite this, no clear suspect emerged until August 2008, when Bruce Ivins was identified as the sole suspect. Ivins worked in an American biodefense lab. He would commit suicide before trial, so his motives remain something of a mystery, although a group of psychiatrists would find a history of mental illness, which they concluded should have prevented his access to dangerous pathogens. Indeed, despite the fact that the FBI effectively closed the case in 2010, many close to Ivins still doubt that he was responsible for the attack.

George Bush immediately announced that in the budget of 2003 an additional $11 bn would be allocated to fight the dangers of biological terrorism. There was also to be enough vaccine available to inoculate all of the US from smallpox (Croft, 2006, p. 129).

In 2003 William Krar was arrested in Noonday, Texas, police having discovered a potentially deadly sodium cyanide bomb at his residence, alongside suitcase bombs and half a million rounds of ammunition, exposing the dangers of chemical weapon attacks from right-wing domestic extremists, although the Bush administration played down the finding of such a large cache of deadly weapons. One of Krar's neighbours in the tiny hamlet of Noonday, Teresa Staples, who rented out three garages to Krar, commented when she saw the FBI agents in biological warfare suits: 'When those guys turned up in spacesuits, I just knew something very bad had been found.'

Fears about bio-terrorism are far from new. Indeed, as far back as 1894 the British magazine *Tit Bits* reported the fictitious claim that there was a plot to release disease into the air or the country's water supply. During the 1990s police discovered Patriots in Minnesota making ricin. They arrested Larry Wayne Harris in 1995, a Patriot who had attempted to procure a bubonic plague toxin, claiming to be a biological weapons researcher. In the same year they charged Patriot Charles Ray Polk with attempted use of a weapon of mass destruction. He attempted to buy 2000 pounds of plastic explosives.

Against such a backdrop it is perhaps unsurprising to note that at the end of October 2003 the Bush Administration received what they believed to be credible information of an even bigger attack than that of 9/11, with the president advised to leave the White House. In the end the date passed without incident (Bush, 2010, p. 159).[66]

A combination of tighter security as well as heightened awareness of the threat of terrorism after 9/11 help to explain the further reduction in terrorist incidents within America. Overseas however, there remained the problem of keeping Americans safe from further attacks. This was graphically driven home when on 12 October 2002 the island of Bali was targeted in a coordinated attack. This was a perfect example of a 'soft target' and one chosen to inflict maximum impact on unsuspecting tourists. Whilst Indonesia has the largest number of Muslims in the world, Bali is over 90 per cent Hindu. A suicide bomber walked into Paddy's Bar and detonated his explosive pack. As tourists ran in panic out onto the narrow streets, a massive truck explosion outside the Sari nightclub created carnage. Some 202 would die, with over two hundred others injured in an attack that instantly overwhelmed the medical facilities. Today a memorial, brightly illuminated at night, stands on the site of the original Paddy's Bar, listing the nationality of victims separately. It memorialises the seven American casualties.[67] What makes this attack more noteworthy is the fact that those brought to justice for the attacks stated that they had specifically targeted those establishments because they believed that they would be able to kill more American tourists (Nyoman, 2007, p. 142), although Australian tourists represented the greatest number killed, with eighty-eight casualties. That America was the central focus was

66 Bush and his wife were called out of bed on the night of 9/11; a false alarm.
67 There were also thirty-eight Indonesian dead, who were mostly Muslim, as well as twenty-three British citizens. Nationals of some twenty-two countries are listed on the memorial.

further demonstrated by the fact that another bomb was detonated a hundred metres from the American consulate, although this did not cause any further casualties.

The group responsible, Jemaah Islamiyah, likely only shared an ideology and sympathy with Al Qaeda, and with the latter group now scattered from their bases in Afghanistan, direct contact seems impractical, meaning that groups were now plotting their own attacks (Burke, 2007, p. 265). On trial, the accused showed little remorse and stated their intention was to remove westerners from the island, as well as taking a stand against the American war on terror. A short audio message from bin Laden on 12 November linked the bombings to a wider campaign and argued Australia had been targeted for supporting the Americans in Afghanistan. A further attack took place in October 2005, which killed twenty people and injured six Americans.[68]

Instead of tackling the threats still posed by groups allied to Al Qaeda or completing actions in Afghanistan, the George Bush administration made its most controversial decision. In March 2003 American and coalition forces moved into Saddam Hussein's Iraq. The main reason given was Hussein's supposed possession of weapons of mass destruction. Croft has argued this incorrect message was fostered by Fox News, which consistently reported that such weapons had been or were about to be uncovered in Iraq (2006, p. 190). No such weapons were ever located. In July 2004 the Senate Select Committee on Intelligence drew attention to highly flawed, exaggerated and misleading information on the potential threat of Saddam Hussein's weapons programmes that led to the invasion. Such reports undermined the case for the invasion being one connected to the war on terror and clearly impacted on Bush's trustworthiness on these issues.

---

68 Part of the aim was achieved in that tourism dropped dramatically after the 2002 and 2005 attacks.

In reality the Administration had made no secret of its desire to topple Saddam Hussein before the events of 9/11 (Hodgson, 2004, p. 279). There were no links between bin Laden and Iraq, although Saddam Hussein had given sanctuary to members of other terrorist groups, and had offered rewards to the families of Palestinian suicide bombers. With no hard evidence to link Hussein to any Al Qaeda faction, the administration reached for highly suspect intelligence stating that Hussein possessed WMDs, which failed to convince various US allies and which soon proved to be false. The takeover of Iraq was quickly achieved, with Bush even appearing on the USS *Abraham Lincoln* at the start of May in front of a large banner that declared 'Mission Accomplished'.

Donald Rumsfeld's memoirs discuss terrorism in some detail. He spends time explaining and justifying the move into Iraq, which he links into the wider terrorist agenda. Having found no direct link to Al Qaeda prior to the war, he declares that the administration did not attempt to mislead over the question of Iraq possessing weapons of mass destruction, but was simply wrong in its assessment (Rumsfeld, 2012, p. 449).

As Gus Martin notes, religious and ethno-nationalist grievances have dominated the Middle East for decades and increasing radicalisation has taken place, however this radicalisation speeded up with the 2003 invasion of Iraq, which saw a large increase in attacks on Western targets in the region. He considers that the new breed of radicalised insurgents are less likely to hesitate to resort to bloodshed and violence.

In the instability that followed the invasion, kidnapping became rife. Around 260 people were kidnapped between the spring of 2004 and 2005, some of whom would end up being held by Al Qaeda operatives (Wilkinson, 2006, p. 117). Even Donald Rumsfeld has acknowledged that Al Qaeda held the initiative in Iraq three years after the American invasion (Rumsfeld, p. 692). The Bush Administration moved to restrict pictures of the caskets of American servicemen killed in Iraq being shown in the US, but they could do little to prevent Al Jazeera showing dead and injured civilians in Iraq. Such pictures inevitably reinforced hatred of the US presence. Despite the growing problems of the war in Iraq, and the failure to locate bin Laden, the war on terror remained an area where Bush scored higher than the Democratic challenger John Kerry in the 2004 elections, helping Bush to secure a second term.

The 9/11 attack inevitably brought significantly increased security checks that have been faced by air travellers ever since. Additional security measures have included the finger printing and photographing of foreign visitors and in 2007 the establishment of the Electronic System for Travel Authorisation (ESTA) for visitors outside of North America to determine eligibility for entrance into the US at least seventy-two hours in advance of travel.

This has not prevented attempts to bring down airliners. In 2006 a plot to destroy planes flying from the United Kingdom to North America using liquid explosives was uncovered. This quickly resulted in liquid restrictions being introduced. A little late perhaps: liquid explosives had been used to target planes ever since the 1930s (Baum, 2016, p. 283).

Just over three months after 9/11, Richard Reid demonstrated that Al Qaeda had not lost interest in the use of aircraft as a tool of terrorism. Despite security concerns, not least because of the absence of checked baggage, Reid was allowed to board a plane from Paris to Miami. During the flight Reid attempted to light a fuse connected to explosives hidden in his shoes but was spotted lighting matches and would be overpowered by passengers, now considerably more alert to the possibly of terrorist actions in flight. Reid would later admit his intention of trying to cripple the American economy at the festive season. A second shoe bomber, Saajid Badat, was also due to attack a plane via the same technique, but did not follow through.

On Christmas Day 2009, Umar Abdulmutallab boarded a plane from Amsterdam to Detroit, without any checked-in luggage and close to landing disappeared to the toilet where he was able to start igniting explosives which he had hidden in his underwear. After a small explosion, which ignited his trousers, he was overpowered by passengers and the plane was able to make an emergency landing in Boston a few minutes later.

It was perhaps inevitable that the Bush administration following 9/11 would be dominated by the War on Terror. Increasingly Bush saw this as his personal mission and even his Farewell Address would talk of preventing another 9/11. Bush's successor, Barack Obama, would not have to place terrorism so high on the political agenda, but debates about terrorism would never be too far from the political surface. As a state senator for Illinois during the events of 9/11, Obama was one of the few politicians who publicly expressed a desire to seek to understand the reasons behind the attacks (Starr-Deelen, 2004, p. 167). Politicians in America have shied away from addressing the reasons that terrorists have given for their attacks. George Bush, whilst attempted to draw a distinction between the terrorists and the larger Muslim population, simply argued that all terrorists are connected by the common ideology of opposing freedom, and American culture (Winkler, 2006, p. 182). Such notions are simple, easy to understand, take away any possible legitimacy from the terrorist actions and certainly succeed in uniting the American public. The problem with such an approach is that it actively misleads the public into believing that terrorists simply attack the US out of jealousy or because of some kind of Medieval anti-democratic mindset. In reality, none of the attacks against America, either internally or externally, can be explained away in such terms. Without a clear understanding of the reasons behind terrorist attacks, there is the danger that they will never be addressed and terrorists will continue to resort to violent methods in order to get their voice heard.

Despite signing an Executive Order in January 2009 to close the prison at Guantanamo Bay over the following year, President Obama hit a wall of intransigence in Congress, which placed strict controls on transferring the detainees and banned the transfer of any of the inmates into the US. They also imposed a rule that any prisoner sent abroad had to be signed off directly by the US Defense Secretary Robert Gates, making closure of the prison all but impossible and blocking one of President Obama's key election pledges.

After nearly a decade of searching, by late 2010 intelligence information suggested that Osama bin Laden had been located in Abbottabad, Pakistan, living just two miles away from the Pakistan Military Academy, the equivalent of America's West Point. Whilst Defence Secretary Robert Gates, still mindful of the failure of the rescue operation in Iran, and worried about inflaming Pakistan, admits he was initially wary of a military assault on the housing complex, he eventually agreed (Gates, 2014, p. 539).

To avoid any possibility that bin Laden could be tipped off, Pakistan was not informed of America's plans in advance, inevitably causing some tension. It was late in the evening on 1 May 2011 but still 56.7 million Americans would tune into hear President Barack Obama announce that Osama bin Laden had been killed in a fire-fight with US Navy SEALs. The President declared that 'justice had been done' leading to emotional celebrations by crowds in New York and Washington. The president hailed 'the most significant achievement to date in our nation's effort to defeat Al Qaeda'.

The reality was also acknowledged that although America had finally removed its most wanted terrorist, nearly two decades after first identifying him as such, the dangers of action from those inspired by him very much remained. Long before his death he was no longer the leader of a group, but a symbol of the international jihad against American imperialism.

Recent events in America have shown that terrorism remains a threat in the United States, as seen with recent bombing attacks and the attempted use of bio-terrorism. In April 2013 an attack on runners during the Boston Marathon once again brought the issue of terrorism centre stage. The attack was carried out by two brothers, Kyrgyzstani-Americans Dzhokhar and Tamerlan Tsarneav. They would claim that their actions were conducted as a reprisal against American foreign policy. Dzhokhar said that they were self-radicalized and unconnected to any outside terrorist groups. In 2016 Omar Mir Seddique's killing of 49 people in Orlando, Florida, was also linked to US foreign policy; the killings were, at the time, the deadliest shooting by a lone gunman in US history.

That year also brought a confirmation that the threats from bio-terrorism remain ever present. James Everett Dutschke posted letters containing ricin to various officials, including President Obama. Curiously, Dutschke, who was given a twenty-five year sentence, sent the poisoned letters for no other reason than to attempt to frame someone else. In October 2018 Navy veteran William Clyde Allen III would be arrested in Utah for a ricin scare via letters he sent to President Trump and the Pentagon. It is a grim fact that no book can ever be-up-to-date in investigating terrorist attacks against the US.

9

REPRESENTATIONS OF TERRORISM

To cover all the ways in which terrorism has been represented in the US media would be a herculean task. Ultimately, Hollywood is 'American culture writ large', even as streaming begins to supersede the silver screen. So powerful are Hollywood images that entertainment has in some ways usurped reality. Mass-mediated depictions of terrorism have a profound impact on people's perceptions of terrorism (Tuman, 2003, p. 115). There have been hundreds of depictions of terrorism on TV[69] and film, which could not all be covered, so this chapter looks at how Hollywood has portrayed the threat of terrorism, both before and after 9/11. These films usually portray crazed terrorists, increasingly Middle Eastern, threatening the West, reinforcing stereotypes and helping to increase the fear of such attacks.

For some, looking at 9/11 through the prism of Hollywood was initially one of the ways of making sense of the incomprehensible

---

69 Notable American TV programmes that have dealt with terrorism issues include *The West Wing* (1999), *24* (2001), *Alias* (2001), *The Agency* (2001), *Spooks* (2002), *Criminal Minds* (2005), *Sleeper Cell* (2005), *Homeland* (2011), *Person of Interest* (2011). *The Looming Tower* (2018) deserves a special mention for going much deeper into the background and reasons behind the attacks.

real-life tragedy that had played out in real time on American TV screens. The attack looked exactly like a scene from a disaster movie.

The *New York Times*, two days after the event wrote:

It may seem trivializing — even obscene — to talk about movies in the same breath as this week's tragedy, but the fact that so many people did was a symptom of our inability to get our minds around this disaster, our inability to find real-life precedents, real-life analogies for what happened in the morning hours of Sept. 11.

On 16 September, Anthony Lane writing in the *New Yorker* magazine pointed out that television commentators struggling to find ways to describe the events of the morning of 9/11 fell back on cinematic references: 'It was like a movie'. 'It was like *Independence Day*.' 'It was like *Die Hard*.' 'No, *Die Hard 2*.' '*Armageddon*.'

As the rise of terrorist threats grew from the 1960s onwards, so too, albeit gradually, did Hollywood's interest in the topic. Clearly, Hollywood has a role in altering how we perceive the issue of terrorism and how we relate to the threats that it poses. After 9/11 several previous events related to the history of America and terrorism, many of which have been covered in this book, were given a cinematic makeover.

The first representation of a terrorist bombing came in 1936 in Alfred Hitchcock's *Sabotage*, which featured a bomb exploding on a London bus. The story itself was based on Joseph Conrad's *Secret Agent* (see chapter seven).

In 1954, Frank Sinatra played a would-be presidential assassin John Baron in the film *Suddenly*. The film came just four years after the attempt to kill President Truman, but the storyline, which involved targeting the president's train, had faint echoes of the 1911 attempt to kill President Taft (see chapter three).

Another notable film of the 1950s was *The FBI Story* starring James Stewart as FBI agent John 'Chip' Hardesty. The film told the story of Hardesty's career, which included investigating the Ku Klux Klan, as well as covering the story of John Gilbert Graham, the man who had duped his own mother into carrying a bomb onto a plane in order to collect the insurance money, events that were covered in chapter four.[70] Also of note, although not a cinematic release, an episode of *Deadline* in 1959 covered the exploits of the 'Mad Bomber' George Metesky.

Since the 1960s James Bond has been fighting terrorism on film. Bond's nemesis Ernst Stavro Blofeld led SPECTRE (Special Executive for Counterintelligence, Terrorism, Revenge and Extortion). However, the motives of Blofeld and other evil geniuses, such as Auric Goldfinger, were very much geared towards greed or power, rather than any specific political motives, something that was true of personifications of terrorists more generally in pre 9/11 films. Fleming's creation may have been battling terrorism since his creation but his opponents are unconcerned with morals or ethics (Black, 2005, p. 52).

The 1970s opened with the film *The Molly Maguires*, directed by Martin Ritt, the film was released in January 1970 and performed poorly at the box office.

In 1973, at the same that Weather Underground were planting bombs, came the film *No Place to Hide*, an early cinematic vehicle for Sylvester Stallone. Here student activists plot to bomb the offices of various companies who conduct business with overseas dictators, but in contacting a known terrorist, they soon attract the attention of the FBI. The film *Running on Empty* (1988) features a family who have been in hiding ever since their anti-war protest attack on a laboratory paralysed a janitor.

---

70 The film had the full approval of J. Edgar Hoover, who also appears in it very briefly.

The 1975 film *The Human Factor* would feature George Kennedy as a NATO computer operator who goes on the hunt for a terrorist gang who are targeting Americans after his family is killed. An impressive cast would also be assembled for the 1977 *Rollercoaster*, where George Segal, Richard Widmark and Henry Fonda take on a crazed bomber who targets children's amusement parks.

If the latter film had little connection to real terrorist events, there were certainly films made that did at least reflect aspects of contemporary history. *Black Sunday* was inspired by the events of the 1972 Munich Olympics. Based on the novel by Thomas Harris, the film followed the more standard Hollywood formula; in this version of history, the Black September group are prevented from carrying out their plan to kill people using blimps.

More terrorist-related films appeared in the 1980s. The 1980 film *The Octagon*, which starred Chuck Norris, actually begins in a terrorist training camp. Norris would be back in action against terrorists again in the 1986 film *Delta Force*, with a stellar cast that included Lee Marvin, Robert Vaugh, Shelley Winters and George Kennedy. Here the Americans are heroes overwhelming the evil Arab hijackers. It was clear that the plot was inspired by the hijacking of TWA Flight 847, which had taken place the previous year. Anti-Islamic themes were also present in the film *To Live and Die in L.A.* (1985) where a suicide bomber has to be overcome to prevent an attack.

Under Siege (1986), as noted by Philip Jenkins (Jenkins, 2006, p. 230) in showing multiple terrorist attacks on the US, including attacking planes and a rocket attack on Washington D.C. potentially orchestrated by a rogue state

Terrorism even took detours into lighter films and comedy. Clearly representing Ronald Reagan's preoccupation with Libyan terrorists, the hugely successful 1985 film *Back to the Future* would see the character of Dr Brown procure plutonium from

Libyan terrorists, who unsuccessfully attempt to shoot him dead. Libyan terrorism would also feature in the 1987 film *Terror Squad*.

The 1988 *Naked Gun* movie, staring Leslie Neilson and once again George Kennedy, opens with the main character Frank Drebin undercover in Beirut at a terrorist conference of rogue states, with the leaders of Cuba, Libya, Uganda, Iran, the PLO, and even the Soviet Union. On the cusp of agreeing to commit to a terrorist act in America, Drebin springs into life, beating up the participants before warning them not to let him catch them Stateside.

An interesting film in relation to terrorism was *True Lies* (1994) directed by James Cameron. Croft argues that it develops a new template for the characterisation of Islamic terrorists intent on using nuclear weapons (Croft, 2006, p. 270). The film played a part in stereotyping Arabs as terrorists. Such personifications were reinforced in the 1996 film *Executive Decision*, where Kurt Russell and Steven Segal team up against a group of heavily stereotyped Muslim terrorists, led by David Suchet, who are attempting to launch an attack on America with chemical weapons launched from a commercial airliner. The film is one of many that repeat crude stereotypes of social and cultural differences, and which push the idea that Islam is closely connected to violence (Jackson, *Terrorism*, 2011, p. 58).

The most intriguing terrorist themed movie of this pre-9/11 era was *The Siege* (1998). The film proved to be remarkably prescient featuring a group of Palestinians who demand the release of an inspirational sheikh, a clear nod to bin Laden, and bomb a series of targets. The overreaction to these events sees a state of siege, where Arabs are locked up in football stadiums and the army begin a brutal campaign of torture and repression (Valantin, 2005, p. 54).

In an article for the Washington Post, Zbigniew Brzezinski, former national security advisor to Jimmy Carter, has argued that the war on terror created a culture of fear within America, which allowed TV serials and films to exploit the latent Islamophobia. Brezezinski stated that there have been occasions when Arab facial stereotypes had been portrayed 'in a manner sadly reminiscent of Nazi anti-Semitic campaigns' (Brzezinski, 2007). Karl Rove (and other advisors) formed a lobbying group, a 'Hollywood 9/11 Coalition' asking around 50 executives in Hollywood to help win the war on terror.

Following 9/11 the Arnold Schwarzenegger film *Collateral Damage* was pulled from release until February 2002 as it featured a fire-fighter caught up in international terrorism. Despite the change of release date, the film performed poorly at the box office.

In addition, somewhat controversially, some films that were in production, such as *Men in Black II*, chose to edit out images of the World Trade Center, something that was seen by some as a capitulation to the terrorists.

9/11 conversely had the effect of moving forward the production of *Black Hawk Down*, a film which sought to recast the events in Somalia in 1993 as a tale of heroism, reminding the viewers of the humanitarian nature of the mission. The film even had the support of the US military via military advisors and access to American military bases (Dixon, 2004, p. 212).

The Sum of All Fears, which was already in production, conveyed a message that deception, assassination and the invasion of privacy were now acceptable practices (Bell-Metereau, 2004, p158) as America reeled from nuclear explosions in Baltimore. The concept of nuclear weapons being smuggled into America was picked up in the film *Bad Company* (2002), which veered awkwardly into comedy and failed to make back its production budget.

Trey Parker and Matt Stone's *Team America: World Police* (2004) was more successful in terms of working in humour in a film that offered up something of a critique of the war on terror, US foreign policies and rogue states, using of old-style hand-operated puppets. The film seemed determined to offend both sides of the terrorism debate, with negative portrayals of both America and the states that have supported terrorism, such as North Korea (Croft, 2006, p. 254). The film at least recouped its budget costs within the US. The same could not be said for the Hugh Grant vehicle *American Dreamz* (2006), where a group of jihadists plot to kill the American president when he agrees to act a guest judge on a panel show.

The renewed interest in terrorism brought with it a renewed interest in former terrorist incidents. *The Death of Klinghoffer* (2003) was based on a John Adams opera about the *Achille Lauro* hijacking. *The Assassination of Richard Nixon* (2004) featuring Sean Penn, revisited the attempt by Samuel Byck to fly a plane into the Whitehouse, a case that received attention in the 9/11 Commission Report. *Without a Paddle* (2004) picks up on America's only unsolved skyjacking, the bizarre case of D. B. Cooper in Nov 1971. *Munich* (2005) saw Steven Spielberg give the big screen treatment to the tragic terrorist events at the 1972 Munich Olympics.

Terrorism featured once again in the Die Hard franchise with the fourth instalment, *Live Free or Die Hard* focussing on cyber-terrorism, some nineteen years after Bruce Willis' character, John McClane, had first taken on 'terrorists' in a Los Angeles skyscraper in 1988, though the terrorist action was simply a ruse for a robbery. In 2013 the fifth movie, *A Good Way to Die Hard* saw the character of McClane caught up in Russia and dealing with terrorists and weapons of mass destruction. All the movies in the series performed well at the US and international box office

Since 2004 the war on terror has been viewed with a more critical eye by various film makers. This reflects the changing attitude of the American public. Crucial to this was the outrage created by media revelations about torture at Abu Ghraib prison. The 'war on terror' was no longer so clearly put forward as simply 'good against evil'. Even as the war on terror was running into problems both at home and abroad, movies that were critical of government policy ran the risk of alienating their audiences or failing to secure funding. Films such as *Syriana* (2005) and *Good Night, and Good Luck* (2005), both vehicles for George Clooney, were made by an independent company.

Given the initial reticence of film makers to produce films related to 9/11, for some years a film goer could have been forgiven for thinking the war on terror had not taken place. There are in fact important exceptions, especially if one takes into account a number of documentaries that were produced soon after, which had a wealth of footage from that morning to call upon. Michael Moore's *Fahrenheit 9/11* was a brave attempt to question aspects of American foreign policy at a time when there remained a high level of support for Bush's handling of the war on terror. Moore had briefly touched on the contradictions of American foreign policy in *Bowling for Columbine*. *Fahrenheit 9/11* proved to be the most successful documentary film of all time in terms of box office, taking some $119 million at the American box office.[71]

It would not be until 2006 that Hollywood felt that there was enough time elapsed for there to be cinematic portrayals of the events of that day. This was never going to be a straightforward task as the film makers had to find ways to create something positive from the tragic events of the day. In the end the focus was on the heroism of the passengers who had brought down United 93 before it reached its intended target and on the fire-fighters who has rushed into the World Trade Center.

Paul Greengrass in *United 93*, the first American film to cover the hijackings, portrays the passengers heroically bring the plane down in Shanksville, Pennsylvania. Having discovered the fates of the other planes, the passengers try to prevent the aircraft being flown into another location, possibly the White House. The focus

---

71 The film would gross $222.4 million worldwide.

was on ordinary people saving others through extraordinary actions. That is not say the film is inaccurate, but is significant that the first film about 9/11 was about American heroism. In a sad reflection of post 9/11 fears, Iraqi-born actor Lewis Alsamari (the UK based actor had played a hijacker) was denied entry to the US to attend the film's premier.

With the death tolls rising in Iraq, major losses for the Republicans in the 2006 midterm elections and the resignation of Donald Rumsfeld, some filmmakers took a more critical tone. Peter Berg's *The Kingdom* (2007) starring Jamie Foxx looked at the attacks on the Khobar complex and raised questions about terrorist motives, even if these motives are not fully brought out. The star-studded *The Good Shepherd*, directed, produced and starring Robert De Niro, alongside Matt Damon and Angelina Jolie, looked at the founding of the CIA but featured a waterboarding scene which drives a Russian defector to his death; waterboarding had been extensively used during the war on terror and defended by George W. Bush during and after his presidency. Both high budget films struggled to recoup their outlays, although Paul Greengrass' *The Bourne Ultimatum* (2007) featured both waterboarding and clear criticism of the intelligence agencies, performed strongly at the box office. Films such as *Safe House* (2012) would also feature waterboarding and a critical look at CIA activities; the lead star, Denzil Washington, even agreed to be waterboarded to experience the trauma.

Rendition in 2007 picked up on one of the most controversial aspects of America's war on terror strategy. Despite an impressive cast, that included Reese Witherspoon, Jake Gillenhaal and Meryl Streep, the film grossed under $10 million at the US box office, although it trebled this internationally. Another highly critical film was Robert Redford's *Lions for Lambs*, which also starred Meryl Streep and Tom Cruise. This film grossed only $15 million at the US box office, although it took over $48 million internationally.

Faring even worse was Paul Haggis' film *In the Valley of Elah*, about the death of an American soldier who returns from Iraq, despite a strong cast that included Tommy Lee Jones, Susan Sarandon, Charlize Theron and Josh Brolin, the film grossed just $6.7m in the US. The critically panned film *Redacted* (2007) by Brian De Palma, based loosely on events surrounded the rape of a fifteen year old Iraqi girl and the murder of her family, made just $65,000 at the US box office and less than $1 million worldwide. The failure of these films in the home markets reveals that Americans were still reticent about major Hollywood productions directly tackling the controversies involved in the war on terror. Heroism remained a safer and more rewarding theme. Even controversial film maker Oliver Stone, better known for straying into conspiracy culture with films such as *JFK* (1991) and *Nixon* (1995), stayed on less contentious ground by focussing on the heroism and survival of two Port Authority Police officers in his film *World Trade Center*, which made close to $100 million more than its production costs when released in 2006.

Most recently terrorist themes have been highly represented in high profile superhero movies. Thomas Pollard has argued that the hugely successful explosion of superhero films such as *Spider-Man*, *Superman*, *Iron Man* and the *Dark Knight*, along with their many sequels, were a response to the threat from terrorism and the need to find superheroes able to destroy evil and return the world to order and stability (Pollard, 2009, p. 206).

CONCLUSION

One of the central themes of this work has been that terrorism has always played a part in American history, predating the founding of the republic. The idea that terrorism began on 9/11, or even that a new era of terrorism began on that date, was a potentially dangerous falsehood that increased the shock and horror of the terrible events of that day.

Whilst many of the events covered have been largely ignored by many history texts, it is also true that in recent years some excellent scholarship has addressed these under-represented aspects of America's history. Recent books on the Preparedness Day bombing and the era of the Galleanists, the Wall Street bomb attack, the attempted assassination of President Truman, the Weather Underground and the other terrorist groups of the 1970s have all shed new light. As noted in the opening chapter, the reasons why 9/11 proved to be so shocking and surprisingly to many was not just the dramatic events of the day, or the unprecedented death toll from a terrorist attack on American soil, it was the shattering of the myth that American was somehow immune to an overseas terrorist attack.

Whilst there is clearly no perfect fit between anarchism and terrorism, radical anarchists did engage in 'propaganda by deed', something that became a lot more practical, and dangerous, with the invention of dynamite. Throughout its history terrorists have been able to take advantage of America's 'openness'. The leading anarchists were able to move to America at a time when they faced repression at home. They were just another small group among the huddled masses increasingly drawn to America, sailing past the Statue of Liberty, who were 'yearning to breathe free'. Once in America they were able to exercise their rights of free speech to call not only for the overthrow of the capitalist system, but the violent overthrow of the American government.

It is difficult to say with certainty just how many anarchists were resident in the US; only very small numbers ever engaged in terrorist acts. The reality was that very few people were killed by anarchist activities in the US. Indeed, many of the anarchists themselves were subject to threats and violence, especially in the wake of President McKinley's death. Whilst many of these leaders were pilloried in the media, then entering an era of mass readership, there would be little significant clampdown upon their activities until after the death of McKinley. As has been seen, until that time there was no belief that the spate of assassinations in Europe could possibly be replicated in the US. The deaths of both President Lincoln and President Garfield were seen as one-off events and no significant changes to presidential security were made until towards the end of the first decade of the twentieth century. The era of the anarchists only came to end in the 1920s when America began a concerted campaign to crack down on anarchists and agitators, including such figures as Emma Goldman, who were deported, often in breach of US law. Though tighter laws had been passed in 1917 and 1918.

This work began with a consideration of what comprises terrorism, given the need to separate out acts of revenge, or murder, and concluded that the most meaningful distillation of the many differing definitions was to see terrorism as violence, or indeed a credible threat of violence, perpetrated or threatened in order to achieve a political objective. It is hard to better the description of Philip Heymann, that terrorism is 'generally a calculated move in a political game' (2000, p. xix).

Terrorism, in spite of, or indeed because of, its extreme tactics, has often proved successful in achieving its aims. To be successful the aims of the terrorists had to be limited, for example the terrorist campaigns to force America out of the Lebanon or Somalia proved highly influential in America's decision to leave those countries (whilst it is accepted that these were military targets, civilians also died). The use of terrorist tactics, including kidnapping, violence and even an early use of the media proved very successful in garnering financial bounty for the Barbary pirates for many years, as chapter two outlined.

In the international arena it is America that decides which states, groups and individuals comprise those who support terrorism. The US has supported many states with poor human rights records and supplied many groups expressly to undermine sometimes democratically elected regimes. Gabriel Kolko has argued that such actions help explain the attacks against America on its own soil, expressing surprise that this did not take place sooner (Kolko, 2006, p. 83).

Terrorism is effectively a weapon of last resort, when other options, such as negotiations, have proved fruitless, and where the perpetrators can often call upon years of frustration, impotence and bitterness to engender support. Terrorism is a means by which a smaller, weaker force can defeat or frustrate a much larger one. Despite all the resources allocated to the war in Vietnam, which at its peak included some 549,000 US service personnel, the Americans were unable to defeat the Vietminh. America's involvement in the war was the biggest single galvanising force that spurred a tide of terrorist groups and actions within the US, as well as the event which provided the first real proof that unconventional asymmetric warfare could defeat even the greatest military power on Earth.

Attempts by terrorist groups to overhaul the political system or economic structure of the US never had any realistic chance of success. As outlined in chapter three, the late nineteenth and early twentieth centuries brought the rise of the anarchist movement (Rapoport's first wave of terrorism), a movement that did seek the overhaul of the American capitalist system. Whilst the impact of the movement was significant, and indeed whilst labour disputes during this era proved to be considerably more violent than in Europe, there was never a time when this movement represented an existential threat to the ruling classes. The anarchists never represented a mass movement and there was no realistic chance the disparate anarchist elements, many of whom were viewed with deep suspicion even by those who shared some sympathy with the cause, could pose a serious threat to the government. This was even more the case in the late 1960s and early 1970s, when despite the prevalence of attacks on American soil peaking in 1970, with 450 recorded, the different radical groups never represented a credible threat to the status quo. Al Qaeda may have damaged the US economically and led it towards external wars, but it could never remove or defeat armies or remove regimes.

Individuals have been able to capitalise on the fear of terrorism: Allan Pinkerton with the Molly Maguires, Michael Schaack with anarchists, and to a lesser extent Deputy Police Commissioner Robert Daley with the Black Liberation Army. Pinkerton and Schaack wrote books which stressed not only the threats posed by these groups, but their own roles in subduing those threats.

Indeed, the existence of such groups not only led to the inevitable government clampdown on their activities but also provided a useful political opportunity to exploit and heighten the public's fears about safety and order to the advantage of those in authority. Presidents Theodore Roosevelt and Richard Nixon often overstated the threats from such groups to bolster their political position. When in May 1970 four students were gunned down by the National Guard at Kent State University, despite being nothing more than innocent bystanders, a Gallup Poll taken very soon after the shootings showed that 58 per cent of respondents blamed the students, 11 per cent blamed the National Guard and 31 per cent expressed no opinion.

Despite the plethora of attacks within the US, especially in the first half of the decade, America did not experience the far more violent terrorist campaign that took place in Germany. The Baader-Meinhof Gang, unlike American groups, linked up with external groups such as the Popular Front for the Liberation of Palestine.

For President Reagan, the rise of overseas terrorism represented not only a real threat to Americans abroad but an opportunity to link terrorist attacks to communism. Reagan was both encouraged to believe and receptive to arguments that the Kremlin supported a worldwide campaign of terrorism, which involved active support for rogue states and terrorist groups. The idea held such attraction that important figures within the Reagan administration took to disseminating 'black propaganda', which was then accepted by the administration as truth. The dangers posed to American citizens and military forces abroad from rogue states or terrorist groups was real, but Reagan would be guilty of overstating the threats, moving the topic to the top of his political agenda in the summer of 1985. After 1986, with Reagan increasingly embroiled in the Iran–Contra scandal, which was tied to the freeing of hostages in Lebanon, the issue of terrorism slipped down the list of priorities.

Reagan's legacy to the history of terrorism would be an unintended one, and would provide perhaps one of the greatest incidences of 'blowback' in modern American, or even world, history. When Reagan made the decision to increase funding and support to the Islamic *mujahideen*, no one imagined that the fighters involved in removing the Soviet Union from Afghanistan would soon begin to apply their military experience and resources into an attack on America.

The end of the Cold War would have a dramatic impact on the threats from terrorism. One advantage of the collapse of the Soviet Union was the ending of terrorist acts by groups who had fought for liberation from Soviet control. The collapse of the Soviet Union took away the rationale for attacks by groups connected to The Jewish Defence League, or those seeking Croatian independence (which was eventually achieved in 1991).

Also crucial in explaining the rise in Islamic terrorism was the invasion of Iraq in 1990, and more specifically the impact of American troops moving into Saudi Arabia, something that the country was initially reticent about, until pushed by the George H. W. Bush administration (Bush & Scowcroft, 1998, pp. 324–30).

Clinton placed a high priority on issues related to terrorism, although there was little recognition that the first attack on the World Trade Center, just weeks into his presidency, would be the precursor to America's future war with Islamic terrorists. There is much debate over whether Clinton could have done more to prevent the events of 9/11 and indeed whether the distractions of his involvement with intern Monica Lewinsky and subsequent impeachment led him to make serious mistakes in dealing with the threat posed by Al Qaeda.

Other factors made terrorism a more formidable threat from the 1990s onwards. The ability of terrorist groups to publicise their messages, to recruit and to raise funds was greatly facilitated by the internet and by new media outlets, especially Al Jazeera.

Globalisation has played a role in stoking terrorism. Groups such as the Weather Underground and the Black Panther movement had opposition to global capitalism as a central tenet. Globalisation has also helped spur right-wing terrorism; with greater migration to the US has come a resurgence of nativism. By far the greatest number of terrorist attacks since the 1970s have been against businesses rather than individuals or government targets, although this is far from the perception given by presidents or the media (Winkler, 2006, p. 196). In part, such attacks can be explained by the expansion of Western values into areas of the world that are opposed to Western culture. American culture – movies, music, business, advertising – has penetrated almost every corner of the globe. There are only two countries in the world where you cannot legally buy Coke Cola, and the US dollar is not only in use as the currency of countries as diverse as Ecuador and Palau, but widely accepted in almost any location. ATM Machines dispense American dollars in Cambodia and Kyrgyzstan. It is not surprising that American culture is countered by a growing number of people who have resented its encroachment, especially if they have failed to experience any additional economic benefit from the globalisation process.

External threats to American citizens have been rising since the 1960s. Since 1979, we have entered what Rapoport termed the 'religious' wave, and we are still in it. In 1993 Samuel Huntington put forward the idea that future conflicts would be less between states than between cultures, a so-called 'Clash of Civilisations'. Whilst the idea seemed problematic if not simplistic, it gained traction following 9/11, not least because it gained support directly from bin Laden (Lawrence, 2005, p. 124).

As outlined in chapter two, racial terrorism has been an aspect of American history since before the American Revolution. Although one of a number of nativist groups, the Ku Klux Klan has proved to be the most resilient, there being distinct incarnations which have engaged with different targets. Each wave of white supremacism has used terrorist tactics. The initial formation of the group after the Civil War would prove hugely effective in its chief aim of preventing the former slaves from assuming any form of political power. After its resurgence in 1915, the Klan changed its focus to represent white Protestants and became an important organisation in both northern and southern states. The main home-grown internal threats have increasingly been moving from left- to right-wing terrorism.

Since the 1960s, by far the biggest rationale for terrorists attacking America has been in order to pressure the US into changing aspects of its foreign policy. Chalmers Johnson has argued that even 9/11 was not an attack on America, but on American foreign policy (2002, p. viii). It is important to remember that the US has been involved in bombing or invading five Islamic countries since 1982. Notable too was the fact that five of the seven states on America's terrorism list were essentially Muslim states. This is not to suggest that anti-Americanism pervades all Islamic states, there is a huge diversity within the Muslim world and fundamental divides such as between Sunni and Shia. Some states place Islam as the ideological underpinning of the state and its laws, other states within the Muslim world are essentially secular. Such diversity demonstrates why bin Laden and others were never able to unite the Islamic world.

American relations with many Islamic countries such as Turkey have traditionally been very strong, indeed, after 9/11 relations with states such as Pakistan, Sudan and Libya improved (Cameron, 2005, p. 139). So too did relations with other non-traditional allies such as Uzbekistan, (useful as a border state with Afghanistan), where America quadrupled aid and moved in troops; although this new closer partnership ended in 2005. In fact, the US established thirteen new bases in nine countries, five of which were Islamic states.

As to rogue states, the rogues' gallery of countries provided by the State Department almost rounds up the usual suspects. Though state terrorism is far less of a reality than it was in the 1980s. The American invasions of Afghanistan and Iraq took them off the list and the death of Colonel Gaddafi removed a former adversary, albeit one who had belatedly renounced state terrorism. As Litwak notes, Cuba does not fit any meaningful American definition of a rogue state, having long since stopped actively supporting terrorism (2000, p. 76). The death of Fidel Castro in 2016 symbolised the passing of another old American foe. However, in April 2019 Trump imposed the most severe sanctions against Cuba since JFK's economic embargo in 1962. The fact that JoAnne Chesimard and also FALN bomber Willie Morales still reside in Cuba is a reminder of Cuba's past support for radical groups. With Syria embroiled in civil war and North Korea no longer having the financial ability or political will to conduct terrorist activities, much of the spotlight still falls on Iran.

That terrorism remains a major issue in America was demonstrated by the emphasis that Donald Trump placed upon it during his presidential campaign. During the first month of his presidency he signed Executive Order 13769, entitled 'Protecting the Nation from Foreign Terrorist Entry into the United States'. The order proved highly controversial as it targeted Muslim countries, with the Supreme Court upholding the ban 5 to 4 in June 2018.

The war on terror has proved to be hugely costly in blood and treasure. The US Department of Defense lists the total number of US troops killed in Iraq during Operation *Iraqi Freedom* as 4410 with nearly 32,000 wounded. A further 2300 have died in Afghanistan during Operation *Enduring Freedom* and Operation *Freedom's Sentinel* with over 20,000 wounded. Regarding the numbers of civilian casualties, *The Lancet* in July 2006 estimated this at over 650,000.

The financial costs of 9/11 that were discussed in chapter eight have been dwarfed by the enormous costs of the wars in Iraq and in Afghanistan, where US and NATO remain in a training and support role, alongside costs arising from Homeland Security and

Veterans Affairs spending. These are beginning to push the total for America's spending on the war on terror towards a staggering $6 trillion. When viewing such figures, it is wise to keep in mind Osama bin Laden's stated plan to 'bleed America to the point of bankruptcy' (Lawrence, 2005, p. 242).

The prevalence of terrorism in terms of news, politics, films, media, books, articles and even computer games leads to the feeling that terrorism is everywhere and the threats to people's safety and security is greater than it actually is. North America has consistently experienced a low number of terrorist attacks when compared with Western Europe, South America, South Asia or the Middle East, the latter region having the largest number of terrorist attacks.

This work will not end with any great prophecies regarding the future of terrorism, save that whilst there will be ebbs and flows in media and public interest, the issue will never be too far from the surface, pushing back into public attention following an attack or during an election campaign. Terrorism can never be eradicated, and terrorists have an almost infinite number of possible targets. It is possible to reduce the number of attacks, and indeed western security forces have had considerable success in that regard. However, as the IRA once noted after a bombing attack in Brighton, which came close to killing Prime Minister Margaret Thatcher, a terrorist group only has to be lucky with one attack, whilst security forces 'have to be lucky always'. Security forces cannot hope to prevent every attack against every possible target in every conceivable place. It is possible to reduce terrorist attacks by taking away some of the forces that galvanise and inspire terrorist recruits. But terrorist cells can exist in a society for decades before being activated and many of those responsible for recent terrorist attacks have not registered on any terrorist database, making it impossible to track and trace every potential suspect. As Paul Wilkinson has noted, the use of overseas bases to hold detainees away from the American legal system has severely damaged its reputation as a champion of the rule of law or protector of human rights (2006, p. 62). Further, the exposed abuses of Abu Ghraib prison, coupled with the growing death toll of Iraqi civilians, pictures of which were broadcast around the Arab world by Al Jazeera and other channels, only fuelled greater anger and resentment against the US and its allies.

Since the 1970s civil liberties have had to compete with public security concerns. Americans have tolerated less freedom to help secure their society, but at a risk of losing some of their long enjoyed freedoms. America has to strike a difficult balance between keeping itself protected from the threat of terrorism and maintaining its traditional values of being a free and open society, as well as keeping values set out in its constitution.

As has been seen in this work, terrorism has been declining overall, with twenty-nine Americans dying in domestic terrorist attacks from 2000-15. In 2017 it was reported that on average two Americans are killed by Jihadist immigrants, five by far-right terrorist, twenty-one by armed toddlers, thirty-one by lightning, sixty-nine by lawnmowers, 737 by getting out of bed and 11,737 are killed by another American.

Despite this context, we should never forget America's long history of dealing with terrorists, and that the threat from terrorism remains very real.

Appendix

REPORT OF THE NATIONAL COMMISSION ON TERRORISM TO CONGRESS, JUNE 2000

COUNTERING THE CHANGING THREAT OF INTERNATIONAL TERRORISM

Pursuant to Public Law 277, 105th Congress

FOREWORD

Six months ago, the National Commission on Terrorism began its Congressionally mandated evaluation of America's laws, policies, and practices for preventing and punishing terrorism directed at American citizens. After a thorough review, the Commission concluded that, although American strategies and policies are basically on the right track, significant aspects of implementation are seriously deficient. Thus, this report does not attempt to describe all American counterterrorism activities, but instead concentrates on problem areas and recommended changes. We wish to note, however, that in the course of our assessment we gained renewed confidence in the abilities and dedication of the Americans who stand on the front lines in the fight against terrorism.

Each of the 10 commissioners approached these issues from a different perspective. If any one commissioner had written the report on his or her own, it might not be identical to that which we are presenting today. However, through a process of careful deliberation, we reached the consensus reflected in this report.

Throughout our deliberations, we were mindful of several important points:

- The imperative to find terrorists and prevent their attacks requires energetic use of all the legal authorities and instruments available.
- Terrorist attacks against America threaten more than the tragic loss of individual lives. Some terrorists hope to provoke a response that undermines our Constitutional system of government. So U.S. leaders must find the appropriate balance by adopting counterterrorism policies which are effective but also respect the democratic traditions which are the bedrock of America's strength.
- Combating terrorism should not be used as a pretext for discrimination against any segment of society. Terrorists often claim to acton behalf of ethnic groups, religions, or even entire nations. These claims are false. Terrorists represent only a minuscule faction of any such group.
- People turn to terrorism for various reasons. Many terrorists act from political, ideological, or religious convictions. Some are simply criminals for hire. Others become terrorists because of perceived oppression or economic deprivation. An astute American foreign policy must take into account the reasons people turn to terror and, where appropriate and feasible, address them. No cause, however, justifies terrorism.

Terrorists attack American targets more often than those of any other country. America's pre-eminent role in the world guarantees that this will continue to be the case, and the threat of attacks creating massive casualties is growing. If the United States is to protect itself, if it is to remain a world leader, this nation must develop and continuously refine sound counterterrorism policies appropriate to the rapidly changing world around us.

Ambassador L. Paul Bremer III
Chairman

Maurice Sonnenberg
Vice Chairman

EXECUTIVE SUMMARY

International terrorism poses an increasingly dangerous and difficult threat to America. This was underscored by the December 1999 arrests in Jordan and at the U.S./Canadian border of foreign nationals who were allegedly planning to attack crowded millenium celebrations. Today's terrorists seek to inflict mass casualties, and they are attempting to do so both overseas and on American soil. They are less dependent on state sponsorship and are, instead, forming loose, transnational affiliations based on religious or ideological affinity and a common hatred of the United States. This makes terrorist attacks more difficult to detect and prevent.

Countering the growing danger of the terrorist threat requires significantly stepping up U.S. efforts. The government must immediately take steps to reinvigorate the collection of intelligence about terrorists' plans, use all available legal avenues to disrupt and prosecute terrorist activities and private sources of support, convince other nations to cease all support for terrorists, and ensure that federal, state, and local officials are prepared for attacks that may result in mass casualties. The Commission has made a number of recommendations to accomplish these objectives:

Priority one is to prevent terrorist attacks. U.S. intelligence and law enforcement communities must use the full scope of their authority to collect intelligence regarding terrorist plans and methods.

- CIA guidelines adopted in 1995 restricting recruitment of unsavory sources should not apply when recruiting counterterrorism sources.
- The Attorney General should ensure that FBI is exercising fully its authority for investigating suspected terrorist groups or individuals, including authority for electronic surveillance.
- Funding for counterterrorism efforts by CIA, NSA, and FBI must be given higher priority to ensure continuation of important operational activity and to close the technology gap that threatens their ability to collect and exploit terrorist communications.
- FBI should establish a cadre of reports officers to distill and disseminate terrorism-related information once it is collected.

U.S. policies must firmly target all states that support terrorists.

- Iran and Syria should be kept on the list of state sponsors until they stop supporting terrorists.
- Afghanistan should be designated a sponsor of terrorism and subjected to all the sanctions applicable to state sponsors.
- The President should impose sanctions on countries that, while not direct sponsors of terrorism, are nevertheless not cooperating fully on counterterrorism. Candidates for consideration include Pakistan and Greece.

Private sources of financial and logistical support for terrorists must be subjected to the full force and sweep of U.S. and international laws.

- All relevant agencies should use every available means, including the full array of criminal, civil, and administrative sanctions to block or disrupt nongovernmental sources of support for international terrorism.
- Congress should promptly ratify and implement the International Convention for the Suppression of the Financing of Terrorism to enhance international cooperative efforts.
- Where criminal prosecution is not possible, the Attorney General should vigorously pursue the expulsion of terrorists from the United States through proceedings which protect both the national security interest in safeguarding classified evidence and the right of the accused to challenge that evidence.

A terrorist attack involving a biological agent, deadly chemicals, or nuclear or radiological material, even if it succeeds only partially, could profoundly affect the entire nation. The government must do more to prepare for such an event.

- The President should direct the preparation of a manual to guide the implementation of existing legal authority in the event of a catastrophic terrorist threat or attack. The President and Congress should determine whether additional legal authority is needed to deal with catastrophic terrorism.
- The Department of Defense must have detailed plans for its role in the event of a catastrophic terrorist attack, including criteria for decisions on transfer of command authority to DoD in extraordinary circumstances.
- Senior officials of all government agencies involved in responding to a catastrophic terrorism threat or crisis should be required to participate in national exercises every year to test capabilities and coordination.
- Congress should make it illegal for anyone not properly certified to possess certain critical pathogens and should enact laws to control the transfer of equipment critical to the development or use of biological agents.
- The President should establish a comprehensive and coordinated long-term research and development program for catastrophic terrorism.
- The Secretary of State should press for an international convention to improve multilateral cooperation on preventing or responding to cyber attacks by terrorists.

The President and Congress should reform the system for reviewing and funding departmental counterterrorism programs to ensure that the

activities and programs of various agencies are part of a comprehensive plan.

- The executive branch official responsible for coordinating counterterrorism efforts acrossthe government should be given a stronger hand in the budget process.
- Congress should develop mechanisms for a comprehensive review of the President's counterterrorism policy and budget.

THE INTERNATIONAL TERRORISM THREAT IS CHANGING

Who are the international terrorists?
What are their motives and how do they get their support?
How can we stop them?

The answers to these questions have changed significantly over the last 25 years. There are dramatically fewer international terrorist incidents than in the mid-eighties. Many of the groups that targeted America's interests, friends, and allies have disappeared. The Soviet bloc, which once provided support to terrorist groups, no longer exists. Countries that once excused terrorism now condemn it. This changed international attitude has led to 12 United Nations conventions targeting terrorist activity and, more importantly, growing, practical international cooperation.

However, if most of the world's countries are firmer in opposing terrorism, some still support terrorists or use terrorism as an element of state policy. Iran is the clearest case. The Revolutionary Guard Corps and the Ministry of intelligence and Security carry out terrorist activities and give direction and support to other terrorists. The regimes of Syria, Sudan, and Afghanistan provide funding, refuge, training bases, and weapons to terrorists. Libya continues to provide support to some Palestinian terrorist groups and to harass expatriate dissidents, and North Korea may still provide weapons to terrorists. Cuba provides safehaven to a number of terrorists. Other states allow terrorist groups to operate on their soil or provide support which, while failing short of state sponsorship, nonetheless gives terrorists important assistance.

The terrorist threat is also changing in ways that make it more dangerous and difficult to counter.

International terrorism once threatened Americans only when they were outside the country. Today international terrorists attack us on our own soil. Just before the millennium, an alert U.S. Customs Service official stopped Ahmad Ressam as he attempted to enter the United States from Canada – apparently to conduct a terrorist attack. This fortuitous arrest should not inspire complacency, however. On an average day, over one million people enter the United States legally and thousands more enter illegally. As the World Trade Center bombing demonstrated, we cannot rely solely on existing border controls and procedures to keep foreign terrorists out of the United States.

Terrorist attacks are becoming more lethal. Most terrorist organizations active in the 1970s and 1980s had clear political objectives. They tried to calibrate their attacks to produce just enough bloodshed to get attention for their cause, but not so much as to alienate public support. Groups like the Irish Republican Army and the Palestine Liberation Organization often sought specific political concessions.

Now, a growing percentage of terrorist attacks are designed to kill as many people as possible. In the 1990s a terrorist incident was almost 20 percent more likely to result in death or injury than an incident two decades ago. The World Trade Center bombing in New York killed six and wounded about 1,000, but the terrorists' goal was to topple the twin towers, killing tens of thousands of people. The thwarted attacks against New York City's infrastructure in 1993 – which included plans to bomb the Lincoln and Holland tunnels – also were intended to cause mass casualties. In 1995, Philippine authorities uncovered a terrorist plot to bring down 11 U.S. airliners in Asia. The circumstances surrounding the millennium border arrests of foreign nationals suggest that the suspects planned to target a large group assembled for a New Year's celebration. Overseas attacks against the United States in recent years have followed the same trend. The bombs that destroyed the military barracks in Saudi Arabia and two U.S. Embassies in Africa inflicted 6,059 casualties. Those arrested in Jordan in late December had also planned attacks designed to kill large numbers.

The trend toward higher casualties reflects, in part, the changing motivation of today's terrorists. Religiously motivated terrorist groups, such as Usama bin Ladin's group, al-Qaida, which is believed to have bombed the U.S. Embassies in Africa, represent a growing trend toward hatred of the United States. Other terrorist groups are driven by visions of a post-apocalyptic future or by ethnic hatred. Such groups may lack a concrete political goal other than to punish their enemies by killing as many of them as possible, seemingly without concern about alienating sympathizers. Increasingly, attacks are less likely to be followed by claims of responsibility or lists of political demands.

The shift in terrorist motives has contributed to a change in the way some international terrorist groups are structured. Because groups based on ideological or religious motives may lack a specific political or nationalistic agenda, they have less need for a hierarchical structure. Instead, they can rely on loose affiliations with like-minded groups from a variety of countries to support their common cause against the United States.

Al-Qaida is the best-known transnational terrorist organization. In addition to pursuing its own terrorist campaign, it calls on numerous militant groups that share some of its ideological beliefs to support its violent campaign against the United States. But neither al-Qaida's extremist politico-religious beliefs nor its leader, Usama bin Ladin, is unique. If al-Qaida and Usama bin Ladin were to disappear tomorrow, the United States would still face potential terrorist threats from a growing number of groups opposed to perceived American hegemony. Moreover, new terrorist threats can suddenly emerge from isolated conspiracies or obscure cults with no previous history of violence.

These more loosely affiliated, transnational terrorist networks are difficult to predict, track, and penetrate. They rely on a variety of sources for funding and logistical support, including self-financing criminal activities such as kidnapping, narcotics, and petty crimes. Their networks of support include both front organizations and legitimate business and nongovernment organizations. They use the Internet as an effective communications channel.

Guns and conventional explosives have so far remained the weapons of choice for most terrorists. Such weapons can cause many casualties and are relatively easy to acquire and use. But some terrorist groups now show interest in acquiring the capability to use chemical, biological, radiological, or nuclear (CBRN) materials. It is difficult to predict the likelihood of a CBRN attack, but most experts agree that today's terrorists are seeking the ability to use such agents in order to cause mass casualties.

Still, these kinds of weapons and materials confront a non-state sponsored terrorist group with significant technical challenges. While lethal chemicals are easy to come by, getting large quantities and weaponizing them for mass casualties is difficult, and only nation states have succeeded in doing so. Biological agents can be acquired in nature or from medical supply houses, but important aspects of handling and dispersion are daunting. To date, only nation states have demonstrated the capability to build radiological and nuclear weapons.

The 1995 release of a chemical agent in the Tokyo subway by the apocalyptic Aum Shinrikyo group demonstrated the difficulties that terrorists face in attempting to use CBRN weapons to produce mass casualties. The group used scores of highly skilled technicians and spent tens of millions of dollars developing a chemical attack that killed fewer people than conventional explosives could have. The same group failed totally in a separate attempt to launch an anthrax attack in Tokyo.

However, if the terrorists' goal is to challenge significantly Americans' sense of safety and confidence, even a small CBRN attack could be successful.

Moreover, terrorists could acquire more deadly CBRN capabilities from a state. Five of the seven nations the United States identifies as state sponsors of terrorism have programs to develop weapons of mass destruction. A state that knowingly provides agents of mass destruction or technology to a terrorist group should worry about losing control of the terrorists' activities and, if the weapons could be traced back to that state, the near certainty of massive retaliation. However, it is always difficult and sometimes dangerous to attempt to predict the actions of a state. Moreover, a state in chaos, or elements within such a state, might run these risks, especially if the United States were engaged in military conflict with that state or if the United States were distracted by a major conflict in another area of the world.

The Commission was particularly concerned about the persistent lack of adequate security and safeguards for the nuclear material in the former Soviet Union (FSU). A Center for Strategic International Studies panel chaired by former Senator Sam Nunn concluded that, despite a decade of effort, the risk of "loose nukes" is greater than ever. Another ominous warning was given in 1995 when Chechen rebels, many of whom fight side-by-side with Islamic terrorists from bin Ladin's camps sympathetic to the Chechen cause, placed radioactive material in a Moscow park.

Cyber attacks are often considered in the same context with CBRN. Respectable experts have published sobering scenarios about the potential impact of a successful cyber attack on the United States. Already, hackers and criminals have exploited some of our vulnerabilities. Certainly, terrorists are making extensive use of the new information technologies, and a conventional terrorist attack along with a coordinated cyber attack could exponentially compound the damage. While the Commission considers cyber security a matter of grave importance, it also notes that the measures needed to protect the United States from cyberattack by terrorists are largely identical to those necessary to protect us from such an attack by a hostile foreign country, criminals, or vandals.

Not all terrorists are the same, but the groups most dangerous to the United States share some characteristics not seen 10 or 20 years ago:

- They operate in the United States as well as abroad.
- Their funding and logistical networks cross borders, are less dependent on state sponsors, and are harder to disrupt with economic sanctions.
- They make use of widely available technologies to communicate quickly and securely.
- Their objectives are more deadly.

This changing nature of the terrorist threat raises the stakes in getting American counterterrorist policies and practices right.

BIBLIOGRAPHY

Chapter 1

Allman, T.D. (2004). *Rogue State: America at War with the World*. New York: Nation Books.

Berkman, A. (1912). *Prison Memoirs of an Anarchist*. New York: Mother Earth Publishing Association.

Blau, J., Brunsma, D.L., Moncada, A., Zimmer, C. (2008). *The Leading Rogue State: The U.S. and Human Rights*. Colorado: Paradigm Publishers.

Blum, W. (2006). *Rogue State*. London: Zed Books.

Borgeson, K., & Valeri, R. (2009). *Terrorism in America*. Sudbury, Mass.: Jones and Bartlett.

Burke, E., Todd, W., & Langford, P. (Eds). (1991). *The Writings and Speeches of Edmund Burke Vol.9, 1: The Revolutionary War 1794-1797*, Oxford: Clarendon Press.

Cameron, F. (2005). *US Foreign Policy After the Cold War: Global Hegemon or Reluctant Sheriff?* (2nd Edition). London: Routledge.

Castro, F. (2006). *Che: A Memoir*. Melbourne: Ocean Press.

Castro, F. (2007). *My Life: Fidel Castro*. London: Allen Lane.

Chomsky, N. (2000). *Rogue States*. London: Pluto.

CIA. (2013). News and Information, Terrorism FAQs. *CIA*. Retrieved from cia.gov

Cooper, H.A. (2001). Terrorism: The Problem of Definition Revisited. *American Behavioural Scientist*, Vol. 44(6): 881-893.

Crenshaw, M. (2000). The Psychology of Terrorism. *Political Psychology*, Vol. 21(2): 405-420.

Crenshaw, M. (2011). *Explaining Terrorism: Causes, Processes and Consequences*. London: Routledge.

Dearden, L. (2017, Oct 6). Stephen Paddock: Isis Insists Las Vegas Shooter Was 'Soldier of Caliphate' as Authorities Probe Gunman's Motive. *Independent*. Retrieved from independent.co.uk.

Dugard, J. (1974). International Terrorism: Problems of Definition. *International Affairs,* Vol. 50(1): 67-81:

FBI. (2019). Terrorism: What We Investigate. Retrieved from FBI.gov.

Fellman, M. (2010). *In the Name of God and Country: Reconsidering Terrorism in American History.* New Haven: Yale University Press.

Foner, E. (2009). *Give Me Liberty!: An American History.* (Seagull 2nd Edition). New York: W.W. Norton.

Gage, B. (2009). *The Day Wall Street Exploded: A Story of America in its First Age of Terrorism.* Oxford: Oxford University Press.

Griset, P., & Mahan, S. (2003). *Terrorism in Perspective.* London: SAGE.

Hewitt, C. (2003). *Understanding Terrorism in America.* London: Routledge.

Hoffman, B. (2006). *Inside Terrorism.* (Revised Edition). New York: Columbia University Press.

Homeland Security. (2018). Inside Threat – Terrorism. *Homeland Security.* Retrieved from dhs.gov.

Homolar, A, (2010). Rebels Without a Conscience: The Evolution of Rogue States Narrative in US Security Policy. *European Journal of International Relations.* 17(4): 705-727.

Hornall T., & Roberts, L. (2018, Dec 28). John Major Government Sent Blistering Notes to Clinton Administration After Gerry Adams Got US Visa, Cabinet Papers Show. *Independent.* Retrieved from independent. co.uk.

Jackson, R. (et al). (2011). *Terrorism: A Critical Introduction.* Basingstoke: Palgrave.

Jackson, R., & Sinclair, S.J. (2012). *Contemporary Debates on Terrorism.* Abingdon: Routledge.

Jenkins, B. Cited in: Whittaker, D.J. (2007). *The Terrorism Reader.* London: Routledge

Johnson, C. (2002). *Blowback: The Costs and Consequences of American Empire.* (New Edition). London: Time Warner.

Jones, A. (2006). *Genocide: A Comprehensive Introduction.* New York, NY: Routledge.

Kiras, J. Cited in: Baylis, J., & Smith, S. (Eds). (2005). *The Globalisation of World Politics.* (Third Edition). Oxford: Oxford University Press.

Kolko, G. (2006). *The Age of War: The United States Confronts the World.* Boulder, Colo.: Lynne Rienner.

Laqueur, W. (1986). Reflections on Terrorism. *Foreign Affairs,* 65(1): 86-100.

Laqueur, W. (1999). *Age of Terrorism.* Oxford: Oxford University Press.

Laqueur, W. (2012). *A History of Terrorism.* (7th Edition). New Brunswick; NJ.: Transaction Publishing.

Laqueur, W. (2003). *No End to War: Terrorism in the Twenty-First Century.* New York: Continuum.

Larabee, A. (2011). Why Historians Should Exercise Caution When Using the Word "Terrorism". *The Journal of American History.* 98(1): 106-110.

Lawrence, B.B. (Ed.) (2005). *Messages to the World: The Statements of Osama Bin Laden.* London: Verso.

Lennon, A.T.J. & Eiss, C. (Eds). (2004). *Reshaping Rogue States: Preemption, Regime Change, and US Policy Toward Iran, Iraq and North Korea.* Cambridge, Mass.: MIT Press.

Martin, G. (2013). *Understanding Terrorism: Challenges, Perspectives, and Issues.* (4th Edition). Thousand Oaks, California: SAGE Publications.

Mindock, C. (2018, Oct 3). National Security Advisor John Bolton Brands Iran 'Rogue Regime' as U.S. Pulls Out of 1955 Treaty. *Independent.* Retrieved from independent.co.uk.

Obama, B. (2013, July 25). Remarks by President Obama and President Truong Tan Sang of Vietnam after bilateral meeting. *The White House.* Retrieved from Obamawhitehouse.archives.gov.

Prestowitz, C. (2004). *Rogue Nation: American Unilateralism and the Failure of Good Intentions.* New York: Basic Books.

Rapoport, D. (2011). Reflections of Terrorism and the American Experience. *The Journal of American History.* Vol. 98(1): 115-120.

Reeve, S. (1999). *The New Jackals.* New Hampshire: Northeastern University.

Sinclair, A. (2013). *An Anatomy of Terror: A History of Terrorism.* Basingstoke: Pan Macmillan.

Takaki, R. (1993). *A Different Mirror: A History of Multicultural America.* Boston: Little Brown and Company.

Thackrah, J.R. (2004). *Dictionary of Terrorism.* London: Routledge.

Tindall, G., & Shi, D. (2016). *America: A Narrative History.* (Brief 10th Edition). New York: W.W. Norton.

Toth, J. (2013). *Sayyid Qutb. The Life and Legacy of an Islamic Intellectual.* Oxford. Oxford University Press.

Wang, A., & Berman, M. (2018, Feb 10). Las Vegas Shooter Was Sober, Autopsy Finds, Leaving His Motives a Mystery. *Washington Post.* Retrieved from washingtonpost.com.

Waxman, O. (2018, July 18). The U.S. Government Had Nelson Mandela on Terrorist Watch Lists Until 2008. *Time.* Retrieved from time.com.

Whittaker, D.J. (2004). *Terrorists and Terrorism in the Modern World.* New York: Routledge.

Whittaker, D.J. (2007). *The Terrorism Reader.* London: Routledge.

Winkler, C.K. (2006). *In the Name of Terrorism: Presidents on Political Violence in the Post-World War II Era.* New York: State University Press of New York.

Yungher. N. (2008). *Terrorism – the Bottom Line.* Upper Saddle River NJ.: Prentice Hall.

Zinn, H. (2005). *A People's History of the United States.* New York: HarperPerennial.

Chapter 2

Adamic, L. (2008). *Dynamite: The Story of Class Violence in America.* (Updated Edition) Edinburgh: AK Press.

Appleton, S. (2000). Trends: Assassinations. *The Public Opinion Quarterly,* 64(4): 495-522.

Bibliography

Ayton, M. (2017). *Plotting to Kill the President: Assassination Attempts from Washington to Hoover.* University of Nebraska Press: Potomac Books.

Bradburn, D. (2008). A Clamor in the Public Mind: Opposition to the Alien and Sedition Acts. *The William and Mary Quarterly.* Third Series, Vol. 65(3): 565-600.

Bradburn, D. (2009). *Jeffersonian America: Citizenship Revolution: Politics and the Creation of the American Union, 1774-1804.* Charlottesville, VA.: University of Virginia Press.

Bulik, M. (2015). *The Sons of the Molly Maguire: The Irish Roots of America's First Labor War.* New York: Fordham University Press.

Burrough, B. (2015). *Days of Rage: America's Radical Underground, the FBI and the Forgotten Age of Revolutionary Violence.* New York: Penguin.

Carlson, J.D., & Ebel, J. (2016). *From Jeremiad to Jihad: Religion, Violence and America.* Berkeley: University of California Press.

Chowder, K. (2000). The Father of American Terrorism. *American Heritage.* Vol. 51(1).

Clarke, J. (1981). American Assassins: An Alternative Typology. *British Journal of Political Science.* Vol. 11(1): 81-104.

Daniels, R. (1988). *Asian America: Chinese and Japanese in the United States since 1850.* Seattle; London: University of Washington Press.

Davidson, J.W., & Lytle, M.H. (1992). *After the Fact: The Art of Historical Detection.* USA: McGraw Hill.

Fellman, M. (2010). *In the Name of God and Country: Reconsidering Terrorism in American History.* New Haven. CT.: Yale University Press.

Finkelman, P. (2011). John Brown: America's First Terrorist? *Prologue Magazine.* Vol. 43(1)

Foner, E. (2009).*Give Me Liberty!: An American History.* (Seagull 2nd Edition). New York: W.W. Norton.

Gilpin, R.B. (2011). *John Brown Still Lives!: America's Long Reckoning with Violence, Equality, and Change.* Chapel Hill: University of North Carolina Press.

Goldberg, D. (1999). *Discontented America: The United States in the 1920s.* Baltimore, Md.: Johns Hopkins University Press.

Hammond, W. (2011). *For the Love of Country.* Naval Institute Press.

Henderson, H. (2001). *Terrorism.* New York: Facts on File.

Hyams, E. (1975). *Terrorists and Terrorism.* London: J.M. Dent & Sons Ltd.

Kenny, K. (1998). *Making Sense of the Molly Maguires.* Oxford: Oxford University Press.

Kumamoto, R. (2014). *The Historical Origins of Terrorism in America 1664-1880.* New York; London: Routledge.

Kydd, A.H., & Walter B.F. (2006). The Strategies of Terrorism. *International Security,* Vol. 31(1): 49-80.

Jennings, M. Cited in: Law, R. (2015). *The Routledge History of Terrorism.* Abingdon: Routledge.

Jones, T. Cited in: Law, R. (2015). *The Routledge History of Terrorism.* Abingdon: Routledge.

Leiner, F.C. (2006). *The End of Barbary Terror: America's 1815 War against the Pirates of North Africa*. Oxford: Oxford University Press.

Lutz, J., & Lutz, B. (2007). *Terrorism in America*. New York: Palgrave.

McCann, J.T. (2006). *Terrorism on American Soil*. Boulder, CO: Sentient Publications.

Neal, S.L. (Ed) (2010). *Religious Intolerance in America: A Documentary History*. Chapel Hill, N.C.: University of North Carolina Press.

Oates, S. (1984). *To Purge This Land with Blood: A Biography of John Brown* (2nd Edition). Amherst: University of Massachusetts Press.

Peskin, L.A. (2009). *Captives and Countrymen: Barbary Slavery and the American Public – 1785-1816*. Baltimore, MD.: Johns Hopkins Press.

Pinkerton National Detection Agency. (2018). Our History. *Pinkerton*. Retrieved from pinkerton.com.

Pinkerton, A. (1877). *The Molly Maguires and the Detectives*. New York: G.W. Carleton & Co.

Robertson, R.G. (2001). *Rotting Face: Smallpox and the American Indian*. Caxton Press: Idaho.

Rohrs, R. (1981). Partisan Politics and the Attempted Assassination of Andrew Jackson. *Journal of the Early Republic*, 1(2): 149-163.

Simon, J.D. (2001). *The Terrorist Trap: America's Experience with Terrorism*. Bloomington: Indiana University Press.

Takaki, R. (1993). *A Different Mirror: A History of Multicultural America*. Boston: Little Brown and Company.

Tindall, G., & Shi, D. (2016). *America: A Narrative History*. (10th Edition). New York: W.W. Norton.

Turner, J. (2012). *Brigham Young: Pioneer Prophet*. Cambridge, Mass.: Belknap Press of Harvard University Press.

Wicks, R.S. & Fositer, F.R. (2005). *Junius and Joseph: Presidential Politics and the Assassination of the First Mormon Prophet*. Utah: USA Press.

Winkler C.K. (2006). *In the Name of Terrorism: Presidents on Political Violence in the Post-World War II Era*. Albany: State University Press of New York.

Winn, K.H. (1989). *Exiles in a Land of Liberty: Mormons in America, 1830-1846*. Chapel Hill: University of North Carolina Press.

Yungher. N. (2008). *Terrorism – the Bottom Line*. Upper Saddle River NJ.: Prentice Hall.

Chapter 3

Adamic, L. (2008). *Dynamite: The Story of Class Violence in America*. (Updated Edition). Edinburgh: AK Press.

Anderson, C.R., (1998). *All American Anarchist: Joseph A. Labadie and the Labor Movement*. Detroit: Wayne State University Press.

Appleton, S. (2000). Trends: Assassinations. *The Public Opinion Quarterly*, 64(4), 495-522.

Avrich, P. (1994). *Anarchist Voices: An Oral History of Anarchism in America*. Princeton NJ. Princeton Press.

Avrich, P., & Avrich, K. (2012). *Sasha and Emma: The Anarchist Odyssey of Alexander Berkman and Emma Goldman.* Cambridge, Mass.: Belknap Press.

Ayton, M. (2017). *Plotting to Kill the President: Assassination Attempts from Washington to Hoover.* University of Nebraska Press: Potomac Books.

Barton, M. (2015). The Global War on Anarchism: The United States and International Anarchist Terrorism 1898-1904. *Diplomatic History.* Vol. 39(2): 303-330.

Black Tom 1916 Bombing. (N/D). *FBI History.* Retrieved from fbi.gov.

Black Tom Explosion. (2019). *Jersey City Past and Present.* Retrieved from njcu.libguides.com.

Borgeson, K., & Valeri, R. (2009). *Terrorism in America.* Sudbury, Mass.: Jones and Bartlett.

Bulik, M. (2015). *The Sons of the Molly Maguire: the Irish Roots of America's First Labor War.* New York: Fordham University Press.

Carlisle, R. (2004). Encyclopedia of Intelligence and Counterintelligence. New York: Routledge.

Childers, J.P. (2013). The Democratic Balance: President McKinley's Assassination as Domestic Trauma. *Quarterly Journal of Speech.* Vol. 99(2):156-79.

Churchwell, S. B. (2018). *Behold America: A History of America First and the American Dream.* London: Bloomsbury Publishing.

Clarke, J. (1981). American Assassins: An Alternative Typology. *British Journal of Political Science.* 11(1): 81-104.

Clymer, J. A. (2002). The 1886 Chicago Haymarket Bombing and the Rhetoric of Terrorism in America. *The Yale Journal of Criticism.* 15(2): 315-344.

Clymer, J.A. (2003). *America's Culture of Terrorism.* Chapel Hill, NC.: University of North Carolina Press.

Crotty, W. S. (1998). Presidential Assassinations. *Society,* 35(2), 99-107.

Daniels, R. (1988). *Asian America: Chinese and Japanese in the United States Since 1850.* Seattle; London: University of Washington Press.

De Grazia, E. (2006). The Haymarket Bomb. *Law and Literature.* 18(3): 283-322.

Drinnon, R. (1961). *Rebel in Paradise: A Biography of Emma Goldman.* Chicago: University of Chicago Press.

Fellman, M. (2010). *In the Name of God and Country: Reconsidering Terrorism in American History.* New Haven. CT.: Yale.

Fine, S. (1955). Anarchism and the Assassination of McKinley. *The American Historical Review,* Vol. 60(4): 777–799.

Foner, P.S. (1977). *The Autobiographies of the Haymarket Martyrs.* New York: Monad Press.

Freeberg, E. (2009). *Democracy's Prisoner: Eugene V. Debs, the Great War, and the Right to Dissent.* Cambridge, Mass.: Harvard University Press.

Gage, B. (2006). Why Violence Matters: Radicalism, Politics, and Class War in the Gilded Age and Progressive Era. *Journal for the Study of Radicalism.* 1(1): 99-109.

Gay K., & Gay, M. (1999). *Encyclopaedia of Political Anarchy.* California. ABC Clio.

Goldman, E. (1970). *Living My Life.* New York: Dover Publications.

Gores, S. (1970). The Attempted Assassination of Teddy Roosevelt. *The Wisconsin Magazine of History*. Vol. 53(4): 269-277.

Gould, L.L. (1980). *The Presidency of William McKinley*. Lawrence: Regents Press.

Graham, H.D., & Gurr T.R. (1979). *Violence in America*. Beverly Hills: Sage.

Green, J. (2006). *Death in the Haymarket*. New York: Anchor Books.

Irving S., & Schwab M. (2012). Sabotage at Black Tom Island: A Wake-Up Call for America, *International Journal of Intelligence and Counter-Intelligence*. 25:2: 367-391.

Irwin, L. (2010, Oct 3). Bombing of The Times in 1910 Set Labor Back a Generation. *Los Angeles Times*. Retrieved from latimes.com.

Irwin, L. (2015). *Deadly Times: The 1910 Bombing of the Los Angeles Times and America's Forgotten Decade of Terror*. Connecticut: Globe Pequot Press.

Jensen, R. (2010). Daggers, Rifles and Dynamite: Anarchist Terrorism in Nineteenth century Europe. *Terrorism and Political Violence*. Vol. 16(1): 116-153.

Jensen, R. (2010). The United States, International Policing and the War against Anarchist Terrorism, 1900-1914. *Terrorism and Political Violence*, 13(1): 15-46.

Jensen, R. (2014). *The Battle against Anarchist Terrorism: An International History, 1878-1934*. Cambridge; New York: Cambridge University Press.

Jensen, R. (2015). Anarchist Terrorism and Global Diasporas, 1878-1914. *Terrorism and Political Violence*. Vol. 27(3): 441-453.

Johnson, J. (2018). *The 1916 Preparedness Day Bombings: Anarchy and Terrorism in Progressive Era America*. New York: Routledge.

Kemp, M. (2018). *Bombs, Bullets and Bread: The Politics of Anarchist Terrorism Worldwide 1866-1926*. North Carolina: McFarland Books.

Kenny, K. (1998). *Making Sense of the Molly Maguires*. Oxford: Oxford University Press.

Kingseed, W. (2001). The Assassination of William McKinley. *American History*. 36(4): 22-30.

Kumamoto, R. (2014). *The Historical Origins of Terrorism in America 1664-1880*. Abingdon: Routledge.

LaFeber, W., Polenberg, R., & Woloch, N. (2013). *The American Century: A History of the United States since the 1890s*. London, New York: M.E. Sharpe.

Larson, S. (1974). The American Federation of Labor and the Preparedness Controversy. *The Historian*. 37(1): 67.

Law, R. (2009). *Terrorism: A History*. Malden, MA: Policy Press.

Law, R. (2015). *The Routledge History of Terrorism*. Abingdon: Routledge.

Lens, S. (1974). *The Labor Wars: From the Molly Maguires to the Sitdowns*. Garden City, N.Y.: Anchor Press.

Lowe, V. (2005). 'Clear and Present Danger': Responses to Terrorism. *The International and Comparative Law Quarterly*. 54(1): 185-196.

Lutz, J., & Lutz, B. (2007). *Terrorism in America*. New York: Palgrave.

Lynd, S., & Grubacic, A. (2008) *Wobblies and Zapatistas*. USA: PM Press.

McCann, J.T. (2006). *Terrorism on American Soil.* Boulder, CO: Sentient Publications.

McRae, D. (2009). *The Old Devil: Clarence Darrow: The World's Greatest Trial Lawyer.* London: Simon and Schuster.

Messer-Kruse, T. (2012). *Haymarket Conspiracy: Transatlantic Anarchist Networks.* Champaign: University of Illinois Press.

Miller, N. (1992). *Theodore Roosevelt: A Life.* New York: Quill, William Morrow.

Mitchell, S. (1941). The Man Who Murdered Garfield. *Proceedings of the Massachusetts Historical Society.* 67: 452-489.

Mitrani, S. (2013). *The Rise of the Chicago Police Department: Class and Conflict, 1850-1894.* Champaign: University of Illinois Press.

Nix, E. (2016, Jul 29). In 1916 German Terrorists Launched An Attack on American Soil. *History.* Retrieved from history.com.

Novak, D. (1954). Anarchism and Individual Terrorism. *The Canadian Journal of Economics and Political Science.* Vol. 20(2): 176-184.

Pietrusza, D. (2007). *1920; The Year of the Six Presidents.* Philadelphia: Basic Books.

Pinkerton, R.A. (1901). Detective Surveillance of Anarchists. *North American Review.* Vol. 173(540): 609-17.

Pope, D. (2001). *American Radicalism.* Malden, Mass.: Blackwell.

Preston, W., & Handlin, O. (1963). *Aliens and Dissenters: Federal Suppression of Radicals, 1903-1933.* New York: Harper & Row.

Reagan, R. (1984). *Ronald Reagan: My Early Life.* Guildford: Sidgwick & Jackson.

Reynolds, D. (2010). *America: Empire of Liberty: A New History.* London: Penguin.

Riffenburgh, B. (2013). *Pinkerton's Great Detective: The Amazing Life of and Times of James McParland.* New York: Viking.

Roberts, S. (2016, Jul 24). An Attack That Turned Out to be German Terrorism Has a Modest Legacy 100 Years Later. *New York Times.* Retrieved from nytimes.com

Simon, J.D. (2001). *The Terrorist Trap: America's Experience with Terrorism.* Bloomington: Indiana University Press.

Simon, J.D. (2008). The Forgotten Terrorists: Lessons from the History of Terrorism. *Terrorism and Political Violence,* Vol. 20(2): 195-214.

Smith, C. (1996). *Urban Disorder and the Shape of Belief.* Chicago: University of Chicago Press.

Strang, D.A. (2013). *Worse Than the Devil: Anarchists, Clarence Darrow and Justice in a Time of Terror.* Madison: University of Wisconsin Press.

Vials, C. (2004). The Despotism of the Popular: Anarchy and Leon Czolgosz at the Turn of the Century. *Americana: The Journal of American Popular Culture from 1900 to the Present.* 3.2.

Wayne Morgan, H. (2003). *William McKinley and his America.* Kent, OH: Kent State University Press.

Witcover, J. *Sabotage at Black Tom: Imperial Germany's Secret War in America 1914-1917*. Chapel Hill N.C.: Algonquin Books of Chapel Hill.

Chapter 4

Adamic, L. (1988). *Dynamite: The Story of Class Violence in America.* (Updated Edition). Edinburgh: AK Press.

Appleton, S. (2000). Trends: Assassinations. *The Public Opinion Quarterly.* 64(4): 495-522.

Ayton, M. (2017). *Plotting to Kill the President: Assassination Attempts from Washington to Hoover.* University of Nebraska Press: Potomac Books.

Baum, P. (2016). *Violence in the Skies: A History of Aircraft Hijacking and Bombing.* Chichester: Summersdale.

Bernstein, A. (2009). *Bath Massacre: America's First School Bombing.* Ann Arbor: University of Michigan Press.

Burcar, C. (2011). *It Happened in Michigan: Remarkable Events that Shaped History.* Rowman and Littlefield: ebook.

Castro, F. (2007). *My Life: Fidel Castro.* London: Allen Lane.

Clarke, J. (1981). American Assassins: An Alternative Typology. *British Journal of Political Science,* 11(1): 81-104.

Clymer, J.A. (2003). *America's Culture of Terrorism.* Chapel Hill, NC: University of North Carolina Press.

Crotty, W. S. (1998). Presidential Assassinations. *Society.* 35(2): 99-107.

Davis, M. (2007). *Buda's Wagon: A Brief History of the Car Bomb.* London: Verso.

Eisenhower, D., & Ferrell, R. (1981). *The Eisenhower Diaries.* New York; London: Norton.

Ewing, C.P. (2006). *Minds on Trial.* New York: Oxford Press.

Finn, C. (2008). *From the Palmer Raids to the Patriot Act.* Boston: Beacon Press.

Gage, B. (2009). *The Day Wall Street Exploded: A Story of America in its First Age of Terrorism.* Oxford: Oxford University Press.

Goldberg, D. (1999). *Discontented America: The United States in the 1920s.* Baltimore, Md.: Johns Hopkins University Press.

González-Cruz, M., Marquez Sola, A., & Terando, L. (2008). Puerto Rican Revolutionary Nationalism: Filiberto Ojeda Ríos and the Macheteros. *Latin American Perspectives.* 35(6): 151-165.

Greenburg, M.M. (2011). *The Mad Bomber of New York.* New York: Union Square Press.

Hamm, Mark, & Ramón Spaaij. The Age of Lone Wolf Terrorism, Columbia University Press, 2017. ProQuest Ebook Central.

Hewitt, C. (2003). *Understanding Terrorism in America.* London: Routledge.

Hunter, S. (2005). *American Gunfight: The Plot to Kill Harry Truman and the Shoot-out that Stopped it.* New York: Simon and Schuster.

Jensen, R. (2014). *The Battle against Anarchist Terrorism: An International History, 1878-1934.* Cambridge; New York: Cambridge University Press.

Johnson, J. (2018). *The 1916 Preparedness Day Bombings: Anarchy and Terrorism in Progressive Era America.* New York: Routledge.

Landes, W. M. (1977). *An Economic Study of U.S. Aircraft Hijacking, 1960-1976*. Cambridge: National Bureau of Economic Research.

Law, R. (Ed). (2015). *The Routledge History of Terrorism*. Abingdon: Routledge.

Lutz, J., & Lutz, B. (2007). *Terrorism in America*. New York: Palgrave.

McCann, J.T. (2006). *Terrorism on American Soil*. Boulder, CO: Sentient Publications.

Miller, M. (2013). *The Foundations of Modern Terrorism: State, Society and the Dynamics of Political Violence*. Cambridge: Cambridge University Press.

Relatives Claim Passenger in 1958 Plane Crash Off Cuba Was a Hijacker. (2008, Nov, 19). *The Guardian*. Retrieved from theguardian.com.

Shappee, N. (1958). Zangara's Attempted Assassination of Franklin D. Roosevelt. *The Florida Historical Quarterly*. 37(2): 101-110.

Simon, J.D. (2001). *The Terrorist Trap: America's Experience with Terrorism*. Bloomington: Indiana University Press.

Simon, J.D. (2008). The Forgotten Terrorists: Lessons from the History of Terrorism. *Terrorism and Political Violence*. Vol. 20(2): 195-214.

Spaaij, R. (2010). The Enigma of Lone-Wolf Terrorism: An Assessment. *Studies in Conflict and Terrorism*. Vol. 33(9): 854-870.

Truman, H., & United States Office of the Federal Register. (1965). *Harry S. Truman, Containing the Public Messages, Speeches and Statements of the President, April 12, 1945 to January 20, 1953*. Public papers of the presidents of the United States, Vol. 6, 1950. Washington, D.C.: U.S. Government Printing Office.

Tuman, J. (2003). *Communicating Terror: The Rhetorical Dimensions of Terrorism*. London: SAGE.

Wade, W. (1986). *The Fiery Cross: The Ku Klux Klan in America*. New York: Simon and Schuster.

Warner, G. (1999). Eisenhower and Castro: US-Cuban relations, 1958-60. *International Affairs*. 75(4): 803-817.

Wilkinson, P. (2006). *Terrorism versus Democracy: The Liberal State Response*. (Revised Edition) London: Routledge.

Winick, C. (1961). How People Perceived 'The Mad Bomber'. *The Public Opinion Quarterly*. Vol. 25(1): 25-38.

Chapter 5

Alpert, J. (1981). *Growing Up Underground*. New York: Morrow.

Ambrose, S. (1989). *Nixon: The Triumph of a Politician, 1962-1972 Vol.2*. New York: Simon and Schuster.

Anderson, J. (1997). *Che Guevara: A Revolutionary Life*. London: Bantam.

Appleton, S. (2000). Trends: Assassinations. *The Public Opinion Quarterly*. 64(4): 495-522.

Ayers, B. (2001). *Fugitive Days: A Memoir*. Boston: Beacon Press.

Baker, A. (2008, Aug 9). Terrorist's Release Reopens Wound of Unsolved Bombing. *New York Times*. Retrieved from nytimes.com.

Beekman, S. (2005). *William Dudley Pelley: A Life in Right-Wing Extremism and the Occult*. Syracuse: Syracuse University Press.

Berger, D., (Ed.) (2010). *The Hidden 1970s: Histories of Radicalism.* New Brunswick: Rutgers University Press.

Burrough, B. (2015). *Days of Rage: America's Radical Underground, the FBI and the Forgotten Age of Revolutionary Violence.* New York: Penguin.

Carter, J. (2010). *White House Diary.* New York: Farrar Straus and Giroux.

Clarke, J. (1981). American Assassins: An Alternative Typology. *British Journal of Political Science.* 11(1): 81-104.

Crenshaw, M. (2011). *Explaining Terrorism: Causes, Processes and Consequences.* London: Routledge.

Deleon, D. (1973). The American as Anarchist: Social Criticism in the 1960s. *American Quarterly.* Vol. 25(5): 516-37.

Eager, P.W. (2008). From Freedom Fighters to Terrorists: Exploring Women and Political Violence. *Women's Rights Law Reporter.* Vol. 31(2-3): 268-285.

Five Shot in U.S. Congress. (1954). Pathe News. Retrieved from youtube.com.

Flynn, D.J. (2008). *A Conservative History of the American Left.* New York: Crown Forum.

Gilbert, D. (2012). *Love and Struggle: My Life in SDS, the Weather Underground and Beyond.* Chicago: PM Press.

Gitlin, T. (1993). *The Sixties: Years of Hope, Days of Rage.* New York: Bantam Books.

González-Cruz, M., et al. (2008). Puerto Rican revolutionary nationalism: Filiberto Ojeda Ríos and the Macheteros. *Latin American Perspectives.* Vol. 35(6): 151–165.

Graham, H.D., & Gurr T.R. (1979). *Violence in America.* Beverly Hills: Sage.

Hewitt, C. (2003). *Understanding Terrorism in America.* London: Routledge.

Hodgson, G. (2004). *More Equal than Others: America from Nixon to the New Century.* Princeton, N.J.: Princeton University Press.

Hoffman, B. (1986). Terrorism in the United States and the Potential Threat to Nuclear Facilities. Santa Monica, CA: RAND Corporation.

Hunter, S. (2005). *American Gunfight: The Plot to Kill Harry Truman and the Shoot-out That Stopped it.* New York: Simon and Schuster.

Jones, B., & O'Donnell, M. (2010). *Sixties Radicalism and Social Movement Activism: Retreat or Resurgence?* London: Anthem Press.

Kalman, L. (2010). *Right Star Rising: A New Politics, 1974-1980.* New York: W.W. Norton.

Kifner, J. (1970, Oct 6). Explosion in Chicago Rips Statue of a Policeman. *New York Times.* Retrieved from nytimes.com.

Kurlansky, M. (2005). *1968: The Year That Rocked the World.* London: Vintage.

Law, R. (2015). *The Routledge History of Terrorism.* Abingdon: Routledge.

Macfarquhar, N. (1999, Aug 23). Clemency Opens Old Scars for Sons of Bombing Victim. *New York Times.* Retrieved from nytimes.com

Malavet, P.A. (2004). *America's Colony: The Political and Cultural Conflict between the United States and Puerto Rico.* New York: NYU Press.

Martin, D, (2010, Aug 3). Lolita Lebron, Puerto Rican Nationalist, dies at 90. *New York Times.* Retrieved from nytimes.com.

Martin, G. (2013). *Understanding Terrorism: Challenges, Perspectives and Issues.* (4th Edition). Thousand Oaks, California: SAGE Publications.

Bibliography

McCann, J.T. (2006). *Terrorism on American Soil*. Boulder, CO: Sentient Publications.

Morris, K.E. (1996). *Jimmy Carter: American Moralist*. Athens and London: University of Georgia Press.

Mount, G. (2006). *895 Days that Changed the World*. Canada: Black Rose Books.

Nacos, B. L. (2010). *Terrorism and Counterterrorism*. (3rd Edition). New York: Pearson Education.

Naftali, T. (2006). *Blind Spot: The Secret History of American Counterterrorism*. New York: Basic Books.

Ness, C.D. (2008). *Female Terrorism and Militancy: Agency Utility and Organisation*. London: Routledge.

Nixon R.M. (1974). *Public Papers of the Presidents 1970*. Washington: United States Printing Office.

Nixon, R. (1979). *The Memoirs of Richard Nixon*. London: Arrow Books.

Perlstein, R. (2014). *The Invisible Bridge: The Fall of Nixon and the Rise of Reagan*. New York: Simon and Schuster.

Roig-Franzia, M. (1984, Feb 2). A Terrorist in the House. *The Washington Post*. Retrieved from washingtonpost.com

Romero, F. (2010, Aug 16). Lolita Lebron. *Time Magazine*. Retrieved from time.com.

Rosenau, W. (2013). 'Our Backs Are against the Wall': The Black Liberation Army and domestic terrorism in 1970s America. *Studies in Conflict and Terrorism*. Vol. 36(2): 176-92.

Rubin, B., & Colp, J. (2008). *Chronologies of Modern Terrorism*. Armonk: M.E. Sharpe.

Rumsfeld, D. (2012). *Known and Unknown: A Memoir*. New York: Sentinel.

Sandbrook, D. (2012). *Mad as Hell: The Crisis of the 1970s and the Rise of the Populist Right*. New York: Anchor Books.

Sefa Dei, G.J., & Simmons, M. (2010). *Fanon and Education: Thinking Through Pedagogical Possibilities*. Oxford: Peter Lang.

Simon, J.D. (2001). *The Terrorist Trap: America's Experience with Terrorism*. Bloomington: Indiana University Press.

Sjoberg, L., & Gentry, C. E. (Eds.). (2011). *Women, Gender, and Terrorism*. Athens: University of Georgia Press.

Slotnik, D.E. (2013, Sep 5). Croatian Hijacker, Dies. *New York Times*. Retrieved from nytimes.com

Stovall, T. (2015). *Transnational France: The Modern History of a Universal Nation*. Boulder: Routledge.

Treaster, J.B. (1974, Dec 13). Officer Wounded in Blast Faces Layoff as a Rookie. *New York Times*. Retrieved from nytimes.com.

Thomas, E. (2016). *Being Nixon: A Man Divided*. New York: Random House.

Varon, J. (2004). *Bringing the War Home – the Weather Underground, the Red Army Faction and Revolutionary Violence in the Sixties and Seventies*. Berkeley: University of California Press.

Wright, S.A. (2007). *Patriots, Politics and the Oklahoma City Bombing.* Cambridge: Cambridge University Press.

Zebich-Knos, M., & Nicol, H. (2005). *Foreign Policy toward Cuba: Isolation or Engagement?* Lanham, Maryland: Lexington Books.

Chapter 6

A Terrorists Giver in Sudan; Free Two Hostages. (1973, Mar 4). *New York Times.* Retrieved from nytimes.com.

Baum, P. (2016). *Violence in the Skies: A History of Aircraft Hijacking and Bombing.* Chichester: Summersdale.

Bush, G. (2011). *Decision Points.* London: Virgin.

Byman, D. (2005). *Deadly Connections: States that Sponsor Terrorism.* Cambridge; New York: Cambridge University Press.

Byrne, M. (2014). *Iran-Contra: Reagan's Scandal and the Unchecked Abuse of Presidential Power.* Lawrence, Kansas: University of Kansas.

Campbell, C., & Rockman, B. (1991). *The Bush Presidency: First Appraisals.* Chatham, N.J.: Chatham House.

Campos, J.H. (2007) *State and Terrorism: National Security and the Mobilisation of Power.* Abingdon: Ashgate.

Carter, J. (1982). *Keeping Faith: Memoirs of a President.* New York; London: Bantam.

Cassese, A. (1989). *Terrorism, Politics and the Law: The Achille Lauro Affair.* Cambridge: Polity.

Chomsky, N. (2000). *Rogue States.* London: Pluto.

Chomsky, N. (2015). *The Culture of Terrorism.* London: Pluto.

Clarke, R. (2003). *Against All Enemies: Inside America's War on Terror.* New York: Free Press.

Colás, A., & Saull, R. (2006). *The War on Terror and the American 'Empire' After the Cold War.* London; New York: Routledge.

Coll, S. (2009). *The Bin Ladens: Oil, Money, Terrorism and the Secret Saudi World.* Penguin.

Ensalaco, M. (2008). *Middle Eastern Terrorism: From Black September to September 11.* Philadelphia: University of Pennsylvania Press.

Farber, D. (2005). *Taken Hostage: The Iranian Hostage Crisis and America's First Encounter with Radical Islam.* Princeton: Princeton University Press.

Freedman, L. (1986). *Terrorism and the International Order.* Abingdon: Routledge & Kegan Paul PLC.

Gates, R.M. (2014). *Duty: Memoirs of a Secretary at War.* Croydon: W.H. Allen.

Gillon, S.M. (2008). *The Pact: Bill Clinton, Newt Gingrich and the Rivalry that Defined a Generation.* Oxford: Oxford University Press.

Glad, B. (2009). *An Outsider in the White House Jimmy Carter, his Advisors, and the Making of American Foreign Policy.* Ithaca: Cornell University Press.

Griset, P., & Mahan, S. (2003). *Terrorism in Perspective.* London: SAGE.

Haun, P. (2015). *Coercion, Survival, and War: Why Weak States Resist the United States.* Retrieved from https://ebookcentral.proquest.com.

Herring, G. (2011). *From Colony to Superpower: U.S. Foreign Relations since 1776*. New York: Oxford University Press.

Heymann, P.B. (1998). *Terrorism and America*. Cambridge, Mass.: MIT Press.

Hodgson, G. (2004). *More Equal than Others: America from Nixon to the New Century*. Princeton, N. J.; Woodstock: Princeton University Press.

Hoffman, B. (2006). *Inside terrorism*. (Revised Edition). New York: Columbia University Press.

Holden, R. (1986). The Contagiousness of Aircraft Hijacking. *American Journal of Sociology*, 91(4): 874-904.

Hyams, E. (1975). *Terrorists and Terrorism*. London: J.M. Dent & Sons Ltd.

Jenkins, P. (2006). *Decade of Nightmares: The End of the Sixties and the Making of Eighties America*. Oxford: Oxford University Press.

Joffee, L. (2004, Mar 11). Abu Abbas. *Guardian*. Retrieved from theguardian.com.

Kernek, S.J., & Thompson K.W. (1993). *Foreign Policy in the Reagan Presidency*. Lanham: University of Virginia.

Kinzer, S. (2008). *All the Shah's Men – An American Coup and the Roots of Middle East Terror*. Hoboken, N.J.: John Wiley.

Klein, J. (2002). *The Natural: The Misunderstood Presidency of Bill Clinton*. London: Coronet Books.

Kurlansky, M. (2005). *1968: The Year that Rocked the World*. London: Vintage.

Kyvig, D.E. (1990). *Reagan and the World*. New York: Praeger.

Laqueur, W. (2012). *A History of Terrorism*. (7th Edition). New Brunswick; NJ.: Transaction Publishing.

Lawrence, B.B. (Ed.) (2005). *Messages to the World: The Statements of Osama Bin Laden*. London: Verso.

Law, R. (2009). *Terrorism: A History*. Malden, MA: Policy Press.

Litwak, R. (2000). *Rogue States and U.S. Foreign Policy: Containment after the Cold War*. Woodrow Wilson Center Press: Distributed by the Johns Hopkins University Press.

Mamdani, M. (2004). *Good Muslim, Bad Muslim: America, the Cold War and the Roots of Terror*. New York: Three Leaves Press.

Marquis, C. (2003, Dec 23). The Struggle for Iraq: Documents; Rumsfeld Made Iraq Overture in 84 Despite Chemical Raids. *New York Times*. Retrieved from nytimes.com.

Miles, H. (2006). *Al-Jazeera. How Arab TV News Challenged the World*. London: Abacus.

Moldea, D. E. (1995). *The Killing of Robert F. Kennedy*. New York: W.W. Norton and Company.

Morgan, I. (2016). *Reagan: American Icon*. London: I.B. Tauris.

Netanyahu, B., (1986). *Terrorism: How the West Can Win*. New York: Farrar Straus and Giroux.

Nixon R.M. (1974) *Public Papers of the Presidents 1970*. Washington: United States Printing Office.

Pargeter, A. (2012). *Libya: The Rise and Fall of Qaddafi*. Yale: Yale University Press.

Patterson, J.T. (2005). *Restless Giant: The United States from Watergate to Bush v Gore*. Oxford: Oxford University Press.

Price, J. C., & Forrest, J. S. (2012). *Practical Aviation Security: Predicting and Preventing Future Threats*. Retrieved from https://ebookcentral.proquest.com

Raab, D. (2008). *Terror in Black September*. Basingstoke: Palgrave.

Reagan, R. (2004). *Speaking My Mind: Selected Speeches*. New York: Simon and Schuster.

Reagan, R. (1985, July 8), Remarks at the Annual Convention of the American Bar Association. Ronald Reagan Presidential Library and Museum. Retrieved from reaganlibrary.gov.

Reagan, R., & Brinkley, D. (2007). *The Reagan Diaries*. London: HarperPress.

Reagan, R., Anderson, A., Skinner, M. (2004). *Reagan: A Life in Letters*. New York: Free Press.

Rossinow, D.C. (2015). *The Reagan Era: A History of the 1980s*. New York: Columbia University Press.

Rubin, B., & Rubin J.C. (2002). *Anti-American Terrorism and the Middle East*. New York: Oxford.

Schaller, M. (1992). *Reckoning with Reagan: America and its President in the 1980s*. New York; Oxford: Oxford University Press.

Scott, J.M. (1996). *Deciding to Intervene. The Reagan Doctrine and American Foreign Policy*. Durham, N.C.: Duke University Press.

Shay, S. (2007). *The Red Sea Terror Triangle*. New Brunswick and London: Transaction Publishers.

Shultz, G.S, (1984, Oct 26). Excerpts From Schultz's Address on International Terrorism. *New York Times*. Retrieved from nytimes.com.

Shultz, G.S. (1993). *Turmoil and Triumph: My Years as Secretary of State*. New York: Charles Scribner's Sons.

Smith, B. (2000). Moving to the Right: The Evolution of Modern American Terrorism. *Global Dialogue*. 2(4): 52-63.

Stanik, J.T. (2003). *El Dorado Canyon: Reagan's Undeclared War with Qaddafi*. Annapolis, Md.: Naval Institute Press.

Starr-Deelen, D. (2014). *Presidential Policies on Terrorism: From Ronald Reagan to Barack Obama*. New York: Palgrave Macmillan.

Sterling: The Terror Network: The Secret War of International Terrorism (Book Review). (1982). *Middle East Journal*. 36(1): 87.

Thomas, E. (2016). *Being Nixon: A Man Divided*. New York: Random House.

Trainor, B.E. (1989, Aug 6). 83 Strike on Lebanon: Hard Lessons for US. *New York Times*. Retrieved from nytimes.com.

Troy, G. (2013). *Morning in America*. Princeton: Princeton University Press.

Wallace, R. (2000). *Lockerbie: The Story and the Lessons*. Westport: Greenwood Press.

Weinberger, C. (1990). *Fighting for Peace: Seven Critical Years at the Pentagon*. London: Michael Joseph.

Wilentz, S. (2009). *The Age of Reagan: A History 1974-2008*. New York: Harper Perennial.

Wilkinson, P. (2006). *Terrorism versus Democracy: The Liberal State Response.* (Revised Edition) London: Routledge.

Wills. D. (2003). *The First War on Terrorism: Counter-terrorism Policy in the Reagan Administration.* Lanham, Md.: Rowman and Littlefield.

Winkler, C.K. (2006). *In the Name of Terrorism: Presidents on Political Violence in the Post-World War II Era.* New York: State University Press of New York.

Chapter 7

9/11 Commission. (2004). *The 9/11 Commission Report.* New York, London: W.W. Norton and Company.

Albright, M, (2003). *Madam Secretary: A Memoir.* New York: Macmillan.

Ambrose, S., & Brinkley, D. (2011). *Rise to Globalism: American Foreign Policy Since 1938.* (9th Edition). New York, NY: Penguin Books.

Barton, E. (1999). *Divide We Stand: A Biography of New York's World Trade Center.* New York: Basic Books.

Baylis, J. (2007). *Strategy in the Contemporary World: An Introduction to Strategic Studies.* (2nd Edition). Oxford: Oxford University Press.

Broad, W.J. (1998, May 26). Sowing Death: A Special Report; How Japan Germ Terror Alerted World. *New York Times.* Retrieved from nytimes.com.

Burke, J. (2007). *Al-Qaeda: The True Story of Radical Islam.* (3rd Edition). London: Penguin.

Bush, G., & Scowcroft, B. (1998). *A World Transformed.* New York: Alfred A. Knopf.

Campbell, J.W. (2015). *1995: The Year the Future Began.* Berkeley: University of California Press.

Clarke, R. (2003). *Against all Enemies: Inside America's War on Terror.* New York: Free Press.

Clinton, B. (2004) *My Life.* New York: Alfred P. Knopf.

Cooley, J.K. (2002). *Unholy Wars, Afghanistan, America and International Terrorism.* London: Pluto.

Davis, M. (2007). *Buda's Wagon: A Brief History of the Car Bomb.* London: Verso.

Dixon, W.W. (Ed.) (2004). *Film and Television after 9/11.* Carbondale: Southern Illinois University Press.

Dowd, M. (1994, Sep 13). Crash at the White House. *New York Times.* Retrieved from nytimes.com

Fouda, Y., & Fielding, N. (2003). *Masterminds of Terror.* Edinburgh: Mainstream Publishing.

Frum, D. (2003). *The Right Man: The Surprise Presidency of George W. Bush.* London: Weidenfeld & Nicolson.

Gibbons, F. (2001, Aug 17). Vidal Praises Oklahoma Bomber for Heroic Aims. *Guardian.* Retrieved from theguardian.com.

Hamm, M.S. (2007). *Terrorism as Crime: From Oklahoma City to Al-Qaeda and Beyond.* New York: New York University Press.

Harden, B. (1997, Feb 25). Shooter Bought Gun by Using New Florida ID. *Washington Post.* Retrieved from washingtonpost.com

Higgitt, R. (2016, Aug 5). The Real Story of the Secret Agent and the Greenwich Observatory Bombing. *The Guardian*. Retrieved from theguardian.com

Gibbs, N., & Allis, S. (1996). Tracking Down the Unabomber. *Time International* (South Pacific Edition). Vol. 147(16): 22-28.

Hewitt, C. (2003). *Understanding Terrorism in America*. London: Routledge.

Heymann, P.B. (1998). *Terrorism and America*. Cambridge, Mass.: MIT Press.

Hoffman, D. (1998). *The Oklahoma City Bombing and the Politics of Terror*. Venice, CA: Feral House.

Lawrence, B.B. (Ed.) (2005). *Messages to the World: The Statements of Osama Bin Laden*. London: Verso.

Linenthal, E. T. (2003). *Unfinished Bombing: Oklahoma City in American Memory*. Oxford: Oxford University Press.

Matlock, J.F. (2010). *Superpower Illusions: How Myths and False Ideologies Led America Astray*. Yale: Yale University Press.

McCann, J.T. (2006). *Terrorism on American Soil*. Boulder, CO: Sentient Publications.

Nacos, B. L. (2010). *Terrorism and Counterterrorism*. (3rd Edition). New York: Pearson Education.

Naftali, T. (2006). *Blind Spot: The Secret History of American Counterterrorism*. New York: Basic Books.

Normani, A.Q. (1996, Sep 10) Clinton Proposes Measures to Combat Terrorism. *Wall Street Journal*. Retrieved from wsj.com.

O'Neil, J. (2006, Jul 7). New York Tunnel Plot is Uncovered in Early Stage. *New York Times*. Retrieved from nytimes.com.

Patterson, J.T. (2005). *Restless Giant: The United States from Watergate to Bush v Gore*. Oxford: Oxford University Press.

Pease, D.E. (2009). *Critical American Studies: New American Exceptionalism*. Minneapolis: University of Minnesota Press.

Reagan, R. (2004). Speaking My Mind: Selected Speeches. Simon and Schuster.

Reeve, S. (1999). *The New Jackals*. New Hampshire: Northeastern University.

Riegler, T. (2016). 'Mirroring Terror': The Impact of 9/11 on Hollywood Cinema. *Imaginations: Journal of Cross-Cultural Media Studies*. Vol. 5(2): 103-119.

Rubin, B., & Colp, J. (2008). *Chronologies of Modern Terrorism*. Armonk: M.E. Sharpe.

Rumsfeld, D. (2012). *Known and Unknown: A Memoir*. New York: Sentinel.

Simon, J.D. (2001). *The Terrorist Trap: America's Experience with Terrorism*. Bloomington: Indiana University Press.

Smith, B. (2000). Moving to the Right: The Evolution of Modern American Terrorism. *Global Dialogue*. 2(4): 52-63.

Spaaij, R. (2010). The Enigma of Lone-Wolf terrorism: An Assessment. *Studies in Conflict and Terrorism*. Vol. 33(9): 854-870.

Starr-Deelen, D. (2014). *Presidential Policies on Terrorism: From Ronald Reagan to Barack Obama*. New York: Palgrave Macmillan.

Testimony Ends in Terror-Bombing Trial. (1995, Aug 31). *New York Times*. Retrieved from nytimes.com

Tsui, C. (2015). Framing the Threat of Catastrophic Terrorism: Genealogy, discourse and President Clinton's Counterterrorism Approach. *International Politics*. 52(1): 66-88.

Wilentz, S. (2009). *The Age of Reagan: A History 1974-2008*. New York: Harper Perennial.

Winkler, C.K. (2006) *In the Name of Terrorism: Presidents on Political Violence in the Post-World War II Era*. New York: State University Press of New York.

World Trade Centre Bomber Stole Student's Identity. (2001, Sep 24). *Wales Online*. Retrieved from walesonline.co.uk

Wright, S.A. (2007). *Patriots, Politics and the Oklahoma City Bombing*. Cambridge: Cambridge University Press.

Zuckoff, M. (2019). *Fall and Rise: The Story of 9/11*. New York: Harper Collins.

Chapter 8

9/11 Commission. (2004). *The 9/11 Commission Report*. New York, London: W.W. Norton and Company.

Ali. T. (2003). *Bush in Babylon*. London: Verso.

Bergen, P. (2011). *Longest War: The Enduring Conflict between America and Al-Qaeda*. New York: Simon and Schuster.

Bloch-Elkon, Y. (2011). The Polls-trends: Public Perceptions and the Threat of International Terrorism After 9/11. *Public Opinion Quarterly*. 75(2): 366-392.

Burke, J. (2007). *Al-Qaeda: The True Story of Radical Islam*. (3rd Ed.). London: Penguin.

Cameron, F. (2005). *US Foreign Policy after the Cold War: Global Hegemon or Reluctant Sheriff?* (2nd Edition). London: Routledge.

Chomsky, N. (2002). *Pirates and Emperors Old and New. Understanding Terrorism in the Real World*. London: Pluto Press.

Colás, A., & Saull, R. (2006). *The War on Terror and the American 'Empire' after the Cold War*. London; New York: Routledge.

Coll, S. (2009). *The Bin Ladens: Oil, Money, Terrorism and the Secret Saudi World*. Penguin.

Croft, S. (2006). *Culture, Crisis and America's War on Terror*. Cambridge: Cambridge University Press.

Frum, D. (2003). *The Right Man: The Surprise Presidency of George W. Bush*. London: Weidenfeld & Nicolson.

Fy 2020 Budget in Brief (2019, Mar 18). *Homeland Security*. Retrieved from dhs.gov

Gershoff, A. (2005). Shaping Public Opinion: The 9-11 Iraq Connection in the Bush Administration Rhetoric. *Perspectives on Politics*. Vol. 3(3): 525-537.

Greenberg, B.S. (2002). *Communication and Terrorism: Public and Media Responses to 9/11*. Cresskill, N.J.: Hampton Press.

Hewitt, C. (2003). *Understanding Terrorism in America*. London: Routledge.

Holloway, D. (2008). *9/11 and the War on Terror*. Edinburgh: Edinburgh University Press.

Holloway, D. (2008). *Cultures of the War on Terror*. Montreal: McGill-Queen's University Press.

Krauthhammer, C. (2001, Sep 12). To War Not to Court. *The Washington Post*. Retrieved from washingtonpost.com

Laqueur, W. (2003). *No End to War: Terrorism in the Twenty-First Century*. New York: Continuum.

Law, R. (Ed.). (2015). *The Routledge History of Terrorism*. Abingdon: Routledge.

Lawrence, B.B. (Ed.) (2005). *Messages to the World: The Statements of Osama Bin Laden*. London: Verso.

McCann, J.T. (2006). *Terrorism on American Soil*. Boulder, CO: Sentient Publications.

Melnick, J. (2009). *9/11 Culture: America under Construction*. Malden, MA. Wiley-Blackwell.

Morey, P. (2011). *Framing Muslims Stereotyping and Representation After 9/11*. Cambridge. Mass.: Harvard University Press.

Morgan, M.J. (2009). *The Impact of 9/11 on the Media, Arts and Entertainment*. New York: Macmillan Palgrave.

Petrovic, P. (Ed.) (2015). *Representing 9/11*. Lanham, Maryland: Rowman and Littlefield.

Prince, S. (2009). *Firestorm: American Film in the Age of Terrorism*. New York: Columbia University Press.

Qutb, S. (2006). *Milestones*. Birmingham: Maktabah Publishers.

Rubin, B., & Colp, J. (2008). *Chronologies of Modern Terrorism*. Armonk: M.E. Sharpe.

Shaheen, J.G. (2008). *Guilty: Hollywood's Verdict on Arabs after 9/11*. Northampton. Mass: Olive Branch Press.

Starr-Deelen, D. (2014). *Presidential Policies on Terrorism: From Ronald Reagan to Barack Obama*. New York: Palgrave Macmillan.

Wheeler, W.D. (2004). *Film and Television after 9/11*. Carbondale: Southern Illinois Press.

Winkler, C.K. (2006). *In the Name of Terrorism: Presidents on Political Violence in the Post-World War II Era*. New York: State University Press of New York.

Wright, L. (2007). *The Looming Tower*. London: Penguin.

Yungher, N. (2008). *Terrorism – the Bottom Line*. Upper Saddle River, NJ: Prentice Hall.

Chapter 9

Akbarzadeh, S., (2000). *Uzbekistan and the United States*. London: Zed Books.

Altman Says Hollywood 'Created Atmosphere' for September 11. (2001, Oct 18). *The Guardian*. Retrieved from theguardian.com.

Baker, P., Cooper, H., Mazzetti, M. (2011, May 1). Bin Laden is Dead, Obama Says. *New York Times*. Retrieved from nytimes.com.

Bart, P. (2001, Sep). Finding Hope amid the Ashes. *Variety, 384*, 1-1, 3.

BBFC. (2018). Casablanca. Retrieved from bbfc.co.uk.

BBFC. (n/d). The 1970s. Retrieved from bbfc.co.uk.

Bergen, P. (2016). *United States of Jihad, Investigating America's Homegrown Terrorists*. New York: Crown Publishers.

Binder, A. (2014, Jan 17). Defendant Admits Sending Letter With Ricin to Obama. *New York Times*. Retrieved from nytimes.com.

Birkenstein, J., Froula, A., & Randell, K. (2010). *Reframing 9/11: Film, Popular Culture and the "War on Terror"*. New York: Continuum.

Black, J. (2005). *The Politics of James Bond*. Lincoln and London. University of Nebraska Press.

Blum, W. (2006) *Rogue State*. London: Zed Books.

Boggs, C., & Pollard, T. (2007). *The Hollywood War Machine: U.S. Militarism and Popular Culture*. Boulder: Paradigm Pub.

Borgeson, K., & Valeri, R. (2009). *Terrorism in America*. Sudbury, Mass.: Jones and Bartlett.

Britton, W. (2005). *Beyond Bond: Spies in Fiction and Film*. Westport, Conn.: Praeger.

Brzezinski, Z, (2007, March 25). Terrorized by 'War on Terror'. *The Washington Post*. Retrieved from washingtonpost.com

Burke, C. (2000, Sep 15). Bush Made Bundle on Movie Violence. *New York Post*. Retrieved from nypost.com.

Carlson, J.D. & Ebel, J. (2016). *From Jeremiad to Jihad: Religion, Violence and America*. Berkeley: University of California Press.

Clay, N. (2017, Feb 22). Older Brother of Terry Nichols Dies in Michigan. *The Oklahoman*. Retrieved from oklahhoman.com.

Cooley, J.K. (2002). *Unholy Wars, Afghanistan, America and International Terrorism*. London: Pluto.

Cooley, J.K. (2005). *An Alliance against Babylon*. London: Pluto.

Crockatt. R. (2003). *America Embattled – September 11, Anti-Americanism and the Global Order*. London and New York: Routledge.

Crockatt, R. (2004). No Common Ground? Islam, Anti-Americanism and the United States. *European Journal of American Culture*. 23(2): 125-142.

Croft, S. (2006). *Culture, Crisis and America's War on Terror*. Cambridge: Cambridge University Press.

De Semlyen, N. (2012, Aug 14). Chuck Norris: In His Own Words. *Empire*. Retrieved from empireonline.com.

Dixon, W.W. (Ed.) (2004). *Film and Television after 9/11*. Carbondale: Southern Illinois University Press.

Duncan, R., & Goddard, J. (2009). *Contemporary America* (3rd Edition) Houndmills, Basingstoke, Hampshire; New York: Palgrave Macmillan.

Dunn, D.H. (2005). Bush, 11 September and the Conflicting Strategies of the War on Terrorism. *Irish Studies in International Affairs*. Vol. 16(1): 11-33.

Edwards, G. (2015). *Overreach: Leadership in the Obama Presidency*. Princeton; Oxford: Princeton University Press.

Enders, W. (2005). After 9/11: Is It All Different Now? *Journal of Conflict Resolution*. Vol. 49(2): 259-277.

Ensalaco, M. (2008). *Middle Eastern Terrorism: From Black September to September 11*. Philadelphia: University of Pennsylvania Press.

Former Canadian Ambassador to Iran Ken Taylor Pleased Ben Affleck Thanked Canada After Winning Best Picture for Argo. (2013, Feb 25). *National Post*. Retrieved from nationalpost.com.

Gates, R.M. (2014). *Duty: Memoirs of a Secretary at War*. London: W.H. Allen.

Gershoff, A. (2005). Shaping Public Opinion: The 9-11 Iraq Connection in the Bush Administration Rhetoric. *Perspectives on Politics*. Vol .3(3), 525-537.

Goodrich, T. (2005). *The Darkest Dawn Lincoln, Booth, and the Great American Tragedy*. Bloomington: Indiana University Press.

Gourevich P., & Morris, E. (2009). *Standard Operating Procedure*. London: Picador Press.

Grisham, L. (2015, Jan 5). Timeline: North Korea and the Sony Pictures hack. *USA Today*. Retrieved from eu.usatoday.com.

Hall, G. (2007). *American Global Strategy and the War on Terrorism*. Aldershot: Ashgate.

Herrington, E., & Taylor, A. (2005). *The Afterlife of John Brown*. London and New York. Palgrave Macmillan.

Hewitt, C. (2003). *Understanding Terrorism in America*. London: Routledge.

Hiro, D. (2002). *War without End: The Rise of Islamist Terrorism and the Global Response*, Abingdon: Routledge.

Hoffman, B. (2015). A First Draft of the History of America's Ongoing Wars on Terrorism. *Studies in Conflict and Terrorism*. Vol. 38(1): 75-83.

Holloway, D. (2008). *9/11 and the War on Terror*. Edinburgh: Edinburgh University Press.

Jackson, R., Smyth, M., Gunning, J., & Jarvis, L. (2011). *Terrorism: A Critical Introduction* Basingstoke: Palgrave Macmillan.

Jewitt. R. (2003). *Captain America and the Crusade against Evil*. Cambridge, Cambridge: University Press.

Johnson, C. (2002). *Blowback: The Costs and Consequences of American Empire*. London: Time Warner.

Kakutani, M. (2001, Sep 13). Critic's Notebook: Struggling to Find Words for a Horror beyond Words. *New York Times*. Retrieved from nytimes.com

Kellner, D. (2009). *Cinema Wars: Hollywood Film and Politics in the Bush-Cheney era*. London: John Wiley.

Lane, A. (2001, Sep 16). This is not a Movie. *The New Yorker*. Retrieved from newyorker.com.

Langman, L (1998). *American Film Cycles: The Silent Era*. Westport, CT: Greenwood Press.

Law, R. (Ed.). (2015). *The Routledge History of Terrorism*. Abingdon: Routledge.

Lebovic, J.H. (2007). *Deterring International Terrorism and Rogue States: US National Security Policy After 9/11*. London; New York: Routledge.

Leffler, M., Legro, J. (2011). *In Uncertain Times: American Foreign Policy after the Berlin Wall and 9/11*. Ithaca: Cornell University Press.

Lennon, A.T.J. & Eiss, C. (Eds). (2004). *Reshaping Rogue States: Preemption, Regime Change, and US Policy toward Iran, Iraq and North Korea*. Cambridge, Mass.: MIT Press.

Bibliography

Leung, R. (2004, May 5). Abuse at Abu Ghraib. *60 Minutes*. Retrieved from cbsnews.com.

Levitas, D. (2003, Dec 13). Our Enemies at Home. *New York Times*. Retrieved from nytimes.com.

Markert, John. (2011). *Post-9/11 Cinema: Through a Lens Darkly*. Lanham, MD.: Scarecrow Press.

Munn, M. (2005). *John Wayne the Man behind the Myth*. New York: Berkley Books.

Pollard, T. Cited in: Morgan, M. (2009). *The Impact of 9/11 on the Media, Arts, and Entertainment*. New York: Palgrave Macmillan.

Philipps, D. (2018, Oct 3). F.B.I. Arrests Utah Man in Ricin Scare at Pentagon. *New York Times*. Retrieved from nytimes.com.

Price, J. C., & Forrest, J. S. (2012). *Practical Aviation Security: Predicting and Preventing future threats*. Retrieved from https://ebookcentral.proquest.com

Prince, S. (2009). *Firestorm: American Film in the Age of Terrorism*. New York: Columbia University Press.

Riegler, T. (2010). Through the Lenses of Hollywood: Depictions of Terrorism in American Movies. *Perspectives on Terrorism*. 4(2): 35-45.

Rommel-Ruiz, W.B. (2011). *American History Goes to the Movies*. New York: Routledge.

Sanger, D.E. (2001, Sep 18). A Nation Challenged: The President; Bin Laden is Wanted in Attacks, Dead or Alive, President Says. *New York Times*. Retrieved from nytimes.com.

Shaheen, J. (2008). *Guilty: Hollywood's Verdict on Arabs after 9/11*. Northampton, Mass.: Olive Branch Press.

Shaheen, J. (2009). *Reel Bad Arabs: How Hollywood Vilifies a People*. (Revised Edition). Northampton, Mass.: Olive Branch Press.

Shane, S. (2011, Mar 23). Panel on Anthrax Inquiry Finds Case Against Ivins Persuasive. *New York Times*. Retrieved from nytimes.com.

Schneider. S.J. Cited in: Dixon, W.W. (Ed.) (2004). *Film and Television after 9/11*. Carbondale: Southern Illinois University Press.

Sjoberg, L., & Gentry, C. E. (Eds.). (2011). *Women, Gender, and Terrorism*. Athens: University of Georgia Press.

Slocum, J. (Ed.). (2005). *Terrorism, Media, Liberation*. New Brunswick, N.J.: Rutgers University Press.

Slocum, J. (2006). *Hollywood and War: The Film Reader*. New York; London: Routledge.

Starr-Deelen, D. (2014). *Presidential Policies on Terrorism: From Ronald Reagan to Barack Obama*. New York: Palgrave Macmillan.

Suedfeld, P. (2007). *Understanding the Bush Doctrine: Psychology and Strategy in an Age of Terrorism*. New York: Routledge.

Tuman, J. (2003). *Communicating Terror: The Rhetorical Dimensions of Terrorism*. London: SAGE.

US Bars United 93 Star From Premier. (2006, Apr 24). *The Guardian*. Retrieved from theguardian.com.

Valantin, J. (2005). *Hollywood, the Pentagon and Washington*. London: Anthem.

Vaughn, S. (1994). *Ronald Reagan in Hollywood: Movies and Politics*. USA: Cambridge University Press.

Washington, D. (2012, 19 Feb). Washington: I Was Waterboarded while Filming Safe House. Interview with Andrew Marr. *BBC*. Retrieved from BBC iplayer.

Winkler, C.K. (2006). *In the Name of Terrorism: Presidents on Political Violence in the Post-World War II Era*. New York: State University Press of New York.

Wright, L. (2007). *The Looming Tower*. London: Penguin.

Zizek Cited in: Slocum, J. (2006). *Hollywood and War: The Film Reader*. New York; London: Routledge

Zuckoff, M. (2019). *Fall and Rise: The Story of 9/11*. New York: Harper Collins.

Conclusion

Armed Toddlers Kill Twice as Many Americans Each Year as Terrorists. (2017, Jan 31). *Euronews*. Retrieved from euronews.com.

Bush, G., & Scowcroft, B. (1998). *A World Transformed*. New York: Alfred A. Knopf.

Cameron, F. (2005). *US Foreign Policy after the Cold War: Global Hegemon or Reluctant Sheriff?* (2nd Edition). London: Routledge.

Heymann, P.B. (1998). *Terrorism and America*. Cambridge, Mass.: MIT Press.

Jackson, R. (et al). (2011). *Terrorism: A Critical Introduction*. Basingstoke: Palgrave.

Johnson, C. (2002). *Blowback: the Costs and Consequences of American Empire*. London: Time Warner.

Kolko, G. (2006). *The Age of War: The United States Confronts the World*. Boulder, Colo.: Lynne Rienner.

Law, R. (Ed.). (2015). *The Routledge History of Terrorism*. Abingdon: Routledge.

Lawrence, B.B. (Ed.) (2005). *Messages to the World: The Statements of Osama Bin Laden*. London: Verso.

Rapoport, D. (2011). Reflections of Terrorism and the American Experience. *The Journal of American History*. Vol. 98(1), 115-120.

Wilkinson, P. (2006). *Terrorism versus Democracy: The Liberal State Response*. (Revised Edition) London: Routledge.

Winkler, C.K. (2006). *In the Name of Terrorism: Presidents on Political Violence in the Post-World War II Era*. New York: State University Press of New York.

INDEX